ROOTED JAZZ DANCE

UNIVERSITY PRESS OF FLORIDA

Florida A&M University, Tallahassee
Florida Atlantic University, Boca Raton
Florida Gulf Coast University, Ft. Myers
Florida International University, Miami
Florida State University, Tallahassee
New College of Florida, Sarasota
University of Central Florida, Orlando
University of Florida, Gainesville
University of North Florida, Jacksonville
University of South Florida, Tampa
University of West Florida, Pensacola

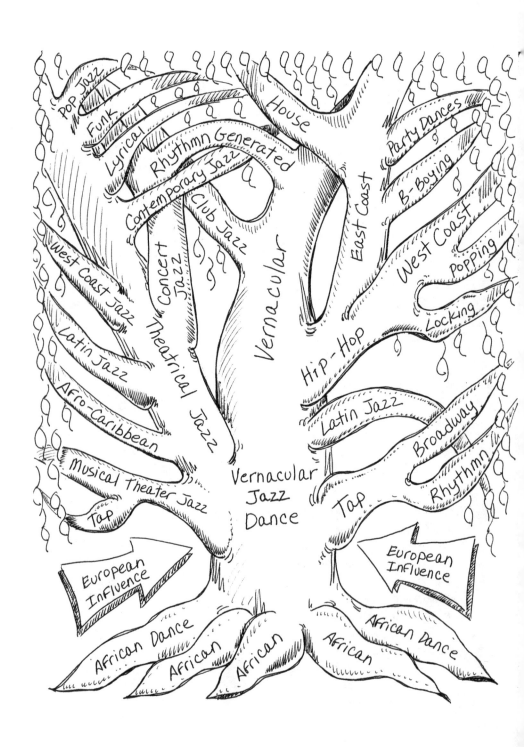

Rooted Jazz Dance

Africanist Aesthetics and Equity in the Twenty-First Century

EDITED BY
Lindsay Guarino,
Carlos R. A. Jones,
and Wendy Oliver

UNIVERSITY PRESS OF FLORIDA
Gainesville · Tallahassee · Tampa · Boca Raton
Pensacola · Orlando · Miami · Jacksonville · Ft. Myers · Sarasota

Publication of this work is made possible by a Sustaining the Humanities through the American Rescue Plan grant from the National Endowment for the Humanities.

Frontispiece: Jazz Dance Tree, by Kimberly Testa.

First cloth printing, 2022
First paperback printing, 2024

29 28 27 26 25 24   6 5 4 3 2 1

Library of Congress Cataloging-in-Publication Data
Names: Guarino, Lindsay, editor. | Jones, Carlos R. A., editor. | Oliver,
   Wendy, editor.
Title: Rooted jazz dance : Africanist aesthetics and equity in the
   twenty-first century / edited by Lindsay Guarino, Carlos R. A. Jones,
   Wendy Oliver.
Description: 1. | Gainesville : University Press of Florida, 2022. |
   Includes bibliographical references and index.
Identifiers: LCCN 2021031918 (print) | LCCN 2021031919 (ebook) | ISBN
   9780813069111 (hardback) | ISBN 9780813057972 (pdf) | ISBN 9780813072111
   (ebook) | ISBN 9780813080765 (pbk.)
Subjects: LCSH: Jazz dance—United States—History. | African American
   dance—History. | African American aesthetics. | Racism—United
   States—History. | BISAC: PERFORMING ARTS / Dance / Jazz | PERFORMING
   ARTS / Dance / History & Criticism
Classification: LCC GV1784 .R66 2022 (print) | LCC GV1784 (ebook) | DDC
   793.30973—dc23
LC record available at https://lccn.loc.gov/2021031918
LC ebook record available at https://lccn.loc.gov/2021031919

The University Press of Florida is the scholarly publishing agency for the State University System of Florida, comprising Florida A&M University, Florida Atlantic University, Florida Gulf Coast University, Florida International University, Florida State University, New College of Florida, University of Central Florida, University of Florida, University of North Florida, University of South Florida, and University of West Florida.

University Press of Florida
2046 NE Waldo Road
Suite 2100
Gainesville, FL 32609
http://upress.ufl.edu

CONTENTS

Dancers Ashley "Colours" Perez and Hollywood Jade of Holla Jazz. Photo by David Hou.

FIGURES

TABLES

Decidedly Jazz Danceworks' Natasha Korney and Kaleb Tekeste (2013). Photo by Trudie Lee Photography. Courtesy of DJD.

PREFACE

This book began as a follow-up to *Jazz Dance: A History of the Roots and Branches*, which looked broadly at twentieth-century jazz dance while investigating its roots. In the years that followed its publication in 2014, conversations within the jazz dance community materialized into a sense that it was time for a more nuanced look at the ways we could identify and honor the Africanist aesthetics and African American continuum of jazz. Furthermore, there was a disconnect between acknowledging the roots of jazz and moving that knowledge into practice. Together as the editors, we imagined a new kind of book on jazz dance: one that stems from a twenty-first-century critical consciousness.

Conversations about jazz are messy. In theory, jazz upholds the enshrined American values of individuality, freedom, democracy, and diversity, appearing to be accessible and available to all. When jazz is positioned in its historical and sociopolitical contexts, however, it becomes evident that it is a mirage. Concealed under the surface is the African American experience, thus, making jazz a dichotomy. This is just like the America we live in: what it is for some, it is not for all.

We first found ourselves entrenched in conversations about racism and ownership while collaborating on *Jazz Dance: A History of the Roots and Branches*. These conversations were frequent among the authors of the book and gained momentum in the years that followed. While some people believed that jazz cannot be considered jazz unless it reflects and embodies its West African roots and the African American experience, others felt that jazz is fluidly evolving and can exist free of limitations. Tangential perspectives weighed the use of jazz music, the presence of ballet versus vernacular movement vocabulary, and whether or not social and improvisational aspects are central to its form.

Jazz Dance was published in 2014 and inspired a National Dance Education Organization (NDEO) conference in the summer of 2016 titled "Jazz Dance: Roots and Branches in Practice." The conversation had shifted by that time so all participants, approximately one hundred dance educators and artists from several countries, were acknowledging and discussing the African roots of jazz.

At that time the atmosphere felt inclusive, making space for jazz styles across the continuum. This "democratic" attitude is made visible in the 2020 documentary *Uprooted: The Journey of Jazz Dance*,[1] where it is made clear that the roots are African and the nature of jazz complex, and yet colonized and codified jazz styles are celebrated and made a visual priority in the film regardless.

What has emerged for many of us in recent years is a restlessness in the form of a new question: Now that we more clearly see the roots, how do we move them into practice? Saying the core is African American but dancing a colonized version of jazz with only traces of Africanist elements felt irresponsible and racially problematic. Many of the authors of this book, most of whom attended the 2016 conference, moved out into their own communities and deepened their practices to unearth the social and kinetic elements of African American vernacular jazz that were often ignored in jazz training. Some had already been doing this for years. For others, the work was new. Many of us came to jazz through training that was colonized, so, regardless of race, there were layers that needed to be peeled away to find authenticity within the jazz form.

The Black and White editors and authors of this book have been negotiating with jazz through our personal lenses, shaped by our racially informed experiences, to chip away and find the truth. In this excavating, two things were discovered: First, that the process of understanding jazz—really and truly seeing and experiencing its magic—involves uprooting racism and looking beneath the training that previously informed our jazz experiences. The more work we do to strip away that which was concealed and altered by Whiteness, the more jazz reveals itself. Second is that there is a potency in authentic community where Black and White[2] members of the jazz community can communicate openly, honestly, and constructively about how they see and experience jazz. For the White members, there is tremendous responsibility in this, as a guest in the form, and also a process of letting go of the values and entitlements that previously seemed to be inclusive for all. For many of the Black members, it involves being heard, seen, and valued as more than equal. Jazz created a gateway for the kind of progress many seek to find in antiracism efforts. Finding the sacred space where jazz is honored as a Black American art form and has the vitality to grow in the twenty-first century, bringing communities together in oral and corporeal realities, proved its limitless potential.

The authors of this book were already writing their chapters when a second NDEO jazz dance conference convened in the summer of 2019, "Jazz Dance: Hybrids, Fusions, Connections, Community." Whereas the first conference embraced the democratic spirit of the first book, the pulse of the 2019

FIGURE 0.1. NDEO's "Jazz Dance: Hybrids, Fusions, Connections, Community" conference, Salve Regina University, August 2019. Photo by Kim Fuller Photography.

conference had shifted. Many were holding tightly onto ballet-based and codified jazz styles, feeling them threatened in conversations about White privilege and colonization. Implicit biases were at the forefront of conversations about vernacular movement as people questioned its value in "formal" training. New questions arose, many of which were framed by the fraught tensions in the American social and political landscape. How could jazz mean such different things for different people? How could jazz be about freedom and democracy if those ideals have never truly been available to the community and culture from which it was born? How can one engage responsibly in jazz if they are not African American? How could one be explicitly antiracist as a jazz dance educator if they have only studied and taught jazz through a colonized lens?

This book is not political, but the issues these authors have investigated have been politicized: Equity. Justice. The Black American Experience. Whiteness. Gender expression. The momentum of the Black Lives Matter movement in the midst of Covid-19 has ushered in a period of deep questioning about what it is to be alive at this specific moment in time, and how our identities shape our realities. In our early conversations discussing the prospect of this new book, our goal was to pick up where *Jazz Dance* left off, giving readers the tools to engage responsibly in a wide range of jazz styles. Over time, our ideas became more focused due to the shifting world around us. Now we can see that this book found its groove because of the complex social and political issues that have saturated our hearts and minds, informing our perspectives on and relationships with jazz. Together, the authors of this book are united in our understanding of jazz dance and in our commitment to dancing, choreographing, and teaching jazz in ways that embody and embrace Africanist aesthetics, and in our efforts to work toward a world that is more just and equitable.

Each of us has taken our own journey to arrive at our current perspectives, as evidenced throughout the pages ahead. Jazz is personal and dynamic; it defines us from the inside out as our circumstances mold us from the outside in. Our journeys will continue as the world changes and as our perspectives shift and evolve. We encourage you to take your individual journey, and we welcome you on our collective one as we approach jazz with care and responsibility, and engage with it from a place of community in celebration of our shared humanity.

NOTES

1. *Uprooted: The Journey of Jazz Dance*, dir. Khadifa Wong (London: On the Rocks Films, 2020).

2. This does not negate or diminish the role of non-Black people of color (POC) in the jazz community but rather acknowledges the critical dialogue between Black and White folks as White people make amends for centuries of cultural theft and appropriation.

In this volume, we, the editors, have made the intentional decision to capitalize Black, Brown, and White when referring to communities of people or specific social practices and codes. We acknowledge that there are different views on using capital versus lowercase letters for these racial identifiers, particularly with the utilization of the capital "W" when referring to White people, ideologies of Whiteness, or White cultural practices. Our choice to use the capital "W" is in support of this book's main theme of restorative practices in creating, teaching, or performing jazz dance. It is our view that restoration can only happen by naming and holding accountable the bodies and systems that have consistently marginalized the original architects of jazz dance. The uppercase "W" is used to signify White as an identity that must be engaged in the discourse on race. This is key, as supremacist ideology seats Whiteness at the center of power, which is the sole driver of the erasure of Black and Brown people, aesthetics, and culture from the jazz dance narrative. The Center for the Study of Social Policy frames the issue as follows:

> To not name "White" as a race is, in fact, an anti-Black act which frames Whiteness as both neutral and the standard. . . . We believe that it is important to call attention to White as a race as a way to understand and give voice to how Whiteness functions in our social and political institutions and our communities. Moreover, the detachment of "White" as a proper noun allows White people to sit out of conversations about race and removes accountability from White people's and White institutions' involvement in racism.[1]

As scholar Kwame Anthony Appiah states, "Black and White are both historically created racial identities," and we should avoid grammatical conventions that encourage us to forget this.[2] In addition to Appiah, Nguyễn, and Pendleton, the American Psychological Association also follows this practice.[3] We agree that moving the conversation forward requires acknowledging the existence of Black, Brown, and White cultural identities through capitalization. Any exceptions to this rule are in quoted material; it is important to note that it is only recently that the capitalization of Black has become best practice. These decisions were made with consideration and care in the hope of restoring Black voices as primary in the creation of jazz dance.

In the same spirit of intentionality and critical awareness, we feel it is important to acknowledge our racial identities. As a Black editor (Jones), I come to this project fully aware of my role and the duality that accompanies that role. I act as welcoming curator of multiple voices while also operating as judicious champion for the Black voice within the content. It is important to state that my role was self-imposed and not assigned. I am not the gatekeeper of all things Black. Rather, my intent is to recognize the effects of colonization on us all and remain open to each author's perspective, yet call upon each of us, myself included, to move the conversation forward while amplifying the voice of the marginalized. As White editors (Guarino and Oliver), we recognize our privilege and also the delicate space we occupy as editors of a book on a Black American art form. We do not aim to position ourselves as experts on Black American culture or antiracism but instead hope to use our privilege to restore jazz by challenging systems of oppression and injustice. We are listening and learning, with immense gratitude for the Black members of our jazz community who are some of our greatest teachers, and commit to continued growth in the future. These pages are a product of true kinship, the result of community and conversation among editors and authors with a deep respect for each other and love for the form that brought us all together: jazz.

NOTES

1. Ann Thúy Nguyễn and Maya Pendleton, "Recognizing Race in Language: Why We Capitalize "Black" and "White," Center for the Study of Social Policy, https://cssp.org/2020/03/recognizing-race-in-language-why-we-capitalize-black-and-white/.

2. Kwame Anthony Appiah, "The Case for Capitalizing the *B* in Black," *The Atlantic*, June 18, 2020, www.theatlantic.com/ideas/archive/2020/06/time-to-capitalize-black-and-white/613159/.

3. American Psychological Association, https://apastyle.apa.org/style-grammar-guidelines/bias-free-language/racial-ethnic-minorities#:~:text=Racial%20and%20ethnic%20groups%20are,Hispanic%2C%E2%80%9D%20and%20so%20on.

Introduction

LINDSAY GUARINO, CARLOS R. A. JONES,
AND WENDY OLIVER

The United States is in a period of recognizing past and present instances of systemic racism. As we write this introduction, protests and riots rage across the country in anguish over the killing of Black citizen George Floyd by a White Minneapolis police officer. Floyd's death is only one in an ongoing litany of Black men and women killed in the name of law enforcement ever since the onset of slavery in 1619. Meanwhile, Covid-19 is tearing through our population, with far more devastating consequences for people of color than for White folks. The unequal treatment of people of color, and African Americans in particular, is a legacy of slavery and the open wounds that remained after Emancipation in the late nineteenth century.

Scholar bell hooks reminds us that "again and again visionary thinkers on the subject of race encourage us to confront directly and honestly the way in which White supremacist ideology informs the lives of everyone in our nation to a greater or lesser degree . . . White supremacist thinking informs the consciousness of everyone irrespective of skin color."[1] hooks goes on to say that if we can accept this truth, then we can move beyond binaries: "Unless we make a conscious effort to change thought and action by honestly naming all the myriad ways white supremacy impinges on daily life, then we cannot shift from a politics of hate and create a new foundation based on a revolution of love."[2] White people in particular need to understand how American culture has developed so that "Whiteness" is invisible, and how that invisibility allows Whiteness to be the dominant sociopolitical and psychic force shaping our society.

Once we understand the pervasive nature of Whiteness, it is vital to acknowledge racism in ourselves and fight against it in every way possible. Activist and author Ibram X. Kendi explains that most people in our society

FIGURE O.2.
Juneteenth celebra-
tion and protest,
June 19, 2020,
Providence, Rhode
Island. Photo by
Wendy Oliver.

today consider themselves "not racist": "What's the problem with being 'not racist'? It is a claim that signifies neutrality . . . But there is no neutrality in the racism struggle . . . [T]he opposite of 'racist' isn't 'not racist.' It's antiracist."[3] Kendi tells us that the key is finding where the power lies to make positive change, and to create policies that can change lives. Kendi's Boston University Center for Antiracist Research does that by bringing together researchers and practitioners across disciplines to better understand and fight racial inequity and injustice.[4] Research, education, advocacy and policy innovation all work hand-in-hand to bring about change.

As Black and White dance educators and artists, the editors of this book feel a responsibility to future and current generations of students, teachers, and artists to address the racism and some of the past injustices within our own field. We may not personally be able to prevent racism across our country, but we can look at instances in our own field where harm has been inflicted and work to correct them. We look at this as a form of reparations.

In June 2019, the 116th U.S. Congress passed the HR40 Bill, which established the Commission to Study and Develop Reparation Proposals for African-Americans Act.[5] Additionally, reparations are a current topic of discussion at some institutions of higher learning, where the use of slave labor to build historic campuses is being acknowledged. Some of the institutions joining the discussion include the University of Virginia, Georgetown University, University of Wisconsin, Madison, and University of Mississippi.[6] Likewise, the dance community needs to uncover, acknowledge, and begin to make reparations to the African American arts community, including the many artists who are the unsung innovators and pioneers of jazz dance. This book is a small step in that direction.

In these pages, we present the obscured story of how normalized Whiteness has permeated our dance culture to such an extent that dance educators, performers, and choreographers have been participating unawares in a misguided appropriation of artistic capital. In order to unpack this dilemma, we describe, analyze, affirm, and celebrate the Africanist aesthetic in jazz dance, which has often been overlooked within the jazz dance world since the mid-twentieth century. This common understanding will help us all be more informed creators, performers, scholars, and teachers; it will continue the narrative of investigating African American forms within dance. In 1993, scholar Sally Banes pointed out Balanchine's use of jazz dance characteristics, noting that, when choreographing *Agon,* "Balanchine specifically borrows from an African-rooted aesthetic, introducing into the classical ballet vocabulary the angular arms, curved torso, percussive footwork, syncopated rhythms, and claps, slaps, and fingersnaps of African American jazz dancing. The music, too, bears traces of jazz influences."[7] Brenda Dixon Gottschild made a similar observation in her influential essay "Stripping the Emperor: The Africanist Presence in American Concert Dance": "The Africanist presence in Balanchine's works is a story of particular and specific motifs . . . from ballets that span the course of his career. In other words, these were not dispensable, decorative touches that marked one or two ballets; rather, they were essential ingredients in his canon."[8] These revelations led the dance world to look more closely at the assumption that American ballet was/is a solely European-based form.

We are continuing in this tradition of revealing and celebrating the Africanist presence in American dance, albeit within the realm of jazz dance. Although some people know that jazz dance has roots in the African diaspora, there is no clear, common understanding of what that means and how it expresses itself physically and emotionally through movement. Many dancers today are unaware that jazz dance comes from Black American people and culture because they have been taught by (mostly) White teachers who do not include historical context as part of their teaching. One way that we editors know of this lack is through our own teaching. Each of us has worked with experienced dance students who are surprised to find out that the history of jazz dance did not start with White artists such as Jack Cole or Bob Fosse. The lack of recognition of the African and African American roots of jazz dance is a product of racism and appropriation, which has influenced the trajectory of the art form.

In our first book, *Jazz Dance: A History of the Roots and Branches* (2014),[9] jazz dance was conceptualized and diagrammed as a tree, with African roots, European influences, and a trunk consisting of African American vernacular dance. There are many different branches extending from the tree, including hip-hop, musical theater, lyrical, and Latin jazz, to name a few. That book focused mainly upon the history of jazz dance and incorporated all branches of the tree, including discussions of the many genres of dance with African roots that are not specifically "jazz." In contrast, this volume does not attempt to look at all forms of dance with African roots but instead examines jazz practices that are "rooted," meaning they clearly acknowledge and incorporate an Africanist aesthetic. For a comprehensive study of early to mid-twentieth-century jazz dance, Marshall Stearns and Jean Stearns's *Jazz Dance: The Story of American Vernacular Dance* is excellent,[10] and there are several others on Black dance in the United States that provide important, detailed historical information and documentation on African diasporic forms.[11]

The same jazz tree appears in this book but is discussed differently. As editors, we are considering the climate and external factors affecting the tree more than the various styles represented in the branches. Picture the jazz tree, planted in American soil on land stolen from Native Americans and laden with the remains of genocidal violence, its roots West African but anchored in America only because of the forced enslavement of Black people. From its origins, the jazz tree has weathered the impacts of a climate saturated with racism. While we cannot change the past, we can change the climate where the tree grows by eradicating White supremacy and providing nourishment for future blossoms to emerge.

In order to change the climate where the jazz tree grows, this book looks closely at jazz dance as an art form, and how it expresses an Africanist aesthetic in a way that is uniquely African American. This book does not offer a comprehensive history of jazz dance but, instead, a particular perspective that is timely for the twenty-first century, as our country collectively examines the history of race in the United States. To aid in this discussion, we have included the poem "I Am Jazz" by Cory Bowles at the end of this introduction, which personifies jazz dance to tell the arc of its history while providing context for the spirit of jazz in the pages that follow.

Identifying Africanist aesthetics as the root, or primary source, for jazz dance offers an important foundation for how jazz can be understood and embodied today. The term "Africanist," as described by scholar Brenda Dixon Gottschild, "includes concepts, practices, attitudes, or forms that have roots/ origins in Africa and the African diaspora."[12] Africanist aesthetics planted the seeds for the movement characteristics unique to jazz: rhythm generated from the inside out, improvisation, personal style, and individuality within community. However, by the time jazz emerged in the 1920s, approximately forty years after Emancipation, it reflected a cultural identity that was distinctly African American. Through centuries of blending Africanist movement aesthetics from disparate African countries and tribes, displaced through enslavement and influenced by European and Latin American aesthetics, the emerging jazz language was complex by nature. This connection between the African roots and the African American vernacular trunk of the jazz tree is described as the "missing link" by author Patricia Cohen in our first book: "Acknowledging the entirety of the genre allows us to establish historical, cultural, social, and kinetic continuity," or what Cohen calls a continuum.[13]

For this reason, aesthetics cannot be discussed apart from their cultural, sociopolitical, and historical contexts. The word "Equity" in the title of this book points to the ways we can value, amplify, and honor African American people and culture through jazz choreography, pedagogy, and curriculum. Furthermore, seeing jazz in relation to the Black American experience illuminates the reasons why jazz has been devalued on concert dance stages and in the academy. To truly see jazz, the entire continuum from its roots to today, is to see racism in America. Identifying the impacts of White supremacy and Western ideology provides an opportunity for revising current practices and examining biases, which elevates jazz as a deserving and valued American art form. Striving toward equity means working toward a future where the Black members of the jazz community feel their ancestors have been fully acknowledged, when authentic community is experienced in dialogue across races, and when jazz dance is fully accepted as an art form no less than its Euro-American counterparts.

Although the gravity of this responsibility is enormous, it also carries the potential for not only cultivating empathy and kinship but for unearthing a fertile and exciting ground for creating and teaching jazz. Tapping into the aesthetic foundation that birthed jazz has the potential to ignite the same

FIGURE 0.3. Holla Jazz rehearsing *Dances with Trane* (2020). Dancers (*left to right*): Tereka Tyler-Davis, Ashley "Colours" Perez, Hollywood Jade. Musicians (*left to right*): Jacob Gorzhaltsan, Ewen Farncombe, Lowell Whitty, Alexander Brown, Tom Richards, Scott Hunter. Photograph by Francesca Chudnoff.

spark responsible for its initial genesis, keeping jazz alive and thriving into the future. Investing in improvisation and individuality opens the door to holistic creative processes and classroom environments, and uniting music, rhythm, and movement together inspires a potentially transcendent experience.

Jazz has been defined as restless, quick to absorb new influences and evolve with the times, ever-American with its eye on the next new thing. Keeping choreography and pedagogy dedicated to this very ingenuity relies on a commitment to the past, to the people and culture forced to adapt and expected to assimilate and remain resilient and creative in the midst of incomprehensible acts of inhumanity. We can continue to let the fluid nature of jazz inspire new innovation, but not without resisting the societal forces that threaten to absorb and obscure African American culture, including its vernacular dance.

ROOTED JAZZ DANCE

Although jazz dance and music are rooted in West African culture, it is the blending of African diasporic and White European movement and music in the United States that created jazz. Marshall Stearns notes in *The Story of Jazz*, "The famous semanticist S. I. Hayakawa is of the opinion that, if the Negro had been fully assimilated, we should have had no jazz; if the Negro had been completely unassimilated, his music would still be more or less African—as in Haiti today—and without much influence on the rest of our music."[14] Jazz exists as a product of the African American experience; when cultures fused in different countries and under different circumstances, even when impacted by colonization and slavery, the resulting forms took on personalities and aesthetic feels unique to the locale.

While it is widely accepted that jazz has West African roots, there are certainly many different ideas about what jazz dance should or could look like since the blending of elements can vary from style to style. In this book, the authors put forward a variety of observations about some core elements of American jazz dance and also use a variety of terms meant to reflect the nuances within the genre. While different authors describe jazz in different ways, "rooted" has emerged as both a descriptive term and unifying perspective among the authors. "Rooted jazz" is not a style of jazz; it is a philosophy that prioritizes an historically informed and culturally responsible way of teaching, choreographing, and performing jazz. The authors in this book do not feel that it is enough to merely acknowledge the roots of jazz as West African. Instead, rooted jazz is a promise to honor the African American experience and essence of jazz in every way possible. Working in a way that is rooted is explicitly antiracist, evident through movement and music choices, language and pedagogy used in the classroom, and shaping of curriculum. It is applicable to every style on the jazz tree.[15] The parameters for dancing, teaching, and choreographing rooted jazz dance are not exclusive to any one people, race, or culture, but they involve a curiosity, respect, and self-awareness—an acknowledgment of who you are and what your connection is to the roots.

To understand where rooted jazz exists, it is first important to note that there is a broad spectrum of dance that includes jazz elements. Melanie George aptly points out in her essay in this volume that "the tradition of Black dance has eschewed the need for clear boundaries between dance forms." Therefore, Black dance companies such as Alvin Ailey American Dance Theatre and Philadanco blend jazz, modern, ballet, and African diasporic styles; often this results in a phenomenon that George calls "jazzy." She defines jazzy as works "that reflect or retain the characteristics of jazz over time without being defined exclusively by jazz." Wendy Oliver uses a similar umbrella term, "jazz-related," in her chapter on professional jazz dance. Jazz-related includes choreographers and companies "who utilize[d] jazz elements in their work, but are typically identified as modern, ballet, or musical theater." Using the labels "jazzy," "jazz-related," and "jazz-influenced" provides a framework for identifying jazz elements where they exist, and for recognizing the far-reaching influence of jazz around the world.

Identifying jazz that is "rooted" is far narrower than the above-mentioned spectrum of jazz by comparison. Rooted jazz dance is tethered to the African American vernacular trunk of the jazz tree, rich in Africanist aesthetics, connected to jazz music, and reflects elements of the Black American experience. A rooted aesthetic cannot be expressed through Eurocentric body placement alone. As Lindsay Guarino explains in chapter 7, "if vernacular movement is absent, as we see in jazz dance when it is reduced to leaps, turns, and leg extensions, then the jazz is absent. Seeing expressive but unaffected bodies moving authentically with rhythm and style, and without ballet-derived posture or technique, is to find vernacular movement." With these terms in mind, consider times when jazz is performed with a lengthened spine, lifted chest and held torso. This aesthetic is not rooted and might be more accurately described as "jazz-influenced." Conversely, rooted jazz can be found outside studios and in social functions, especially in Black American communities where dance is passed down as corporeal knowledge and tradition. Author LaTasha Barnes explains this in her chapter, where she calls her family her first "performance educators."

Moncell Durden opens his chapter by questioning the title "vernacular jazz," since that is the original jazz dance and should be called simply "jazz." Everything that came after would then need a descriptive adjective, such as "theatrical jazz" or "West Coast jazz." Durden closes by reiterating that "jazz dance is rooted in the vernacular expression of tap, eccentric dance, Lindy Hop, and solo dances such as the Charleston and the Mooch." Jazz that lacks a strong foundation in the Africanist aesthetic is not jazz but rather "jazz approximation." When jazz incorporates a preponderance of Eurocentric rather than Afrocentric aesthetics, it is not rooted; when jazz is primarily vernacular-bodied and rich in Africanist aesthetics, it is rooted.

Julie Kerr-Berry focuses upon the Africanist elements within jazz dance, which are fundamental to rootedness. Interestingly, some styles that are not always thought of as jazz are inherently more rooted than many contemporary jazz styles today. In identifying examples of various characteristics, she describes call-and-response, coupled with improvisation, as common among tap dancers, and cites the Hoofers Club in Harlem as a place where friendly challenges took place. In the twenty-first century, we recognize tap and jazz as two entirely separate dance forms, but in the 1920s through the 1940s, they were evolving side by side, both based on West African roots. Constance Valis Hill's book *Brotherhood in Rhythm: The Jazz Tap Dancing of the Nicholas Brothers* states: "Jazz tap dance developed in direct relationship to jazz music in the twenties, thirties, and forties, sharing rhythmic motifs, polyrhythms, multiple meters, elements of swing . . . and structured improvisation." The Nicholas Brothers danced to the jazz music of that era, "for jazz dance cannot and did not exist isolated from its musical counterpart."[16] Thus, tap dance of the jazz era and subsequent tap styles that retain the foundational qualities of jazz can be considered a type of rooted jazz dance.

The idea that some dance is "rooted jazz" whereas other approaches may be "jazzy," "jazz-related," or "jazz-influenced" is emblematic of the notion that jazz dance includes some core principles; assessing the rootedness depends on how each element is expressed in relationship to the jazz continuum. It is important to note, as Carlos Jones explains in chapter 6, that "inquiry into an African element through written form is the antithesis of its original practice . . . Regardless, the conversation is necessary to get to the task of demystifying jazz dance technique." Rooting jazz practices, or what Jones describes as "a call to the exiled origins," is not a methodology or a guaranteed formula for creating jazz—jazz is much more elusive than that. Regardless, Africanist elements are discussed throughout this book in a variety of ways to help identify the touchstones for embarking on a journey to find jazz. When Julie Kerr-Berry outlines foundational Africanist elements of jazz in her chapter, such as "cool," "call-and-response," "improvisation," and "get-down," she offers examples for each. Lindsay Guarino expands this list by recalling Pat Cohen's list of social and kinetic elements from *Jazz Dance: A History of the Roots and Branches,* which includes elements such as "joyousness," "confrontational attitude," "community," and "embellishment," among others. Guarino adds jazz-specific elements such as "jazz and jazz-influenced music," "groove," and "jazz energy" to help assess the proximity of jazz to its roots via the African American vernacular continuum, noting that jazz does not emerge from Africanist elements alone and that there are elements of the African American experience that are distinct and essential to the jazz language. References to the works of scholars Robert Farris Thompson, Brenda Dixon Gottschild, Marshall Stearns and Jean Stearns, and Jacqui Malone are cited by authors throughout this book for the ways they have identified and described Africanist elements in their seminal texts. All combined, discussion of these elements provides inroads to finding, through personal and communal exploration, the essence of jazz. Expressing each Africanist and African American element through the jazz-dancing body—whether consciously (intentional decolonization) or not (trusting lived experience and retaining cultural tradition)—is the act of responsible (rooted) jazz practices.

BOOK OVERVIEW

The book is divided into five major parts, the first of which is "The Place of Jazz Dance in Twenty-First-Century North America." This section, with four chapters, starts with a broad overview of jazz dance and some of the controversies embedded within it. Chapter 1 gives an overview of jazz dance today, looking at the array of jazz styles, companies, and groups practicing and performing this dance genre. A look at how jazz dance is valued in our culture follows in chapter 2, as measured by numbers such as dance company budgets and prizes awarded in the field. Chapter 3 is a look at how jazz dance fractured from its roots due to racism, Eurocentric biases, and White privilege, and how that has led to a lack of understanding among jazz dance practitioners about the roots of the art form. Chapter 4 concludes the section with a focus on the issue of appropriation by examining some specific styles and steps that were created in the Black dance community, then adapted and adopted by the White community without attribution.

Part II, "Analyzing Aesthetics," focuses on the Africanist elements of jazz dance, and their presence, or lack thereof, in jazz choreography of the twentieth and twenty-first century. First, chapter 5 describes and analyzes specific Africanist elements with examples to elevate the reader's understanding of each term. Chapter 6 questions the meaning of the term "technique" as applied to jazz dance, offering a way of understanding technique specific to the jazz form along with an example of specific technical elements. Finally, chapter 7 offers an approach for viewing and analyzing jazz dance, giving readers the tools to determine how "rooted" any given piece of choreography might be.

Part III, "Choreography and Performance of Jazz Dance," is divided into two sections. The first includes a group of four artist statements about choreography and performance in this art form. Each artist gives an individual perspective on how they approach their work, what inspires them, and how they relate to the Africanist elements embedded within their artistry. The second section offers rooted perspectives on making and performing jazz, including the Black experience in jazz dance, the expectations of females within jazz dance aesthetics and performance, and fundamentals of jazz choreography.

Part IV, "Teaching Jazz Dance," focuses on pedagogy in the studio, classroom, and beyond. Chapters focus on topics including vernacular jazz dance, teaching jazz rooted in African cultural values, culturally relevant jazz dance pedagogy, teaching rooted jazz dance in the public high school, teaching a Black dance form as a White instructor, creating a jazz dance lecture-demonstration for touring in the community, and decolonizing jazz dance history.

The authors in this section are performers, choreographers, scholars, artistic directors, department chairs, and dance educators teaching at a variety of institutions including private studios, public schools, and universities, across the United States and Canada, and bring practice-based expertise to their discussions, offering exciting ideas for implementation.

The final section, part V, "The Future of Jazz Dance," comprises two chapters. The first follows three different themes, including the discussion of jazz as a Black American art form; interconnections between jazz music and jazz dance; and the future of jazz studies in the academy. The second chapter is a personal statement by choreographer and teacher Carlos Jones, explaining his understanding of how race and colonization have shaped his own development as an artist, and how he has come to terms with that. He closes with a call for change for all those in the jazz dance field.

This book is intended for all who love jazz dance and want to learn more about its contested and complex history, as well as its practice today. It particularly supports those who choreograph, perform, and teach jazz dance in the twenty-first century, and those who are seeking a deeper understanding of Africanist aesthetic principles and jazz in connection to Black American culture. We offer the reader a variety of author perspectives that are linked through their intention to honor the West African and African American roots of jazz dance, and further, to create positive change through exposing and acknowledging the role of race and racism in the development of this art form.

NOTES

1. bell hooks, "Racism," in *Writing Beyond Race: Living Theory and Practice* (New York: Routledge, 2013), 11.

2. Ibid., 12.

3. Ibram X. Kendi, *How to Be an Antiracist* (New York: One World, 2019), 9.

4. Boston University Center for Antiracist Research website, https://www.bu.edu/antiracism-center/.

5. U.S. Congress website, www.congress.gov/bill/116th-congress/house-bill/40.

6. Mariah Bohanon, "Research and Reconciliation: Some Universities Work to Ensure an Inclusive Future by Acknowledging Their Inequitable Pasts," *Insight into Diversity Magazine,* October 18, 2018, www.insightintodiversity.com/research-and-reconciliation-some-universities-work-to-ensure-an-inclusive-future-by-acknowledging-their-inequitable-pasts/.

7. Sally Banes, "Modern Ballet," in *Dancing Women: Female Bodies on Stage* (New York: Routledge, 1998), 195. Banes references her earlier publication "Balanchine and Black Dance," *Choreography and Dance* 3, no. 3 (1993).

8. Brenda Dixon Gottschild, "Stripping the Emperor: The Africanist Presence in American Concert Dance," in *Moving History/Dancing Cultures,* ed. Ann Dils and Ann Cooper Albright (Middletown, CT: Wesleyan University Press, 2001), 339.

9. Lindsay Guarino and Wendy Oliver, eds., *Jazz Dance: A History of the Roots and Branches* (Gainesville: University Press of Florida, 2014).

10. Marshall Stearns and Jean Stearns, *Jazz Dance: The Story of American Vernacular Dance* (New York: Macmillan, 1968).

11. See, for example, Thomas DeFrantz, *Dancing Many Drums* (Madison: University of Wisconsin Press, 2002); Jacqui Malone, *Steppin' on the Blues: The Visible Rhythms of African American Dance* (Champaign: University of Illinois Press, 1996); Lynne Fauley Emery, *Black Dance: From 1619 to Today* (Trenton, NJ: Princeton Book Company, 1989); and John Perpener, *African American Concert Dance: The Harlem Renaissance and Beyond* (Champaign: University of Illinois Press, 2005).

12. Brenda Dixon Gottschild, *The Black Dancing Body* (New York: Palgrave Macmillan, 2003), xiii.

13. Patricia Cohen, "Jazz Dance as a Continuum," in *Jazz Dance: A History of the Roots and Branches* (Gainesville: University Press of Florida, 2014), 3–7.

14. Marshall W. Stearns, "Jazz and the Role of the Negro," in *The Story of Jazz* (New York: Oxford University Press: 1956), 308.

15. Establishing a rooted connection requires more effort in some styles—like lyrical jazz—than others.

16. Constance Valis Hill, *Brotherhood in Rhythm: The Jazz Tap Dancing of the Nicholas Brothers* (New York: Oxford University Press, 2000), 4.

I Am Jazz

CORY BOWLES

I am Jazz.
I am The Beginning.
I am West Africa . . .

I am the soul, expression, life, drum, can you hear it?
Ceremonial, grounded, uplifting, invoking spirits.
Come near it, I'm infectious. Sophisticated, rhythm complex.
I am the current through the body when foot flexed and ground connects.
I am both music and dancer combined,
Intertwined . . . The first of my kind.
I speak through the rhythm and sing with my torso
My mantra, my force is
"Dance on bended knee lest you be mistaken for a corpse."

I am Jazz.
I am The Raid . . .
When Europeans invade, and move our bodies for trade,
We meet Irish sailors and make sounds with our feet . . .
Way down below ship decks in darkness I still manage to glow . . .
And grow
And what do you know . . .
I'm sowing seeds for tap,
But we'll come back to that.
For now hit new land and my hands are clapping.
I season myself with Caribbean and Latin
And gain satisfaction through
Hips, body, love, lust and passion. Sexy, hot, and spicy.

A new recipe . . .
But still me

I am Jazz.
I am Tradition . . .
I am the transition
With musicality, vitality, growth, maturation.
I am a slave dancing in secret on plantations.
Where upstairs and downstairs mix at sundown, to sarcastically comment.
My cakewalks, my sound is accented on downbeats,
All rally spirits through call-and-response.
Sweet chariots Swing Low, my grace is amazing.
I am West African and European successfully phasing
And still . . .
I move on

In time I find
I'm now free. Inclined to do what I choose.
No longer in chains and sung out in fields. I move

To New Orleans and reflect on my blues.
My blues.
Yeah,
The blues with all sorts of new hues.
You know me as the one who still uses West African grooves.
And stories return,
That strike nerves.
Singing about my baby
Leaving and such
Mmmhmm. Oh yeah.

But wait . . . I'm in two places at once.
Cause over there I got
Horns and brass bands and much
Celebration and clutter and bang
I'm Marching in the saints
And becoming ragtime.
I strut.
Got my turkey trot. Light-hearted chaos
Cluttered with creativity joining my blues . . .

And we fuse.
New page.
A new rage, a new entity as . . .
I am reborn
A new era of jazz.

I am Jazz.
I am an Era . . .
I am Political . . .
I am Outspoken.
And I Charleston and strut like there ain't no tomorrow.
I pluck from all cultures.
Stay true, trust and borrow,
And take it to the stage they brand me as vaudeville.
While I bring down the house they go nuts, they applaud 'till.
They decide that they'll take me and make me their own.
Not borrow,
But steal.
Not real, but all wrong.
I fight for integrity
While they're taking me and making me stiff.
Freezing my torso, and locking my hips.

There's too many I can't stop it I'm losing control.

Lose all my movement
But I still got my soul.
So gather my belongings and open up a new shop.
I take my partner by the hand and do the Lindy Hop.

Now, we the cats in the corner of
The Savoy ballroom where the big bands will swing,
And the songbirds will sing as we do our thing
On the floor until we can dance no more.
But
No more . . .
Is because
We all go to war.
I am empty,
Alone with no dancers . . .

No music shows.
They tax my dance floor
And my dance halls close.
My dance
Is now song.
My song is now music.
My music is changing.
I find new ways to use it

I am Jazz.
I will not stop . . .
I am in clubs
Where they listen to me and christen me with the name Be-bop.
Where I'm faster
And innovative.
Hard to contain.
Improvise and realize my aesthetic
Has transferred fully into music that's kinetic and frenetic . . .
And magnetic.
Using my scat . . .
I'm sometimes confusing
But cruising,
With no choice but to move once again.
And get low.
Like real low.
Grounded.
Hoofing.
Talking to the floor.
To ground making sound with my feet once more.
I am percussive.

I am drum. I am rhythm.

I am shuffle ball change. I am flap.
I am drop roll heel.
A new instrument.
My body.
My tap.
Like that.
And that.

But not that.
See that?
It's lost all the riff
Taking me to places I'm not comfortable with.
And that right there's another false image of me.
Where they forgot how to feel and they only see . . .
The pedagogy.
Meaning steps and rules in studios and schools,
That fuse out my soul, my roots and my tools.
Line us up like fools. I can't even speak
When I see them incorporate some other technique
Of image and look.
It seems they forgot
That soul and feeling just can't be taught.
And they got me lined up in chorus line fashion
In kick lines and Broadway where I'm losing passion
Losing my roots.
My flavourful mixture now watered-down juice
With unnatural taste, a waste, a disgrace.
A history in danger of being erased.
When we improvised through music and song. Don't you get it?
When the body would go where the music would let it.
When elements combined traditions whose echoes are residual and
Celebrate each voice as one individual.
But I will not give up.
I move on and mature.
My change . . .
My next phase again

I am Jazz
I am New York . . .
I am rediscovered, and recovered, from being smothered.
Given new life with nuance,
Contractions, knee slides, isolations, runs.
They name them the fathers; they are really my sons.
I am Robbins, Mattox, Luigi, Cole, Thelonious, Dizzy, Ray, Wynton,
    Maceo . . .
I am Jazz.
My family is well over a dozen.

Allow me to introduce you to my cousins:
Hip-Hop. R&B. Funk. Rock 'n' Roll.
No need for straight lines,
My lines are straight soul
Bring this back.
Bring it back.
Bring it back.

Man what happened to my beats, my drums, my torso, my hips?
I don't ever remember asking for glitter and glitz.
And these bits with straight lines where body is stiff.
Man, I'm calling it quits
If it goes like this.
And I hate to diss,
But where is the bliss?
When the music's in my body like a slow sexy kiss?
Where rumba's not ballroom but down to the earth?
Where a clave and bell call and pelvis have worth?
Now I'm picking pieces since my spirit was lost.
A former list of critical bits.
Has now been crossed.
The cost is no less than
Tearing me apart.
Deteriorates my body . . . especially the heart.
No spirit no groove . . .
I can't take it anymore!

I am Jazz.
I am ever-changing.
I am rearranging.
I am celebration but . . .
I am a wanderer
With very few homes.
I find one of them here
Where those close to me won't let my soul disappear.
With joy and love, essentials and the beat,
A node where all my fundamentals meet.
So they can celebrate through me, giving my life new start.
It's a funny place to find jazz.

But you can tell
These people have it in their hearts.
I am Jazz.
We are Jazz.
You ... Me ... Everybody
Now ...
Feel it.

NOTE

In 2009, Decidedly Jazz Danceworks commissioned Bowles to write "I Am Jazz" for their twenty-fifth anniversary celebration.

Decidedly Jazz Danceworks in rehearsal (2016). Photo by Noel Begin. Courtesy of DJD.

I

The Place of Jazz Dance in Twenty-First-Century North America

Jazz dance, rooted in African diasporic movement, has been used to describe disparate forms and styles of dance, many of which were explored in the book *Jazz Dance: A History of the Roots and Branches* (2014). Moving the conversation forward into the twenty-first century, part I of this book focuses on different aspects of jazz dance as an art form in North America today, rooting contemporary jazz dance in its social, cultural, and historical contexts. Each of the four chapters investigates and reveals some truths about this contested and complex art form.

Melanie George begins with survey of the viability of jazz dance in the twenty-first century, with a focus on authentic, concert, and commercial styles in performance, educational institutions, and the media. George argues for the importance of context and nuance when considering any dance style called jazz, differentiating rooted jazz dance from dance that is jazz-influenced, or jazz in name only, for the overall health and long-term survival of the form.

In chapter 2, Wendy Oliver looks at the status of professional jazz dance today with a review of jazz companies and their budgets, grants and awards received, and summer dance festivals and intensives. In a culture that equates success with money and awards, jazz dance has never had equal standing with other, Whiter, dance forms.

Lindsay Guarino's chapter 3 analyzes articles on jazz dance written in the early to mid-twentieth century to investigate how Whiteness led the jazz dance continuum to fracture from its origins in African American people and culture. Guarino interrogates the master narrative through an antiracist lens, explaining that jazz will not be fully valued or understood until we recognize and repudiate the systems and ideologies that marginalize African American people and culture.

In chapter 4, E. Moncell Durden identifies "Afro-kinetic memory" as the movement and cultural knowledge that is inherently passed down from one generation to the next, linking roots in West Africa to African American vernacular dance throughout history. He elucidates this by tracing the evolution of the Camel Walk and the Charleston, and explains how Whiteness threatens the jazz form by erasing essential Africanist characteristics from the aesthetic.

All four chapters form a context for the remainder of the book, which centers Black American experience, artistry, and aesthetic principles as the core of jazz dance today.

An Overview of Jazz Dance
in the Twenty-First Century

MELANIE GEORGE

Jazz is temporal, somehow managing to be both timely and timeless in every era. From its earliest days in the early twentieth century, while rooted in West African elements, jazz music and its accompanying dances were consistently positioned by creators, critics, and fans as art for the progressive and adventurous. The work of the individuals who rose to prominence in this era reflects a preoccupation with the coexistence of what is and what can be. Fitting, as this is the proposition of the great American experiment, a nation theoretically founded on the principle of democracy for the collective and the individual. More than a century after the birth of jazz, we have come to understand that experimentation does not come without cost and casualty. For every pioneering movement and popular style, there are names of individual contributors relegated to the margins or forgotten altogether. The network of steps and styles is sometimes reconfigured to suit overly neat narratives that are often grounded in colonist values that date back to the earliest encounters of White people and enslaved Africans. The history and evolution of jazz is rich . . . and problematic, but jazz survives, and thrives, because of, not in spite of, its many changes.

Jazz is at a crossroads of our own making, on a path toward reconciling the democratic nature of a form that purposefully makes space for a variety of perspectives, while also attempting a cooperative alliance to increase visibility and representation in the academy, the club, and on stage and screen. This push and pull between the vanguard and the old guard is not unique to jazz, but it seems notable given the history of the form. Jazz music scholars Gerald Early and Ingrid Monson captured this sentiment in their 2019 essay "Why Jazz Still Matters": "But if jazz was, at one point in its history, about freeing oneself from artificial and arbitrary constraints in both popular and classical music, about freeing society from its restrictions and repressions, then, for many of its fans and practitioners, it has now become about preserving and conserving a tradition, an ideology, a set of standards, a form of practice. Today, jazz is an art that can satisfy the compulsions of the liberationist and the conservative, of those who seek change and of those who prefer stasis."[1] This duality is not inherently problematic, as the coexistence of stasis and shift has created an opportunity for dance educators and scholars to realign or debunk historical narratives toward decolonizing the history of the form. In the chronicling of origin and evolution, the Africanist roots of jazz were sublimated in favor of an alternate, ahistorical narrative that asserts that "real" jazz technique and training begins with White male practitioners in the 1930s, and favors ballet-influenced styles within the academy and onstage. This has been damaging to the proposition of jazz as equal in rigor and value as other dance forms. The Western dance training model promotes ballet as essential to all training, and fundamental to learning jazz. In academia, African diasporic dance forms are often electives within the curriculum, whereas ballet and modern technique courses are required.[2] This is a feat of trickery, where modern and ballet are simultaneously deemed essential to our culture while being absent of cultural designation. Obviously, this is false, as ballet bears the markings of its European cultural leanings as clearly as any other dance form. Ballet cannot be the foundation of a form that originated from an entirely different culture. Moreover, if the existence of jazz demands studying other forms concurrently to be competent, what could possibly make jazz essential to any curriculum? This lens has been replicated in academia and the private sector, in all forms of media, and in many of our history texts. As we reconcile fallacy, erasure, and the inherent White supremacy of that narrative, we are required to consider what we value about jazz dance. It takes nothing away from the contributions of the architects of ballet and modern-influenced theatrical and concert jazz dance to rightfully acknowledge the true origins of the form and the marginalization of Black and Brown people within it. The movement toward decolonizing practices in jazz pedagogy and scholarship is an indicator of the health and progressiveness of present-day jazz.

When considering jazz dance today, we see that the range of activity is divided into subsets, with communities demarcated by branches of the jazz family tree, and little to no cross-pollination among the different populations. The authentic jazz dancers are not in dialogue with the classical jazz dancers, who have relatively limited contact with the tap and street dance communities. In an effort to locate jazz dance in the United States and abroad, I conducted research over a sixteen-month period from 2017 to 2018, with the intent of creating a comprehensive directory of jazz dance activity in the United States and abroad for students, educators, artists, and enthusiasts. I was most interested in updating the list of dance companies in the appendix of *Jazz Dance: A History of the Roots and Branches*.[3] Since the publication of that book in 2014, new dance companies and events have been established while others have disbanded, and some organizations have dropped jazz as an identifier of their work altogether.

Research indicates the Lindy Hop community is, perhaps, the most active of all the branches of the tree. The scene extends beyond America's borders to encompass a large international network of teachers, performers, and aficionados, due in large part to decades of teaching at Sweden's Herräng Dance Camp by Lindy Hop legends Frankie Manning and Norma Miller. Like the environments from which authentic jazz arises, the lines between amateur and professional are purposefully blurred. The community contains a mix of recreational hobbyists and professional dancers who spend large portions of the year touring from event to event. Several U.S. cities maintain networks of "dances" and "exchanges" for local enthusiasts. Larger, annual Lindy Hop events are primarily organized as weekend "camps" that include a mix of workshops, master classes, competitions, and social gatherings meant to foster the spirit of the

FIGURE 1.1. Hyunjung Choi and Nicolas Deniau at the Bordeaux Swing Festival, October 2018. Photograph by Tommaso Giuntini.

ballrooms in 1930s Harlem. In addition to weekly events across the globe, like New York City's Frim Fram Jam, there are more than twenty weekend events occurring in a calendar year throughout the contiguous United States, and at least an additional ten taking place in France, Canada, Slovenia, Argentina, and Mexico. Of note is the growing scene in Seoul, Korea, where there are no fewer than twenty venues with dedicated swing dance events.[4] White dancers dominate the global Lindy Hop scene, which is couched in nostalgia for an earlier America rather than an exploration of the Black American culture from which the dance originates. One cannot help but notice parallels between the demographics of the contemporary Lindy Hop scene and the erasure of Blackness within jazz dance overall, which defaulted to centering White artists in the historical narrative following World War II.

Lindy Hop is far less represented in the roster of professional jazz dance companies. Among the few are Caleb Teicher & Company (New York), HellaBlack Lindy Hop (New York and Los Angeles), Wild Rhythm Dance Company (New York), Holla Jazz (Toronto), and the Harlem Hotshots (Stockholm). This is not to imply that there is a lack of performers. In the Lindy Hop world, professionals tend to maintain autonomy from companies, in part because there is less call for company performances, though they may establish a partnership with another dancer for the purpose of lead/follow choreography. Exchanges of partners and collectives are fluid within the form, and, thus, the presentation of performance reflects similar values. Jazz dance companies are predominantly comprised of concert, classical, and rhythm-generated jazz styles and are concentrated in the United States, with a handful of exceptions in France, England, Canada, and Japan. These include established companies that were formed twenty or more years ago—including Joel Hall Dancers (Chicago, est. 1974), Decidedly Jazz Danceworks (Calgary, est. 1984), JazzAntiqua Dance & Music Ensemble (Los Angeles, est. 1993)—and newer companies such as Big Muddy Dance Company (St. Louis), formed within the past ten years. Since the publication of *Jazz Dance: A History of the Roots and Branches*, at least one long-established company, River North Dance Chicago, ceased operation. Due to the financial costs of supporting a company of dancers, more artists are choosing to work from a project-based model rather than maintaining dancers under contract throughout a calendar year.[5] However, even when considering project-based productions, jazz dance companies are less represented in the dance field than in years past.

A related phenomenon is the trend of removing "jazz" from company names and literature. Though jazz still appears in the descriptions of the company history and aesthetic, as of 2009, Giordano Jazz Dance Chicago,

FIGURE 1.2. Dancers Ashley "Colours" Perez and Hollywood Jade of Holla Jazz. Photo by David Hou.

the oldest operating concert jazz dance company in the United States, is now Giordano Dance Chicago. Jump Rhythm® Jazz Project became Jump Rhythm® in 2015. Les Ballet Jazz de Montréal (est. 1972) frequently uses the initials "BJM" in lieu of their full name and, like Hubbard Street Dance Chicago (est. 1977), no longer references jazz in the description of their aesthetic. Each of these companies has been established for well over thirty years; the youngest is Jump Rhythm®, which was formed in 1990. Sustaining a company over multiple decades inevitably means encountering leadership and, possibly, vision and mission changes. When one factors in the shifting tides of jazz inside and outside of its community, there are predictable reasons why a company would adapt language to reflect the times. However, it feels significant that four of the aforementioned companies are based in Chicago, a historical location for the development of jazz music, and the city that was once considered the hub for concert jazz dance in mid- to late twentieth-century America. More significant is the cultural and commercial cachet of the word "jazz," or lack thereof. It is a declarative statement on the value of jazz when a company divorces the term from their aesthetic, regardless of the works performed in their repertory. Rebranding is a decisive choice that, when considered collectively among these companies, speaks volumes on the perception of worth of the word, the marketing prospects of the form, and the standing of jazz in the field of contemporary dance. Bob Boross alludes to this in the 2020 documentary on the history of jazz dance, *Uprooted: The Journey of Jazz Dance*: "Jazz has been told not to be jazz. Jazz is now considered to be a liability." Chet Walker expands on that sentiment in the next scene by sharing the difficulties he encounters in promoting his work: "I was told if you put contemporary in front of it, I could help you out, but I couldn't do that. Jazz should stand by itself, but there's no funding."[6] While multiple elements can play into the decision to remove jazz from a company title, when examined in relationship to the ever-increasing absence of jazz in curricula and programming, the end result is the same. Jazz, in word and form, is less prominent.

In stark contrast to the number of Lindy Hop events, my research identified only eleven jazz-specific "intensives" and "showcases" that serve concert, theatrical, and commercial jazz dancers in North America, South America, and Europe. There was insufficient evidence of similar events advertised globally in other parts of the world. Though jazz is included in the dance convention circuit, contemporary dance dominates those forums. There is no single dance convention I could identify that is devoted exclusively to jazz dance. It should also be noted that the primary audience for Lindy Hop events and jazz dance intensives is adults, but the dance convention circuit is designed for dancers eighteen years and under. The convention dance world provides a direct conduit to commercial and theatrical dance worlds, with overlapping teachers and choreographers among all three industries. For example, Emmy Award–winning choreographer Travis Wall emerged from his mother's competition-based dance studio in Florida to perform on Broadway as a preteen and later compete on the reality competition show *So You Think You Can Dance*. Since his appearance on the television program in 2006, Wall has gone on to choreograph for television, film, and Off-Broadway; teach regularly on the competition circuit; and cofound a touring dance company, Shaping Sound. Wall's work has alternately been described as contemporary, contemporary jazz, and jazz. He is not alone in this mutable definition, as several contemporary jazz choreographers appear to subscribe to a mélange approach to the inclusion of various dance forms and styles in their work. Like Wall and his contemporary jazz dance peers, theatrical jazz choreographers toggle between Hollywood, New York City, and London's West End to present work onstage and onscreen. Throughout its fifteen years on the air, *So You Think You Can Dance* has featured the jazz choreography of Broadway choreographers Andy Blankenbuehler (*Hamilton, In the Heights*), Sonya Tayeh (*Moulin Rouge*), and Joshua Bergasse (*On the Town*), among others. Like jazz itself, contemporary jazz encompasses an array of aesthetics. What makes contemporary jazz difficult to pinpoint is what defines it as contemporary. Trends in contemporary jazz reflect the tradition in jazz dance of constantly evolving stylistically. However, critics of the form may argue that while contemporary jazz is most in line with what is new, it is not necessarily aligned with what is jazz. Nick Lazzarini, another successful *So You Think You Can Dance* alumnus and co-founder of Shaping Sound, alluded to this when he stated, "Jazz is what people used to do in music videos; commercial dance started with jazz."[7]

As the landscape of jazz changes, so too does its environment. I liken these changes to the concept of dynamic alignment in somatic education. Dynamic alignment posits that change in one aspect of a structure requires the whole entity to shift and adapt.[8] As jazz is never fixed, our understanding of where jazz lives and who is keeping it alive adapts too. These are issues unique to jazz, and not at all associated with the state of modern dance and ballet. This is yet another flaw in the proposition that the establishment and health of jazz is rooted in its development through a Euro-American lens. This power differential is at odds with the democratic nature of the form, and disenfranchises a whole section of the family tree, particularly those branches tied to vernacular practices.

In a 2015 article for *Dance Teacher* magazine, journalist Rachel Zar posed the question, "Is Jazz Dance Dead?"[9] This is not a new or novel question. Like its sister form, tap, the health and survival of jazz is regularly questioned. The conventional wisdom of the article implies that the inherent complexity of the form, the lack of willingness to stay fixed in vocabulary or era, contributes to its impending demise. Though the article does not go so far as firmly stating that the time for jazz has come and gone, posing the question in print contributes to the narrative that though it may not be dead, it is certainly ill. To be sure, jazz will continue to be in dire straits if its survival is rooted in artists who no longer choose to claim it, and relies on the support of those who question its relevance in a contemporary dance world.

If legacy jazz companies are no longer claiming jazz, who can we look to for jazz in the twenty-first century? Though not consistently labeled as jazz, the elements are present in the work of artists in concert and vernacular dance worlds. An obvious connection is in the arenas of hip-hop, house dance, and tap. These forms are included in the family tree, and openly acknowledge the lineage from West African, Caribbean, and authentic jazz dance to the movement vocabulary, performance values, and social elements. Concert dance artists such as tap dancers Dormeisha and Michelle Dorrance, and street and social dancer Ephrat Asherie are investigating the lineage of these forms in evening-length works designed to make the bond between jazz and diasporic traditions transparent for audiences. Lesser acknowledged, but no less evident, is the embodiment of jazz aesthetics in the work of companies considered to be modern or contemporary art, as exhibited in the repertory of Camille A. Brown and Dancers and Urban Bush Women. The tradition of Black Dance has eschewed the need for clear boundaries between dance forms. Dancers must be conversant in multiple forms to work both in and outside of the world of Black Dance. The most seminal work in the Black Dance canon, Alvin Ailey's *Revelations,* demonstrates this in the seamless triumvirate of the techniques of Lester Horton and Katherine Dunham, and vernacular movement found in the Black church. When looked at through the lens of signature jazz characteristics, we recognize that along with their esteemed modern dance works, choreographers such as Dunham, Ailey, Talley Beatty, Donald McKayle, Eleo Pomare, Louis Johnson, Dianne McIntyre, Fred Benjamin, and Billy Wilson created jazz dance repertory. From that tradition sprouts works such as Rennie Harris's *Lazarus*, Camille A. Brown's *Mr. TOL E. RAncE*, and Urban Bush Women's *Walkin' with Trane,* which employ vernacular jazz traditions to support the narrative underpinnings of the work, but because they also use the tools of modern dance composition, and in Harris's work hip-hop and house dance, they are often identified by the aesthetics of these other dance forms.

To properly contextualize the multiple identities within these and other works, I propose the framework of Jazz versus Jazzy, with jazz being works and artists that voluntarily identify with jazz dance, and jazzy being those that reflect or retain the characteristics of jazz over time without being defined exclusively by jazz. In this definition, I am making a distinction between retaining jazz characteristics within an evolving movement aesthetic (jazzy) versus simply quoting from the styles or movement vocabulary of jazz (neither jazz nor jazzy). In movement that is jazzy, lineage is embodied and honored as an influence on the dancing. To be conversant in jazz and, by extension, jazziness is to be deeply rooted in the physicality and performance values of the dance, which has its own rules of "phonetics," "grammar," and "syntax" that identify it as being truly from jazz. When we broaden our lens to consider the inherent jazziness in dance today, we see it liberally present in the work of Black and Brown choreographers, whose training models include concurrent study of Africanist and Eurocentric dance vocabularies. We would have less cause to lament the lack of jazz dance visibility if there were a greater willingness to reconsider and claim the vast performance landscape in which both jazz and jazziness are present.

While events and companies represent a divide among the branches of the tree, academia is an environment where styles, artists, and techniques converge. Of the forty-four postsecondary dance programs in the United States identified as integrating jazz dance into the curriculum, all report teaching multiple styles to students.[10] Though this represents a small percentage of the more than two hundred undergraduate dance programs in higher education within the United States, the breadth of jazz representation within an individual curriculum bodes well for evolving jazz pedagogy.[11] This is also indicative of shifts in pop culture. In an earlier era, when jazz dance training was essential for work as a contemporary and commercial dancer, curricula trended heavily toward classical, theatrical, and commercial jazz, with emphasis on the techniques of Gus Giordano, Luigi, Matt Mattox, and Frank Hatchett. As hip-hop entered the academy and usurped jazz as America's dominant popular dance style, room was created for jazz dance educators to include vernacular, African diasporic styles, and older theatrical styles that do not inherently align with commercial dance prospects. Ironically, the decrease in popularity facilitated greater depth of jazz stylization because the training model is no longer defined exclusively through the narrow lens of commercial vocabulary. As a result, vernacular and authentic jazz training, which was absent from most curricula in the late twentieth century and early 2000s, has found its way back into jazz classrooms on college campuses.

Development of new styles tends toward fusion forms, by blending jazz with hip-hop and contemporary modern dance. Owing to modern dance's tradition of associating techniques with the name of the creator rather than titles reflective of the philosophy of the movement, these hybrid styles tend to be identified with the purveyor. Of note are outliers Combat Jazz (Sonya Tayeh), Postjazz (PearlAnn Porter), and Neo-jazz (devised by myself). A blend of contemporary, classicism, and "Detroit house 3am club," Tayeh defines her style as "warrior-like," "staccato, aggressive, and engaged, even when it's slow."[12] Conversely, Porter's Postjazz lingers in the abstract by mixing the diametrically opposed forms of jazz and postmodern dance. Porter and her collaborator musician John Lambert describe Postjazz as "a movement theory of mindfulness in which we seek to honestly identify how we feel in our moment."[13] Defined as "a historically informed, contemporary technique," Neo-jazz sits firmly in the traditions of jazz roots.[14] Its movement elements are aligned with the Africanist characteristics of jazz dance, with emphasis on weight, rhythm, musicality, movement isolation, improvisation, and community. To invoke the term "jazz" as an identifying characteristic of new or old styles is a strong statement during a time when notable others are purposely discarding it. It embodies the maverick spirit at the heart of jazz.

In answer to the question posed in that *Dance Teacher* article, No, jazz dance is not dead. Jazz in the twenty-first century is a mix of roots and fruits of the form, traditions, progressions, and transgressions. Like the country that birthed it, jazz and its citizens are having tough conversations on systems of oppression and the health and well-being of the form. These are needed conversations for responsible and just pedagogy and performance. Our role, as educators, choreographers, dancers, and dancer-lovers, is to contextualize its past and present. This endeavor does not impede creativity within the form; it imbues it with weight and depth. Like a gumbo, jazz dance today is rich, nourishing, and complex.

NOTES

1. Gerald Early and Ingrid Monson, "Why Jazz Still Matters," *Daedalus* 148, no. 2 (2019): 5–12.

2. Kim Chandler Vaccaro, "Jazz Dance in Higher Education," in *Jazz Dance: A History of the Roots and Branches*, ed. Lindsay Guarino and Wendy Oliver, 207–16 (Gainesville: University Press of Florida, 2014).

3. Lindsay Guarino and Wendy Oliver, "Appendix: A Sampling of Twenty-First-Century Jazz Dance Companies," in *Jazz Dance: A History of the Roots and Branches,* 289–94 (Gainesville: University Press of Florida, 2014).

4. "Weekly Social Dances," JP & Michelle, https://sites.google.com/view/jpmichelle/data/swing-dance-in-seoul?authuser=0.

5. Nancy Wozny, "Your Career: Should You Start a Dance Company?," *Dance Magazine*, July 1, 2015, www.dancemagazine.com/your_career_should_you_start_a_company-2306965150.html.

6. *Uprooted: The Journey of Jazz Dance*, dir. Khadifa Wong, documentary film (New York: On the Rocks Films, 2020).

7. Rachel Zar, "Is Jazz Dance Dead? 7 Experts Share Some Perspective," *Dance Teacher,* July 4, 2017, www.dance-teacher.com/7-experts-answer-the-question-is-jazz-dance-dead-2449804652.html?rebelltitem=3#rebelltitem3.

8. Laura L. Cox and Karen Studd, *Everybody Is a Body* (Indianapolis, IN: Dog Ear, 2019), 45–47.

9. Zar, "Is Jazz Dance Dead?"

10. "Directory," Jazz Dance Direct, Jazz Is . . . Dance Project, https://jazzdancedirect.com/directory.

11. "Dance Magazine College Guide," *Dance Magazine,* www.dancemagazine.com/dance-magazine-college-guide-2306965513.html.

12. Jen Jones Donatelli, "Sonya Tayeh Is a Dance Force to Be Reckoned With," *Dance Teacher*, January 14, 2018, www.dance-teacher.com/combat-force-2392314081.html; Kathryn Holmes, "25 to Watch," *Dance Magazine*, July 28, 2009, https://web.archive.org/web/20120323072524/http:/www.dancemagazine.com/issues/January-2009/25-To-Watch.

13. "The Pillow Project: Story," Pillow Project, www.pillowproject.org/story.

14. Melanie George, "Pas de bou-SLAY!: Making the Case for Neo-jazz as a Contemporary Jazz Technique," manuscript, 2017.

2

Professional Jazz Dance in North America

WENDY OLIVER

Since its inception in the Jazz Age of the 1920s–1940s, jazz and "jazz-related" dance has been well-received in U.S. popular culture, as evidenced by the amazing popularity of vernacular jazz dance in Harlem clubs and elsewhere during that time period and beyond.[1] Since then, jazz has branched out in a number of different ways, remaining popular in some settings but often marginalized within the concert dance world and academe.[2] The reasons for this are complex, interwoven with the history of race as well as with artistic achievement and popular culture in the United States. Before exploring the underlying reasons behind the status of jazz dance in contemporary culture, it will be helpful to examine some facts and figures regarding this art form as it exists within the professional dance world.

One way to determine the status of jazz dance in the professional dance world is to look at the number, size, and budgets of professional and semi-professional jazz dance companies. The number of jazz dance companies in North America today is quite small relative to modern, contemporary, and ballet companies, as shown in a variety of dance company lists that can be found online (Dance USA,[3] Wikipedia,[4] Gaynor Minden,[5] and Jazz Dance Direct).[6] Another barometer of jazz dance status is the number of awards and grants given to jazz dance artists and companies.

Summer dance festivals and intensives are another measure of the success and popularity of jazz dance in the professional and preprofessional world. These festivals and intensives are intended to boost the skills of students in a short period of time and expose them to the life and work of professionals in the field. They also give professional choreographers and teachers an opportunity to build their reputations and to create new works.

All of these elements within the milieu and culture of jazz dance combine to paint a multilayered, nuanced portrait of a dance genre that is not yet fully recognized or understood. The data gathered will reveal the specific ways in which twenty-first-century jazz dance is both visible and invisible in the professional dance world.

PROFESSIONAL JAZZ DANCE COMPANIES

Jazz dance companies are relatively rare in the United States and Canada as compared to modern/contemporary and ballet companies. A January 6, 2020, search on the Gaynor Minden website showed that in North America, there were 340 companies in the modern/contemporary category, 323 ballet companies, and 34 jazz companies.[7] In a Wikipedia listing labeled "List of Dance Companies," there were 58 ballet companies, 43 contemporary or modern, and 5 jazz companies.[8] Although these two listings of dance companies are undoubtedly incomplete, the proportions make clear that there are far fewer jazz companies than ballet or modern/contemporary companies in North America.

In order to do a more thorough job of identifying, locating, and verifying nonprofit jazz dance companies in North America, internet research was conducted on a number of sites. The companies were initially identified on one of the following websites under the search term "jazz dance companies": Dance Informa,[9] Dance USA,[10] Gaynor Minden,[11] Jazz Dance Direct,[12] or Wikipedia,[13] and were then verified by checking their individual company websites. Each of these companies was in operation as of January 6, 2020. In order to qualify as a jazz company, the words "jazz" or "swing" had to appear somewhere either in the name of the company or the description of their work. They did not need to be dedicated solely to jazz dance to qualify for this list. Because new companies are constantly in the process of forming, while others are folding, this number can only be a snapshot in time. The number of companies found was 40; they were located across the United States (37) and Canada (3). Several of these companies have been in existence for more than twenty-five years, including, but not limited to: American Dance Machine, Les Ballets Jazz de Montréal, Decidedly Jazz Danceworks, Giordano Dance Chicago, Interweave Dance Theatre, JazzAntiqua Dance and Music Ensemble, Jazz Xchange, Joel Hall Dancers, Jump Rhythm® Jazz Project, Koresh Company, Odyssey Dance, and Savage Jazz. This is an outstanding accomplishment and shows that jazz dance companies can and do survive and thrive in North America over the long term.

In 2015, Dance USA published financial figures from fiscal year 2014 for many nonprofit dance companies in the United States (no more recent figures

FIGURE 2.1. Decidedly Jazz Danceworks in rehearsal (2016). Photo by Noel Bégin. Courtesy of DJD.

have been released). At that time, there were only three jazz dance companies with budgets over $100,000. They were Giordano Dance Chicago, River North Dance Chicago, and Odyssey Dance Theatre, with the largest of these three budgets at $1,305,526. However, Decidedly Jazz Danceworks in Calgary, Canada, had a FY 2014 budget of $2.8 million, with government funding of $389,000;[14] this is a sizeable budget, which dwarfs all of its U.S. jazz dance counterparts.

Since 2014, River North has closed its doors, leaving only two U.S. jazz dance companies in that budget range. On the other hand, there are many ballet companies with budgets over $100,000, and in fact, the 15 companies with the largest budgets out of the entire group of about 400 U.S. companies in the survey were ballet companies. All 15 companies had budgets of over $7 million in FY 2014. Three of these are American Ballet Theatre ($43,423,540); San Francisco Ballet ($51,614,245); and New York City Ballet ($66,481,713). While there were some well-funded contemporary/modern companies, none in this particular survey broke the $7 million mark.[15]

These figures likely confirm that ballet is the most dominant, well-funded dance form in the United States when it comes to not-for-profit, professional dance companies. Without an examination of the budgets of all other types of dance companies in North America, this cannot be definitively stated, but it is a reasonable conjecture, given the evidence available. This reflects the fact that European-based artistic culture has held a place of privilege in the United

States, even as it developed side by side with the culture of African Americans since enslaved Africans were first brought to this country. Ballet companies today such as American Ballet Theatre, San Francisco Ballet, and Boston Ballet all enjoy national and international reputations. American Ballet Theatre currently has eighty-five professional dancers in the company, not including apprentices. Clearly, a very large budget is necessary to support such a huge number of dancers, and this is only possible with a well-oiled fundraising apparatus, support from foundations, substantial ticket prices, and many donors. Jazz dance companies are typically much smaller in scale; for example, Giordano Dance Chicago has ten dancers in its main company, with additional associate company members.[16] The reasons for the disparity in status of ballet and jazz dance in the United States are beyond the scope of this chapter, but more information concerning this theme will be developed throughout the book.

AWARDS AND GRANTS

This section looks at seven different national dance and arts awards to determine the number of recipients in the field of jazz dance, broadly defined. For the purposes of this study, the term "jazz dance" includes various permutations of the form including vernacular, theatrical, Broadway, and concert styles. Also included are some artists (e.g., Katherine Dunham, Donald McKayle, Alvin Ailey, Jerome Robbins) and companies who utilize(d) jazz elements in their work but are typically identified as modern, ballet, or musical theater choreographers. Although tap has African roots and is strongly related to jazz dance, it was excluded for the purposes of this research since it has its own distinct technique and culture within the dance world.

The raw data were gathered from the websites of each of the awarding or granting organizations, from the inception of each award until the present, as available. The lists of awardees were then reviewed to identify jazz dance artists, as either dancers or choreographers.

The awards are listed from the oldest to the newest.

Capezio Dance Awards

New York City, 1952–present, with a total of 80 awards given over sixty-seven years. These 4 awardees amount to 5 percent of the recipients.[17]

1963 Donald McKayle
1976 Jerome Robbins

1991 Katherine Dunham
2003 Alvin Ailey

Dance Magazine Award

New York City, 1954–present, with a total of 244 awards given over sixty-five years. These 14 awardees listed represent approximately 5.7 percent of all Dance Magazine awards.[18]

1957 Jerome Robbins
1958 Gene Kelly
1959 Fred Astaire
1962 Gwen Verdon
1963 Bob Fosse
1969 Katherine Dunham
1972 Judith Jamison
1975 Alvin Ailey
1982 Lee Theodore
2000 Ann Reinking
2005 Donald McKayle
2006 Joan Myers Brown
2007 Bebe Neuwirth
2019 Caleb Teicher

Kennedy Center for Performing Arts Lifetime Achievement Awards

Washington, D.C., 1978–present, with a total of 221 awards given over forty-one years. Of the 221 awards, 34 went to dance artists, and of those 34, 7 were jazz dance related. Therefore, 20.5 percent of Kennedy Center dance awards went to people involved in jazz-related dance.[19]

1978 Fred Astaire
1981 Jerome Robbins
1983 Katherine Dunham
1988 Alvin Ailey
1999 Judith Jamison
2002 Chita Rivera
2015 Rita Moreno

Samuel H. Scripps American Dance Festival Award

Durham, North Carolina, 1981–present, with a total of 41 awards given over thirty-eight years, only 3 of which could be interpreted as jazz-related dance, which is 7.3 percent.[20]

1986 Katherine Dunham
1987 Alvin Ailey
1992 Donald McKayle

National Medal of the Arts

Washington, D.C., 1985–2015; 2019 (President Trump declined to name awardees from 2016 to 2018) with a total of 339 awards given over thirty-one years; 33 of these were given to dancers, choreographers, or dance producers. Of the 33, 7, or 21 percent, were for jazz-related dance.[21]

1988 Jerome Robbins
1989 Katherine Dunham
1994 Gene Kelly
1998 Gwen Verdon
2001 Alvin Ailey Dance Foundation; Judith Jamison
2009 Rita Moreno
2012 Joan Myers Brown

National Endowment of the Arts

Washington, D.C., 1965–2019; 6,814 awards to dance. Of these, 99 (or approximately 1.5 percent) went toward jazz-related endeavors, many of which were to commission jazz music as accompaniment for dances.[22]

A sample of the 99 recipients includes: Alabama Dance Council, Alonzo King LINES Ballet, Alvin Ailey Dance Foundation, Inc., American Tap Dance Foundation, Ballet Hispanico of New York, Jazz Tap Ensemble, Jazzdance (Danny Buraczeski), Urban Bush Women, and Washington Ballet.

Note: some of these groups received more than one grant.

Of all the 99 companies, only two specifically identified themselves as jazz dance companies: Jazz Tap Ensemble and JazzDance (Danny Buraczeski). The remainder were ballet, modern, and tap companies, or umbrella organizations such as festivals or universities. The grant money to nonjazz companies went mainly toward commissioning jazz music for new choreography.

MacArthur Foundation "Genius Grants": Chicago, 1981 to present

There have been a total of 1,014 MacArthur Fellows[23] over thirty-eight years. These grants are given to people in all disciplines within the arts, humanities, sciences, and beyond. A total of 20 fellowships have gone to dancer/choreographers; none, however, have gone to jazz dance artists. The closest was a grant to Michelle Dorrance, a tap artist, in 2015. Most dance recipients have been contemporary/modern choreographers such as Merce Cunningham (1985, modern), Elizabeth Streb (1997, modern), and Okwui Okpokwalisi (2018, interdisciplinary).

Discussion

The above dance and arts awards were given by a group of well-known, prestigious, mostly East Coast organizations. It is apparent that this East Coast–centric group tended to select awardees from the East Coast, and particularly New York City. The exception to this trend appears to be the National Endowment for the Arts and the MacArthur Foundation, which have both awarded grants widely across the country. It is interesting that Chicago jazz choreographer Gus Giordano (1923–2008) does not appear in any of these lists. Giordano was highly acclaimed nationally and internationally for his work, especially during the later twentieth century.[24] Therefore, it should not be assumed that high-quality jazz dance artists, broadly defined, were/are not working in other areas of the United States, as this example indicates. The names above are clearly not a complete listing of all who have achieved excellence within jazz dance in the United States; it is important to consider what names of groups and individuals might be missing from the awards. Those selecting the awards were possibly unaware of the existence of jazz dance companies and artists outside New York, or alternatively, may not have seen jazz artists as equally deserving of awards as their ballet and modern counterparts.

In addition to Giordano, other "big-name" jazz dance artists from the mid- to late twentieth century included Pepsi Bethel, Jack Cole, Matt Mattox, Bob Fosse, Peter Gennaro, Frank Hatchett, Luigi, and Lynn Simonson. Only one of these New York–based artists—Fosse—was recognized by the awarding institutions in this survey. It is possible that these artists were overlooked for a variety of reasons, including a lack of work choreographed for the concert stage.[25] Some, like Hatchett, Luigi, and Simonson, were/are known primarily as teachers. Yet, one cannot help but wonder if their categorization as jazz dance artists left them outside the circle of possible awardees.

Looking at the names on the lists, we see a variety of artists, some of whom might not claim the name "jazz dancer" or "jazz choreographer" for themselves. For instance, Katherine Dunham (1909–2006) distanced herself from the term "jazz" in her earlier days, as noted by dance scholar Susan Manning: "Although Negro dancers did not necessarily exclude jazz from their programs, they did distinguish between their own practice and jazz dancing. In 1938, Katherine Dunham told an interviewer: '[My plans are] to develop a technique that will be as important to the White man as to the Negro . . . to take *our* dance out of the burlesque—to make of it a more dignified art.'"[26] However, two years later, Dunham created a highly successful Broadway show, *Tropics and Le Jazz Hot* (1940), where she specifically featured vernacular jazz dances of the American South.

Donald McKayle was known primarily as a modern dance choreographer who dealt with social justice themes, but he was also a jazz dancer, working with Broadway choreographers Jack Cole, Peter Gennaro, and Jerome Robbins.[27] And while Chita Rivera and Rita Moreno are known as Broadway dancers and actors, what they performed was theatrical jazz dance, in a variety of shows including *West Side Story, Chicago,* and *Kiss of the Spider Woman.*

Despite my casting a wide net when searching for jazz dance artists within the lists of awardees, the numbers indicate that overall, jazz-related dance artists receive far fewer awards than ballet and modern dance artists. For the oldest award, the Capezio Award, there have been a total of 80 awardees, 4 of whom fall into this "jazz-related" category, which is approximately 5 percent. The Dance Magazine Award list shows that 14 out of 244 awards went to jazz-related artists. The Kennedy Center Awards have honored 9 jazz-related artists for lifetime achievement, out of a total of 221 (approximately 4 percent). The Samuel Scripps Award has been given to 4 individuals out of 42 (approximately 9.5 percent), and the National Medal of the Arts has gone to ten jazz dance-related artists/groups out of a total of 338 awards, or about 3 percent. For the National Endowment for the Arts, 1.5 percent of dance awards have gone to jazz-related endeavors, many for creation of jazz music scores. Finally, the MacArthur Foundation Grant has been awarded once to a tap dance artist, but never to a jazz dance artist. It is important to note that some of these artists won multiple awards, with Katherine Dunham taking the lead with 5 awards, and Jerome Robbins and Alvin Ailey receiving 4 each. This reinforces the value of their work in the arts community but also reduces the actual number of different artists recognized within the field of jazz dance.

Aggregating the figures shows the stark contrast among dance genres. The National Endowment for the Arts data were omitted as part of the aggregation, since those awards were entirely for organizations rather than for individuals. The total number of awards given to jazz-related artists is 43, out of a total of 446 dance-specific awards, which amounts to 9.6 percent. For comparison's sake, the percentage of ballet artists who received awards is about 31 percent, and the percentage of contemporary/modern awardees is also about 31 percent. The remainder of dance awards went to tap dancers, other styles of dancers, and dance producers. This balance of awards shows that both ballet and modern/contemporary dancers are better known and better rewarded than other types of dance in the United States. It is also true, as shown earlier, that there are fewer jazz dance artists and companies in North America than ballet and modern/contemporary companies, which makes it less likely that a jazz dance artist would have the opportunity to be recognized, statistically speaking.

Another interesting data point within the awards discussion is how many people of color received these honors, across different dance genres. Within the Capezio Awards, 14 of 67 winners (20.1 percent) were people of color. For the Kennedy Center Awards, a total of 33 dancers received the awards; 12 (36.3 percent) were people of color. The Samuel Scripps Award has gone to a total of 43 dance artists, and 14 (32.5 percent) of them were people of color. Of 240 Dance Magazine Awards, 46 went to artists of color (19.2 percent). The National Medal of the Arts has been awarded to 33 dance artists, and 14 of those went to artists of color (42.4 percent). MacArthur "Genius Grants" have been awarded to 22 dancers, 8 of whom are of color (36.3 percent). Looking at the composite picture of these six awards, the average percentage granted to dance artists of color is 31.1. Therefore, the percentage of dance artists of color receiving awards is significantly higher than the number of jazz dance artists of any race receiving awards (9.6 percent), since dance artists of color receive awards in all genres of dance. Within the aggregated jazz dance awards, the recipients were 60 percent artists of color, mostly African Americans.

SUMMER DANCE FESTIVALS/INTENSIVES

Summer dance festivals and intensives take place across North America, but only certain ones offer jazz dance as an area of focus. These festivals and intensives can be prestigious venues for professional dance artists to teach, develop their work, and build their reputations. Some of the best-known jazz and commercial dance intensives, along with year-round professional training, are offered in New York City, Los Angeles, and Chicago. Broadway Dance Center in New York has a four-month intensive program for pre-professionals, "whether your dreams include Broadway or Beyoncé."[28] The overall faculty there includes 13 permanent jazz teachers, along with more than 27 guest jazz teachers. In addition to dance technique classes, they offer mock auditions and an end-of-term industry showcase. Steps on Broadway also prepares students for a professional career with a four-week summer study option, Theater Dance/Jazz session.[29] In addition to training, they offer performance and networking opportunities with current professionals.

Another New York training opportunity is the Rockettes Conservatory, a three-week intensive in tap, jazz, and ballet, which is available by invitation.[30] Graduates of the program are encouraged to audition, usually in August, for a spot in the Rockettes Christmas show. The Joffrey NYC Jazz and Contemporary Summer Intensive is open to students age eight and up, and includes courses in contemporary, jazz, street jazz, modern, hip-hop, theater dance, ballet, and repertory.[31]

Millennium Dance Complex in Los Angeles is known for its commercial dance training, which is available year-round as well as in intensive formats.[32] Their curriculum offers jazz, jazz funk, ballet, contemporary, hip-hop, tap, and breaking, as well as classes in auditioning and dancing for videos. Likewise, The Edge in L.A. is a feeder for professional dance auditions including music tours, television shows, commercials, videos, industrials, and cruise ships.[33] Their studio offers four levels of jazz dance, jazz funk, contemporary jazz, ballet, contemporary, tap, theater dance, and more.

One midwestern jazz intensive takes place at the Giordano School in Chicago.[34] Gus Giordano founded his company in 1963 and also established this popular school, now directed by his daughter, Amy Giordano. Classes for the Giordano Dance Chicago Summer Intensives include Giordano jazz technique, Giordano repertory, ballet, floor barre, contemporary, musical theater, jazz funk, and hip-hop. The website for the 2020 Chicago summer intensive also mentions "hip-hop, Bollywood, and Latin Pulse" classes.

It is also important to notice where jazz dance is missing. For instance, two of the more historical, long-standing summer dance festivals are the American Dance Festival, in Durham, North Carolina, and Jacob's Pillow Festival in Becket, Massachusetts. Since each of these festivals was created by modern dancers or organizations affiliated with them, it stands to reason that each has a focus toward modern dance. The American Dance Festival, originally known as the Bennington School of Dance and created in 1934, was the site of summer workshops by Martha Graham, Doris Humphrey, Hanya Holm, and Charles Weidman.[35] It eventually grew to encompass much more diversity of style and genres, including jazz dance. In 2019, there were a total of 42 courses offered; 4 were African-based dance, but only one faculty member taught a course labeled "jazz" in the summer intensive.[36]

The website for the Jacob's Pillow Festival in Becket, Massachusetts, advertised for summer 2020 summer intensives including Contemporary Ballet, Street & Club Dances, Contemporary, and Musical Theatre and Dance.[37] Each of these two-week sessions is headed by celebrity artist(s) within the field. The only mention of jazz dance is found within the description of the Musical Theatre and Dance workshop, where it is mentioned as one of the dance genres that students study.

What is evident from this cursory examination of a handful of summer intensives is that jazz dance is offered consistently in commercial intensives and studios, with much less representation in the nonprofit dance world. In order to find jazz dance, one needs to search for festivals or intensives labeled "jazz dance," "theater dance," or "commercial dance." Even then, most likely, the curriculum will also include a significant amount of ballet and modern/contemporary dance, as shown in the examples of the Joffrey NYC Jazz and Contemporary Intensive and the Giordano Dance Chicago Intensive.

Conclusion

Just as White culture has been viewed as "neutral" or "aracial" in the United States, ballet has often been viewed that way as well. Ballet is often assumed as a norm or a standard for what dance is; the language of ballet is used in modern dance and jazz classes as well. Its European roots took hold here in the early twentieth century, concurrently but separately from the African-based forms of dance, of jazz and tap. Today, these African-rooted forms are popular in the dance studio, but they are not always visible on the professional performance stage. This has been reinforced by academe, which overall, has not been inclusive of jazz dance.

The great preponderance of professional dance companies in North America are either ballet or modern/contemporary companies. Jazz dance companies are far fewer in number. The largest U.S. dance company budgets by far, as evidenced by IRS tax reports for FY 2014, belong to ballet companies, which may have as many as 85 dancers, plus administrators and other specialists, on their payrolls. The U.S. jazz-related company in this survey with the largest budget (Odyssey Dance Theatre of Orem, Utah) had a budget that was only approximately 1.5 percent of the largest ballet's budget (New York City Ballet), and Canada's Decidedly Jazz Danceworks' budget was only about 4 percent of the New York City Ballet's budget.

However, success in dance is not determined mainly by money, but by factors including longevity, community relationships, and artistic impact. Where longevity is concerned, many jazz dance companies have passed the twenty-five-year mark, showing their staying power in the dance world. Although it is not possible to measure community impact in a precise way, a review of the websites of jazz dance companies with longevity indicates a high level of involvement with their surrounding communities and beyond. As for artistic impact, one can view the awards and accolades given to these jazz company directors and choreographers by reading their biographies and related news articles.

Dance awards from seven organizations were surveyed from 1952 to 2019. The bulk of awards for the seven organizations surveyed have gone to ballet and modern dance artists and organizations. Overall, slightly under 10 percent of awards have gone to jazz-related dancers/choreographers. Most dance award recipients were from New York and the East Coast, or spent time performing there, which correlates with the fact that five of the award-giving organizations are located on the East Coast. Interestingly, five jazz dance organizations are or were located in Chicago, almost certainly reducing the possibility of their receiving any of the awards surveyed.

A small sample of intensive workshops labeled "jazz" or "commercial" was reviewed. These workshops, billed mainly as "preprofessional" workshops, prepare young dancers (teenage through young adult) for careers as professional dancers. Workshops and studios offering multiple levels of jazz dance classes included Broadway Dance Center, Steps on Broadway (both in New York), as well as The Edge in Los Angeles. Two prestigious, nationally known summer dance intensives, Jacob's Pillow and American Dance Festival, had very little jazz dance in their 2019 or 2020 seasons or curriculums. Although there are jazz dance workshops available in a variety of cities across the country, they tend to highlight ballet and other forms of dance along with jazz dance, implying that jazz is not enough training on its own for a professional performer.

Taken altogether, this research shows that although jazz dance has a solid, long-term presence in the North American nonprofit dance world, it is often overshadowed by ballet and modern dance, becoming invisible. It is problematic that there are comparatively few jazz dance companies to carry on the important tradition of jazz dance, and even fewer that emphasize its African roots. Additionally, the paucity of awards going to jazz dance artists suggests that they were/are seen as "less worthy" of distinction by some of the United States' most prestigious institutions. Many of the award recipients included here, such as Katherine Dunham and Alvin Ailey, were known primarily as modern dancers, which afforded them the opportunity to be regarded as serious artists.[38] Moving forward, it is important to make jazz dance companies and artists more visible through performances, workshops, publications, and the media. Award-granting institutions should be educated about the value and historical significance of jazz dance, so that it can be more fully honored and appreciated throughout the dance world.

NOTES

1. Marshall Stearns and Jean Stearns, *Jazz Dance: The Story of American Vernacular Dance* (New York: Da Capo, 1994).

2. Kim Chandler Vacarro, "Jazz Dance in Higher Education," in *Jazz Dance: A History of the Roots and Branches,* ed. Lindsay Guarino and Wendy Oliver, 207–16 (Gainesville: University Press of Florida, 2014).

3. "Dance USA Directory of Not-for-Profit Dance Ensembles," Dance USA, www.danceusa.org/danceusa-directory-dance-ensembles.

4. "List of Dance Companies," Wikipedia, https://en.wikipedia.org/wiki/Lis_of_dance_companies.

5. "More Dance Companies," Gaynor Minden, https://dancer.com/ballet-info/online-resources/more-dance-companies.

6. "Dance Companies," Jazz Dance Direct, www.Jazzdancedirect.com.

7. "More Dance Companies."

8. "List of Dance Companies."

9. "Dance Companies," Dance Informa, https://danceinforma.us/directories/dance-companies.

10. "Dance USA Directory of Not-for-Profit Dance Ensembles."

11. "More Dance Companies."

12. "Dance Companies."

13. "List of Dance Companies."

14. Decidedly Jazz Danceworks, personal correspondence with the author, May 28, 2020.

15. "Dance USA Directory of Not-for-Profit Dance Ensembles."

16. Giordano Dance Chicago, www.giordanodance.org/dancers.

17. Capezio Dance Awards, www.capezio.com/foundation.

18. Dance Magazine Awards.

19. Kennedy Center for the Performing Arts Lifetime Achievement Awards, www.kennedy-center.org/pages/specialevents/honors.

20. https://americandancefestival.org/wp-content/uploads/2014/06/7-ADF-Timeline.pdf.

21. National Medal of the Arts, www.arts.gov/honors/medals/year-all.

22. National Endowment for the Arts, category "dance," keyword "jazz," https://apps.nea.gov/grantsearch/.

23. MacArthur Foundation Fellows, www.macfound.org/fellows/search/all.

24. Judith Hamera and Gus Giordano, "The Rehearsal, and the Critical Utility of Forgotten Dance Triumphs," *Theatre Journal*, 71–72, E–1, https://jhuptheatre.org/theatre-journal/online-content/issue/volume-71-issue-2-june-2019/gus-giordano-rehearsal-and, DOI: https://doi.org/10/1353/tj.2019.0055.

25. Teal Darkenwald, "Jack Cole and Theatrical Jazz Dance," in *Jazz Dance: A History of the Roots and Branches*, ed. Lindsay Guarino and Wendy Oliver (Gainesville: University Press of Florida, 2014), 84.

26. Susan Manning, *Modern Dance, Negro Dance* (Minneapolis: University of Minnesota, 2004), xiv.

27. Bob Boross, "Donald McKayle, Jazz Dance Then and Now," in *Jazz Dance: A History of the Roots and Branches*, ed. Lindsay Guarino and Wendy Oliver (Gainesville: University Press of Florida, 2014), 127.

28. www.broadwaydancecenter.com/schedule.

29. www.stepsnyc.com/professional-training-programs/summer-study-nyc/.

30. www.rockettes.com/dancer-development/.

31. https://summer.joffreyballetschool.com/nyc-jazz-intensive/.

32. https://millenniumdancecomplex.com/the-certificate-program/.

33. www.edgepac.com/.

34. https://guslegacy.org/summer.

35. American Dance Festival History, https://americandancefestival.org/wp-content/uploads/2013/02/ADF-History.pdf

36. https://americandancefestival.org/education.

37. Ibid.

38. John Perpener, *African-American Concert Dance: The Harlem Renaissance and Beyond* (Champaign: University of Illinois Press, 2001), 18, 179.

Whiteness and the Fractured
Jazz Dance Continuum

LINDSAY GUARINO

> The price one pays for pursuing any profession, or calling, is an intimate knowledge of
> its ugly side.
> James Baldwin

Looking at jazz today through the lens of critical racial and cultural consciousness brings into focus the ways it has been shaped by Whiteness. Since the
origins of jazz, which can be traced to the first cultural interchanges between
Europeans and enslaved Africans on ships crossing the Middle Passage to today,[1] White culture has maintained its perceived superiority as the dominant
culture. It is the perspective of this author, a White female, that the development of racial and cultural consciousness is necessary to see jazz dance clearly
and engage with it responsibly. Turning a critical eye toward the master narrative and the way jazz dance has operated as a system that perpetuated racism, it appears that there is the opportunity to reinterpret history and make
reparations to the people who created and innovated this uniquely African
American music and dance form.

The most mainstream narrative of jazz dance history is obscured when the
lens shifts to consider who the storytellers have been, what biases may have
been present, and what parts of the narrative were left behind. Knowing that
jazz is a descendant of African lineage and is rooted in African American vernacular music and dance, it begs questioning why the most prominent figures
in jazz dance history are White male teachers and choreographers from the
1940s–1980s. It does not diminish the contributions of Jack Cole, Matt Mattox, Luigi, Gus Giordano, or Bob Fosse to question why they are often regarded as "the innovators" or "pioneers" of jazz dance.[2] Instead, it makes space

for deeper investigation into who and what was left out when history was written, and also offers insight into why jazz dance is such an enigma today.

The act of reinterpreting history is challenging at best. On the surface, what has been written and recorded into history is accepted as fact by many. Underneath recorded history lie complex stories of peoples and places, some of which have been elevated while others have been altered or dismissed as cultural ideologies positioned people into a timeline that makes up our past. The biases of those documenting history often remain invisible through writing that is race-neutral, thus enabling a cultural hegemony to form in the collective narrative. In America this has proven to be problematic as the narrative has been driven by Whiteness, a construct that contemporary social scientists believe "is not objective or biologically significant but constructed by social sentiment and power struggle,"[3] with identifiable impacts that privilege White persons above persons of color.[4] This is apparent in the way those elevated in published history are White, while the roles of persons of color are diminished or eliminated. Consequently, the master narrative is not challenged easily as it requires racial consciousness on the part of the reader, and for the dominant culture to step aside and relinquish the same superiority and entitlement that has served them.

Using the word "racism" to contextualize what is happening when one person or group consistently chooses a set of values or beliefs over another might seem threatening, as Robin DiAngelo describes in her book *White Fragility*: "If, however, I understand racism as a system into which I was socialized, I can receive feedback on my problematic racial patterns as a helpful way to support my learning and growth. One of the greatest social fears for a White person is being told that something that we have said or done is racially problematic."[5] Identifying the impacts of Whiteness on jazz is especially complicated when considering that jazz dance was colonized from the moment it was first enacted by White bodies. As Brenda Dixon Gottschild so cogently put it: "Because white-skin privilege confers a degree of power upon the most well-intentioned of its carriers, a benign act of cultural borrowing can have the effect of a calculated theft."[6] From nineteenth-century minstrel shows with White performers in blackface, to Jazz Era social dances appropriated by mainstream popular culture, to mid-twentieth-century choreographers who positioned ballet at the forefront of the jazz form, jazz was systematically stripped of its culture and aesthetic groundings. Today, jazz "belongs" to American culture so that anyone with the means to open a studio or be hired as a dance teacher is deemed qualified to teach jazz, thus disseminating jazz dance history and shaping current perspectives without accountability.[7] If one is teaching or choreographing jazz without acknowledging its African American origins, without relationships with Black Americans or respect for their culture, and with no thought of engaging critically with the topic of race,[8] is that not perpetuating a system of racism? Recognizing implicit bias and decolonizing jazz practices involves self-examination that can be deeply humbling and trying as the ego and entitlements are sacrificed. By lifting the good/bad binary which positions all individuals as either racist (intentionally malicious) or not racist (inherently good), there is an opportunity for evaluating one's own relationship to jazz dance and seeing jazz history through a revisionist lens. According to antiracism scholar and historian Ibram X. Kendi: "'Racist' and 'antiracist' are like peelable name tags that are placed and replaced based on what someone is doing or not doing, supporting or expressing in each moment. These are not permanent tattoos. No one becomes a racist or antiracist. We can only strive to be one or the other."[9] Striving to be antiracist in jazz dance requires the humility to admit when ideas and actions are racist, and a willingness to self-correct through intentionality and sustained effort.

TRANSMISSION AND OPPRESSION OF AFRICANIST AESTHETICS

Enslavement led to a transmission of movement aesthetics that lasted for centuries: African diasporic to European; European to African diasporic. While this exchange of cultural ideas appears fluid on the surface, there existed an imbalance where White ownership and oppression allowed for White persons to take, claim, and appropriate without respect or attribution. As Nikole Hannah-Jones wrote in a *New York Times* article for "The 1619 Project," "They had been made black by those people who believed that they were white, and where they were heading, black equaled 'slave,' and slavery in America required turning human beings into property by stripping them of every element that made them individuals."[10] The enslaved forged a new culture in the absence of their native cultures, languages, and religions, but, according to jazz dance scholar Carlos Jones, by the time jazz emerged as a distinct form in the 1920s, "the movement vocabulary, aesthetic sensibility, and cultural understanding of the black race were gradually and systematically being diluted, recast, or expunged."[11] Cultural biases both overt and covert, in a country defined by racial inequity, resulted in a fractured continuum where European aesthetics were elevated and Africanist pushed aside or dismissed altogether. In the construction of American aesthetics, the answer to the questions, Who decided what was valid? What was good? What was challenging? What was appropriate? has always been the same: White people.[12]

What White people did not innately understand in their misinformed interpretations of African American music and dance was its spiritual power; the transcendent nature of physical movement was not something that could be understood through intellect alone. Rhythm and movement were synonymous with African American existence, from the mundane to the extraordinary.[13] On this point, Brenda Dixon Gottschild says: "By dint of its worldliness it can take us to otherworldly realms . . . It makes good sense that we use our ordinary physical bodies as a means to transport us to extraordinary flights of the spirit."[14] Black singers, dancers, and musicians found creative ingenuity and artistic brilliance by employing the depths of the African American experience. Turning into the body was a gateway to liberation and democracy through freedom of the spirit. In this heightened state, the physical body gave the spirit a way of dealing with a most inhumane reality.[15] Calling African American music and dance primitive or licentious, as they were often described by White ministers and educators in the Jazz Era,[16] exemplifies the way cultural and racial stereotypes distort reality. African American music and dance was a complex blend of *being* driven by survival, escapism, and protest, all of which are embedded in the core aesthetic values of jazz. But the White person could not see what they could not know, or what they did not *want* to know, and so the fusion of aesthetics claimed by Whiteness resulted in a superficial type of mimicry that most often did not capture the essence of the source.

What the White American eye did see and write into history follows a type of pattern, as observed primarily in *Anthology of American Jazz Dance*, a collection of writings from 1929 to 1974 by predominantly White authors.[17] It is important to note the weight these perspectives held in shaping perceptions on jazz dance in the mid-twentieth century when taking into account that these views persisted and might even be regarded by some as benign or valid today. Thomas F. DeFrantz explains in *Dancing Many Drums: Excavations in African American Dance* that "racist attitudes permeate early writing about African diasporic culture in America."[18] An analysis of primary sources from the *Anthology* alongside contemporary scholarship from antiracist perspectives brings the following events and biases that shaped jazz dance into focus:

- Dehumanization of African American people and culture in an effort to maintain White supremacy.
- White Americans co-opt the roots to assert ownership of jazz innovation, thus obscuring the roots so it becomes unclear that the origins are Africanist.

- European aesthetics and White American cultural values are the lens through which American art is appraised, paving the way for White Americans to credit White men as the "innovators" and/or "fathers" of jazz and further disenfranchise African American jazz artists.
- The resulting colonized and codified theatrical jazz styles position ballet at the forefront and retain little connection to jazz aesthetics and values, and yet are still devalued and marginalized by concert dance audiences, critics, and in the academy.

While these actions and attitudes overlap and do not necessarily follow a chronological timeline, they do provide a crude arc of recorded jazz dance history under the influence of Whiteness. This list outlines the fracturing of the jazz aesthetic; its Africanist foundation was unstable from the beginning due to the hostile social climate. Today, for many dancers and audiences alike, it takes a certain retraining of the eye, or shifting the cultural lens, to understand and value jazz outside of ballet ideology.

DEHUMANIZATION OF AFRICAN AMERICANS

Long before the birth of jazz, White patriarchal views saw Black bodies through racial stereotypes where black was associated with "evil and menace," and white with "innocence and goodness."[19] Black people were often described as skill-less, vulgar, and unevolved; these early stereotypes are later reinforced in the language used by White people in their descriptions of jazz. Pope Pius spoke out in 1927 "of the discordant cacophony, arrhythmic howls and wild cries" of this new music: "To listen to the music and see the dances puts one in a profound malaise."[20] In 1929, dance critic John Martin wrote: "The jazz dance is purely physical manifestation. Its origin is coarse and its purpose crude; its effect is upon the sense, not upon the motions or the intellect. Such is obviously not the stuff of which concerts are made."[21] Modern dancer Isadora Duncan made clear where she positioned jazz within the American dance canon when she said: "It seems to me monstrous that any one should believe that the jazz rhythm expresses America. Jazz rhythm expresses the primitive savage."[22] Despite these negative visceral reactions to the nature of jazz, White Americans readily consumed Black American art and culture while fashioning it to their likeness. According to jazz critic and musicologist Marshall Stearns: "The attitude of many white men toward the Negro is ambivalent, a combination of attraction and repulsion, of acceptance and rejection. The Negro is alternately thought of, for example, as a loyal servant and a threatening beast."[23] This paradoxical negotiation between acceptance and rejection made space for White people, in their privileged position, to usurp and commodify jazz, skewing it toward the aesthetics considered more polite and acceptable (White) and away from what they considered primitive and savage (Black). This resulted in African American movement becoming more mainstream American, but also watered down—polyrhythms but with less sophistication, individuality but with conformity, movement from the hips/pelvis but with restraint.

Distorted perceptions and misrepresentations of African, diasporic, and African American art are fixed in the fabric of American society because racism, according to many critical race theorists and social scientists, as explained in the book *Critical Race Theory*, "is pervasive, systemic and deeply ingrained."[24] In America, where the writers of the Constitution regarded enslaved Africans as three-fifths human, it's no surprise that jazz, "with its African sensibilities, had to wrestle with the pervasive ideologies espoused by the principles and contexts of white superiority."[25] Gus Giordano, frequently called the "Godfather of Jazz Dance," all but dismissed the aesthetic value of West African movement when he published the *Anthology of American Jazz Dance* in 1978. In the introduction, he wrote: "The jazz dance came to America by the way of the slaves . . . This lazy movement of legs, feet, arms, and head also included body parts connected to the vertebrae—pelvis, rib-cage, and shoulders."[26] Describing laziness rather than the rhythmic exuberance and ephebism characteristic of West African and African American movement is symptomatic of the way the master narrative was upheld over time. Furthermore, Giordano stated: "Even at this time jazz dance is not a basic dance technique. It needs the fundamentals of ballet and modern dance to bring out the greatness in the jazz dancer. A dancer cannot run until he had learned to walk. The American professional dancer must become a total dancer; he must know all of the dance forms or his growth might be stunted by the ballet corps or the Las Vegas chorus line."[27] Centuries of dehumanizing attacks on African Americans paved the way for Whiteness to shape the narrative and trajectory of jazz dance, and record it into written history as evident throughout the *Anthology of American Jazz Dance*.

Co-opting Jazz Innovation and Obscuring the Roots

Nick LaRocca, a cornetist and trumpeter of Italian descent, claimed to have made the first jazz recording in 1917 and argued that his music was "strictly a white man's music."[28] According to LaRocca: "Black people had nothing to do with it. The Negro did not make any music equal to white man, at any time."[29] It might be inferred that efforts to co-opt ownership and obscure the roots were driven by the need for White people to find their own cultural identity, separate from Europe, as American culture critic Gerald Early suggests in the Ken Burns documentary *Jazz*.[30] Whereas LaRocca's actions were overtly racist, there were leagues of White people more quietly contributing to the uprooting of jazz by authenticating new narratives from the White perspective. Jazz today is celebrated as "American" and not "Black American," a consequence of "race-neutrality,"[31] which, deep in American identity reflects White nationalism and the resentment toward the success of a Black American cultural product. In 1980, writer and activist Audre Lorde said, "We have all been programmed to respond to the human differences between us with fear and loathing and to handle that difference in one of three ways: ignore it, and if that is not possible, copy it if we think it is dominant, or destroy it if we think it is subordinate."[32] Jazz, a Black American art with universal appeal, was copied—but not without disenfranchising its Black founders and innovators.

Writings by White authors from the Jazz Era offer evidence of the many ways recorded jazz history is steeped in White supremacy. In an article titled "Jazz Dancing," W. Adolphe Roberts writes: "Little by little, however—from the bottom, up—the Negro rhythms made headway. It must not be thought for an instant that they remained purely African. They adapted themselves with extraordinary rapidity and sensitiveness to the American tempo. The black folk perceived our energy-worship, our love of mechanical speed, and they mimicked it with gusto."[33] Clearly, the word "our" is indicative of being White and American, and "the American tempo" implies that a propensity for energy and speed is a distinctly White idea. Not only does Roberts position African Americans at "the bottom," but he implies that White attributes are more valued or important, which is why they would be "mimicked." By asserting dominance, White Americans were able to position themselves as superior while co-opting the roots of jazz.

In this same article, the author recounts a visit to see Bill Robinson and Adelaide Hall in *Blackbirds of 1928*, "an all-white creation for an all-black cast,"[34] and asks Robinson to expound on his claim that "Negro jazz dancing" had become a school. Roberts writes: "But they were unable to find words to describe it. The thing exists, but it has no nomenclature."[35] Roberts continues by explaining how Robinson demonstrated movements to elucidate their belonging to African American culture and lineage. Robinson defends himself by saying: "All these have been supposed to be white tap dances which I adopted and ragged . . . But the truth is, I never took a lesson in my life. I

FIGURE 3.1. Bill Robinson (Bojangles), *Blackbirds of 1928*. Photo by Vandamm Studio ©Billy Rose Theatre Division, The New York Public Library for the Performing Arts.

never consciously imitated a white performer."[36] Roberts concludes the article by disputing Africanist aesthetics as central to jazz dance: "So much for the purely Negro aspects of the new technique. I think I have made it clear that I regard jazz dancing as having become the expression of white as well as black America."[37] In this statement, Roberts strips Robinson of ownership and authenticity, and roots the White influence as equal or perhaps even greater than its Africanist counterpart.

In a 1945 article titled "More Respect for the Clown," also reprinted in *Anthology of American Jazz Dance*, Mura Dehn analyzes the jazz aesthetic. She astutely describes the elusive rhythms at the heart of African dance and jazz dance, specifically in the way rhythm drives the movement. Dehn also describes what she sees as a second important feature in jazz and African dance, which is the state of the body before movement begins. By starting in complete relaxation, polyrhythms can emerge—pushing and pulling between tension and release. Because she recognizes the shared aesthetic groundings with a keen sense of clarity, it is a surprise that she comes to the following conclusion: "After tracing the Negro dance to its origin, I have concluded that jazz is an American dance, for which the American white population furnishes the basic form as to movement, and the Negro adapts it, endowing it with that vital significance which makes our rather pale and uninteresting folk and social dancing into an art-form whose power is a contagious one all over the world."[38] This statement again uproots the Africanist origins of jazz. This very point was discredited in 2014 by the authors in *Jazz Dance: A History of the Roots and Branches*, who collectively positioned African dance as the root of the jazz tree,[39] and specifically by dance scholar Takiyah Nur Amin in her chapter titled "The African Origins of an American Art Form." By tracing the traditions and aesthetic markers of African-derived movement, she demonstrates that "the dominant aesthetic inclinations of jazz dance are decidedly Africanist; it becomes clear that other cultural influences and dance styles found today within the lexicon of jazz dance were affixed to African idioms and movement approaches in order for the dance form we call jazz to emerge."[40]

Unpacking jazz history through a revisionist lens provides a clearer picture for why jazz is rarely taught in connection to its history. The complexities of slavery and African American identity are viewed through a narrow lens, one that more often than not excludes an examination of how White people became White.[41] Seeing the impacts of White power and privilege in the jazz continuum reveals a more complete picture of jazz dance history, making visible the inhumanity of enslavers, the post-Emancipation acceptance of Jim Crow–era laws and stereotypes, and the overarching willingness to turn a blind eye to pain, suffering, and injustice. Because this type of self-examination is "scary" for the White person, it is deftly hidden under the surface,[42] always there but rarely recognized as the reason why jazz has never been considered equal to its ballet and modern counterparts.

American Values, White Privilege, and Codification

The fusion of cultures and aesthetics on colonized American soil was subjugated by the developing values that are now recognizable as distinctly American. Emerging as an aesthetic and value system unto itself, these cultural ideals were directives in the trajectory of jazz dance. American culture prides itself on product and achievement, individualism and meritocracy. "Anyone" can live the "American Dream" if they work hard enough. In a society constructed under the guise of White supremacy, what became codified was deemed more important than what existed outside of those constructs. Codification, a temporal means for disseminating a prescribed technique, cannot exist in West African dance. It would negate the creative energy and spiritual force that inspires its very movement and makes the sacred barely distinguishable from the secular.[43] Furthermore, deep structure differences are evident in these unique aesthetic languages, whereas Europeanist "movement exists to produce the (finished) work; in the Africanist view, the work exists to produce the movement."[44] While codification might be considered a logical approach to the former, it threatens the nature of the latter. But in mid-twentieth-century America, where ballet and modern were codified resulting in a tangible and lasting legacy for those who worked to *produce* and *achieve* driven by *individuality* and *meritocracy*, it is no surprise that jazz dance would be approached with the same Western Cartesian mind-set.

Author Ta-Nehisi Coates, in his book *Between the World and Me*, sees the American Dream under a cloak of sadness; he had dreamed of it but knew it was not his for the taking: "But this has never been an option because the Dream rests on our backs, the bedding made from our bodies."[45] As Carlos Jones describes in *Jazz Dance: A History of the Roots and Branches*, the opportunities available to the likes of Jack Cole, who was later named the "Father of Jazz Dance,"[46] never would have been afforded to his Black contemporaries, like Katherine Dunham.[47] The freedom and mobility implied within the American Dream did not exist in a segregated America.

The privilege afforded to White men paved the way for artists such as Cole and Jerome Robbins to *produce* and *achieve* in the 1940s, 1950s and 1960s, and for other White male artists to follow, codifying jazz to reflect and disseminate their individual styles. When describing Cole in an article written by Michael Smuin in 1960, he calls him "the most creative and demanding choreographer in the jazz dance medium." Smuin discusses the great progress he sees in the jazz idiom, pointing to White jazz musicians such as Leonard Bernstein, Robert Prince, and Rolf Liebermann as elevating the form and giving jazz dancers the promise of achievement at the level of classical ballet. "The best Jazz dancers are the ones that have had a basic ballet training," he claims, and then states: "Ballet movements and Jazz movements are so closely related that it is hard to say, 'This is Ballet' or 'This is Jazz.' Many times the music is the only difference."[48] In his article, Smuin effectively undermines the entire African

American bedrock of jazz music and dance by naming Western aesthetics as both superior and foundational. Formally acknowledging the significance of White jazz artists who draw from a ballet base while ignoring their Black contemporaries is racially and culturally problematic, and values colonization over authenticity.

What is most familiarly known as jazz dance today is born of this influence, a fusion style with ballet at its base, developed by and for White people through a process of flattening the Africanist aesthetics and erasing its historical and cultural contexts. Some jazz scholars feel that this jazz style could have—or, perhaps, should have—been called something different altogether.[49] But it wasn't, and this new Euro-American hybrid became the "jazz" that was subsequently taught in studios worldwide with teachers perpetuating the myth that ballet is the foundation of jazz technique.

Furthermore, the social and vernacular aspects of jazz were largely divorced from the new "modern jazz" style in this fusion.[50] Codification favored structure and specificity, leaving no space for the social aspects that gave birth to jazz. Ironically, Jack Cole never claimed the jazz label for this very reason; he preferred "Broadway Commercial" as the more accurate nomenclature. Cole said: "[Jazz is] what we used to see in the dance halls in the twenties and thirties, that is what real jazz dance is . . . All stemming from African dance, and all filled with authentic feeling."[51] Those who followed Cole looked to him as the father of jazz regardless, thus forging ahead on a fractured continuum driven by White American idealism. In the words of Matt Mattox, the desire for codification and Eurocentric classicism is clear: "This jazz form, particularly the one I use, very definitely comes from the pure art form of modern dance. Everything I know in relation to the dynamics, the composition, and the delivery of the jazz form of dance comes from Jack Cole and from the knowledge I have learned by watching such great artists as Martha Graham and a number of her disciples."[52] In Giordano's writing, the disdain for the vernacular is apparent: "Jazz is not the rock 'n' roll hip movement taught in many neighborhood studios. It is not a basic dance that you start learning as a child. It is not the gyrations of a teenager, a bandleader or a guitar player. It is not a hillbilly clap dance. It is not effeminate or flippant or 'arty.'"[53] When Cole, Mattox, Giordano, and others were positioned at the center of jazz dance, it in effect negated the Black cultural values that imbued jazz with a social, spontaneous spirit. Whereas Black American jazz placed community (not the individual) and improvisation (not codification) at the center, the resulting White American interpretation moved the social and vernacular impetus to the periphery.

To be clear, this analysis is intended to shift the lens for how jazz today is understood and defined in its historical, social, and cultural contexts. As outlined above, some artists who became synonymous with jazz recognized their form was different and did not apply the label to their work. Those who did claim jazz were a product of normalized Whiteness in mid-twentieth-century America, reflecting widely held biases that were (and still are) systemic across the American dance landscape. The fact that they were labeled "fathers" and "pioneers" says more about the systems that privilege White people and the internalized biases that cloud perception than it does about the men themselves. While this conversation might feel threatening to some, Dixon Gottschild explains that, with Whiteness, "the only way out is through."[54] Examining history through an antiracist lens is a historically accurate and culturally sensitive way of looking at our past, understanding our present, and moving toward a more equitable future.

CONCLUSION

The creation of Whiteness and the resulting implicit biases have shaped jazz dance history and laid the accepted norms for seeing and understanding jazz dance today. Looking critically at jazz history, and specifically identifying instances in written records where White supremacist views led to the fracturing of the jazz continuum, offers opportunities for better understanding the Black American experience. Imani Perry, author and professor of African American studies at Princeton University, believes that Whiteness created differentiations between us, yet humans are innately capable of deep identification with other people.[55] To be White and dance jazz, today, requires humility, empathy, and a shift of consciousness to interrupt conventions reflecting Whiteness rather than jazz.

This author sees this critical lens as the only way for jazz to claim its rightful and lasting place in the American dance landscape. Lifting the veil of racism that shaped American aesthetic preferences offers the opportunity to rethink why jazz has been lesser-regarded than other Western dance styles, and to reposition it as an equal. While unraveling the constructs that have shaped our identities is no easy feat, we are not trapped in them, nor should we be ashamed of them. In the words of diversity, equity and inclusion consultant and author Tayo Rockson: "Be ashamed of the systems that disempower people based on their identities. When you understand the complexities of your identities and the privilege you have as an ally you're able to understand who agents of oppression are and identify overt and covert forms of oppression. It's up to you to decide whether you'll push through discomfort to do something about what you learned."[56]

This chapter began with a quote by American novelist, playwright, and activist James Baldwin. While a study of jazz dance always takes us back to the conversation of racism, seeing the "ugly side" is also an opportunity for White people to make amends for past wrongs. In understanding what Whiteness as a filter concealed, altered, and oppressed, we can begin to make reparations and honor the people and culture responsible for the great African American creation we call jazz.

Notes

1. Marshall Stearns and Jean Stearns, *Jazz Dance: The Story of American Vernacular Dance* (New York: Macmillan, 1968), 16–17.

2. These are commonly used labels, as noted throughout the *Anthology of American Jazz Dance* (1978) and *Jazz Dance: A History of the Roots and Branches* (2014).

3. Richard Delgado and Jean Stefancic, *Critical Race Theory* (New York: New York University Press, 2017), 85.

4. Michael Eric Dyson, foreword to *White Fragility,* by Robin DiAngelo (Boston: Beacon, 2018), ix–xi.

5. Robin DiAngelo, *White Fragility* (Boston: Beacon, 2018), 4.

6. Brenda Dixon Gottschild, *The Black Dancing Body* (New York: Palgrave Macmillan, 2003), 21.

7. Lindsay Guarino, "Jazz Dance Training via Private Studios, Competitions, and Conventions," in *Jazz Dance: A History of the Roots and Branches,* ed. Guarino and Wendy Oliver (Gainesville: University Press of Florida, 2014), 197–98.

8. DiAngelo, *White Fragility,* 8.

9. Ibram X. Kendi, *How to Be an Antiracist* (New York: One World, 2019), 23.

10. Nikole Hannah-Jones, "Our Democracy's Founding Ideals Were False When They Were Written: Black Americans Have Fought to Make Them True," in "The 1619 Project," *New York Times,* August 14, 2019, www.nytimes.com/interactive/2019/08/14/magazine/black-history-american-democracy.html.

11. Carlos Jones, "Jazz Dance and Racism," in *Jazz Dance: A History of the Roots and Branches,* ed. Lindsay Guarino and Wendy Oliver (Gainesville: University Press of Florida, 2014), 234.

12. See DiAngelo, *White Fragility,* 31, where she provides a racial breakdown of the people who control American institutions.

13. Dixon Gottschild, *The Black Dancing Body,* 15.

14. Ibid.

15. Ibid.

16. Marshall W. Stearns, *The Story of Jazz* (New York: Oxford University Press, 1956), 309.

17. This edited volume served as an important point of analysis when considering, as scholar Thomas F. DeFrantz noted in *Dancing Many Drums: Excavations in African American Dance*, ed. DeFrantz (Madison: University of Wisconsin Press, 2002), 11–13, the almost complete void of written scholarship on African American vernacular dance until the late twentieth century aside from Marshall Stearns and Jean Stearns's *Jazz Dance* (1964), which he describes as curiously apolitical, and Lynne Fauley Emery's *Black Dance in the United States from 1619 to 1970* (1972).

18. Thomas F. DeFrantz, "African American Dance: A Complex History," in *Dancing Many Drums: Excavations in African American Dance*, ed. DeFrantz (Madison: University of Wisconsin Press, 2002), 3.

19. Delgado and Stefancic, *Critical Race Theory*, 85–86.

20. Anna Harwell Celenza, *Jazz Italian Style: From Its Origins in New Orleans to Fascist Italy and Sinatra* (Cambridge: Cambridge University Press, 2017), 91.

21. John Martin, "The Dance: When Jazz Becomes," in *Anthology of American Jazz Dance*, ed. Gus Giordano (Evanston, IL: Orion, 1978), 7.

22. W. Adolphe Roberts, "Jazz Dancing," in *Anthology of American Jazz Dance*, ed. Gus Giordano (Evanston, IL: Orion, 1978), 5.

23. Marshall W. Stearns, "Jazz and the Role of the Negro," in *The Story of Jazz* (New York: Oxford University Press, 1956), 313.

24. Delgado and Stefancic, *Critical Race Theory*, 91.

25. Tamara Thomas, "Making the Case for True Engagement with Jazz Dance," *Journal of Dance Education* 19, no. 3 (August 2019): 98–107.

26. Gus Giordano, introduction to *Anthology of American Jazz Dance*, ed. Giordano (Evanston, IL: Orion, 1978), v.

27. Ibid.

28. Gerald Horne, *Jazz and Justice: Racism and the Political Economy of the Music* (New York: Monthly Review Press, 2019), 19.

29. Ken Burns, *Jazz,* episode 1, "Gumbo" (PBS, 2000).

30. Ibid.

31. Kendi, *How to Be an Antiracist,* 20.

32. Audre Lorde, "Age, Race, Class, and Sex: Women Redefining Difference," in *Sister Outsider: Essays and Speeches* (Freedom, CA: Crossing Press, 1984), 115.

33. Roberts, "Jazz Dancing," 3.

34. *Blackbirds of 1928*, Library of Congress, http://memory.loc.gov/diglib/ihas/loc.music.tda.3245/default.html.

35. Roberts, "Jazz Dancing," 4.

36. Ibid.

37. Ibid.

38. Mura Dehn, "More Respect for the Clown," in *Anthology of American Jazz Dance*, ed. Gus Giordano (Evanston, IL: Orion, 1978), 26.

39. Wendy Oliver, introduction to *Jazz Dance: A History of the Roots and Branches*, ed. Lindsay Guarino and Oliver (Gainesville: University Press of Florida, 2014), xvi.

40. Takiyah Nur Amin, "The African Origins of an American Art Form," in *Jazz Dance: A History of the Roots and Branches*, ed. Lindsay Guarino and Wendy Oliver (Gainesville: University Press of Florida, 2014), 42–43.

41. Serene Jones, interview by Krista Tippett, "On Grace," podcast audio, *On Being with Krista Tippett*, December 5, 2019, https://podcasts.apple.com/us/podcast/on-being-with-krista-tippett/id150892556?i=1000458771992.

42. Ibid.

43. Stuckey, "Christian Conversion," 41–43, where he describes spirituality as central to African dance, even when secular, and the way this is contradictory to Euro-American ideology.

44. Brenda Dixon Gottschild, *Digging the Africanist Presence in American Performance* (Westport, CT: Praeger, 1996), 9.

45. Ta-Nehisi Coates, *Between the World and Me* (New York: Spiegel and Grau, 2015), 10–12.

46. A frequently used label; one instance can be found in a quote by Leticia Jay on page 65 of *Anthology of American Jazz Dance*.

47. Carlos Jones, "Jazz Dance and Racism," 237.

48. Michael Smuin, "Jazz and the Dance," in *Anthology of American Jazz Dance*, ed. Gus Giordano (Evanston, IL: Orion, 1978), 54.

49. Lindsay Guarino and Wendy Oliver, *Jazz Dance: A History of the Roots and Branches* (Gainesville: University Press of Florida, 2014), xvii, 26.

50. Jill Flanders Crosby and Michèle Moss, "Jazz Dance from Emancipation to 1970," in *Jazz Dance: A History of the Roots and Branches,* ed. Lindsay Guarino and Wendy Oliver (Gainesville: University Press of Florida, 2014), 55.

51. Clayton Cole, "It's Gone Silly," in *Anthology of American Jazz Dance*, ed. Gus Giordano (Evanston, IL: Orion, 1978), 73.

52. Matt Mattox, "In Jazz Dance," in *Anthology of American Jazz Dance*, ed. Gus Giordano (Evanston, IL: Orion, 1978), 100.

53. Jack A. Miller, "Modern Jazz Dance Midwest," in *Anthology of American Jazz Dance*, ed. Gus Giordano (Evanston, IL: Orion, 1978), 60.

54. Dixon Gottschild, *The Black Dancing Body,* 10.

55. Imani Perry, interview by Krista Tippett, "More Beautiful," podcast audio, *On Being with Krista Tippett*, September 26, 2019, https://podcasts.apple.com/us/podcast/on-being-with-krista-tippett/id150892556?i=1000451365360.

56. Tayo Rockson, interview by Jen Kinney, "Sustainable Diversity and Inclusion Practices with Tayo Rockson," podcast audio, *Speaking of Racism,* December 9, 2019, https://podcasts.apple.com/us/podcast/speaking-of-racism/id1448794346?i=1000459054415.

This research was supported by a grant from the McAuley Institute for Mercy Education, Salve Regina University, and the Lilly Fellows Program.

.... *4*

The Morphology of Afro-Kinetic Memory

A Provocative Analysis of Marginalized Jazz Dance

E. MONCELL DURDEN

This article builds on the work of dancer/scholar Joe Nash's 1994 article "The Real Thing" by addressing how jazz dance practice continues to value White-ness over movement and cultural knowledge of the Africanist aesthetic.[1] This chapter delves deeply into this culturally sensitive and ethnically contentious material. For instance, the fact that works by White dancers are labeled "jazz dance," while jazz dance by Black dancers such as Mable Lee, Marie Bryant, Norma Miller, Jeni LeGon, and Madeline Jackson goes unsung and is inappropriately encumbered with words like "authentic" or "vernacular." The dance of these pioneers is jazz. No qualifier is needed.

Upon Googling the phrase "jazz dance," one is presented with an extensive collection of images and videos displaying characteristics reflecting European aesthetics. What is visible in the photos and the choreography is a hybrid dance resembling modern and ballet, yet labeled jazz. While some jazz chore-ographers and educators work in grounded movement, asymmetry, and poly-rhythms, chiefly associated with the Black jazz dance aesthetic, it seems that jazz has been given a new identity. In a 1959 interview, jazz critic and musicol-ogist Marshall Stearns pointed out that "much of the modern contemporary dance seen on the stage and television in the 50s [and] presented as jazz dance was more related to ballet or modern." He continued, "We seem to be los-ing the jazz dance, that it was disappearing, and was being replaced or led by Hindu and ballet movement, almost anything but real authentic jazz dance."[2]

Today when someone takes a jazz dance class, they typically learn French ballet terms as the definitive way to describe jazz dance. As well, any steps learned are restructured through a Eurocentric lens. Students are unaware of how the steps were originally performed or how they may have been morphed

63

or co-opted and altered. This White shaping of jazz dance is the opposite of the way early twentieth-century African Americans created jazz dance. Black dance throughout the African diaspora is rooted in functional rituals that celebrate significant milestones in life: spiritual worship, healing, or celebration, for example. The dances have meaning and are reflected in the context of a lived experience. The dances are not solely about style and technique but also about feeling and evoking the energy and spirit of the ancestors. They are an affirmation of Black joy, the cultural identity of Black people dancing, and through tonal-vibrations and spiritual-aesthetic expression, are about taking care of each other. The original Black roots of jazz have morphed into Chicago stepping, the Philly-bop and hip-hop and other Black dance aesthetics, not into the Broadway/concert styles of White dancers.

Pulling at the Roots

> The deep structure within a culture is found in the retention of characteristics of behavior that are not effected by time and geography; surface structure is effected by time and geography.
>
> Cheryl Willis, "Tap Dance: Manifestations of the African Aesthetic"

Jazz dance offers passage into the traditions, structures, expressions, folklore, rituals, characteristics, and the heritage of displaced peoples from the continent of Africa, carried forth as the "deep structure" described above. These practices have survived, cross-pollinated, and morphed into America's first dances, post colonization. At its inception, jazz dance is first and foremost motivated by the music. When taking classes in traditional African dance forms, you experience live drumming where the music provides the spirit and feel of the movement, driving the sensation of dancing. If you went into an African dance class and they played a pop song, you might question the validity of the class and the instructor. The music and the movement should go hand in hand. Many jazz dance classes are using pop music, house music, or rock music, which does not provide the energy, spirit, or feel of the movement that was created to jazz music. And while some classes will provide jazz music, they don't always offer a kinesthetic comprehension of the movement and its roots.

Pat Cohen makes a robust point in *Jazz Dance: A History of the Roots and Branches* by stating that the teaching of jazz dance should be anchored in the acknowledgment of West African roots.[3] Acknowledgment is necessary, but should that also include some kind of lived experience? The experience, embodiment, and quality of life of West Africans may not be inhabited by most people teaching jazz dance. Even African Americans don't know what it means to be an African living on the continent and how their lived experience informs their dance, but we do know what it feels like to be viewed with contempt while products of our cultural heritage, aesthetics, and stylizations are approximated, appropriated, codified, commodified, and monetized by those of a different lived experience.

While multiple ethnicities can all coexist in the same environment sharing a type of lived experience, there still exist different ideologies, interests, or traditions. Holding space to feel empathy doesn't mean one has to agree, but one should be able to appreciate the meanings and values held by another person. The characteristics of behavior in African American dance, polyrhythms, polycentrism, and improvisation, to name a few, have been documented and circulated for hundreds of years by people who were dismissive or ignorant of their origins because of their ethnocentric bias. These biases continue to imbue and stain the ethos of the American psyche and denounce the very aesthetics celebrated in jazz music and dance. Author Mark Knowles cites recorded instances where Jazz was viewed as barbaric, unrefined, primitive and jungle music designed for naked wriggling savages.[4] When addressing the Charleston, the archbishop of Eastern Poland declared, "Dancing the Charleston is an unpardonable sin!"[5] Some European societies once viewed improvisation as unrefined and used reductive adjectives to address the physicality of our corporeal oratories, and not intellectually, using words like rapid, attack, sharp, rhythmic, energetic, and sensual. The National Dancing Masters' Association adopted this rule: "Don't permit vulgar, cheap jazz music to be played. Such music almost forces dancers to use jerky half steps and invites immoral variations. It is useless to expect to find refined dancing when the music lacks all refinement, for, after all, what is dancing but an interpretation of music?"[6]

FORM, STYLE, AND THE MORPHOLOGY

If it wasn't for black people, we would all still be doing the minuet and the polka . . . I strongly believe that most of the innovative dance came out of the black community.

Joan Myers Brown, interview

Since 1850 there has been little change in Europe; all further innovations have come from the United States, Cuba, or South America.

Agnes de Mille, quoted in *Jazz Dance: The Story of American Vernacular Dance*

Our bodies carry all the stored memories, emotions, beliefs, attitudes, and vibrations of our personal history, lineage and culture.

Sharon Moloney, *Activate Your Female Power*

Jazz dance is a form of movement born out of the lived experience of African Americans, as Joan Myers Brown, Agnes de Mille, and Sharon Moloney indicate in the statements above. At its inception, jazz dance allowed individuals to express their feelings about the social, political, and economic environment they experienced. Included were their spiritual practices and cultural beliefs. Their interaction and response to their community informed their aspirations. A growing conversation that I have started among the hip-hop community is the difference between form and style, and how deep structure and cultural heritage are present in both; where one resides deep in structure, the other is at the surface structure. A form is a maintained structure, which allows individuals to find their style. Forms carry with them the cultural legacy of the people, and the aesthetic remains constant, whereas the style or gesture may shift as individualism is applied.

Unlike jazz dance originally created by Black dancers, where the form was maintained amid styling that was individual and reflective of their lived experience, the styles of dances led by White choreographers and teachers subtracted the original form. They began teaching their stylings, which were then codified into a form that did not resemble the original form of jazz dance. By contrast, African American people have maintained the form and have shifted our styling, reflecting our social, cultural, political, environmental, and spiritual practice throughout time. A clear example of form versus style is the Tacky Annie of the 1920s, the 1960s dance the Dog, and the 2015 hip-hop dance Nae Nae, three dances that have a root step in common. The body's structural alignment allows for the root step to maintain a consistency while at the same time leaves space for individuation. The root structure of the legs is the same, but the individual expression in the arms and torso is different and speaks to the social climate of the time. This is what I refer to as the "morphology of Afro-kinetic memory"—a cultural awareness that shifts from generation to generation. It is a well-informed, knowledgeable perception providing particular and familiar emotional states, and atmospheric association to place and people, containing a verbal, musical, kinesthetic communication practice. There is a continuation of cultural heritage, a reflection of Black identity, innovation of a new generation, and nods to the future. Daniel J. Levitin suggests that "our brains learn a kind of musical grammar that is specific to the music of our culture, just as we learn to speak the language of our culture,"[7] and also mentions that the linguistics and musical distinctions of the culture we are born into shape our neural pathways and allow us to internalize a set of rules common to that musical tradition. These cultural rules and common practices speak to why morphology can only happen from within a culture. It's what keeps jazz, jazz.

THE MORPHOLOGY OF THE CAMEL WALK

Another way to examine form versus style, or how style or gesture may shift but the cultural aesthetics remain present, is to look at the morphology of the Camel Walk. The origins of the Camel Walk are believed to have lineage in popular traditional social dance of the Akan people of Ghana known as the Adowa.[8] It is performed at cultural ceremonies like festivals, funerals, engagements, and other celebrations. Two movements from the Adowa may have survived the Middle Passage and reappeared around the end of the nineteenth century. The earliest example of this step on film is Thomas Edison's October 6, 1894, footage titled the "Pickaninny Dance the Passing Show" featuring Joe Rastus, Denny Toliver, and Walter Wilkins.[9] They are the first African Americans to ever appear in front of a motion picture camera. These are grown men, and the fact that they are referred to as pickaninnies is problematic but not the focus of this article. The three men demonstrate a series of tap and social dance steps like Fall off the Log, then a Breakdown, performed by Toliver. Wilkins is even more impressive as he lays down some shuffles, crossovers, stomps, and flaps, all while playing the harmonica, but it is Brown who begins Patting Juba after a brief diagonal pass through the center in which he demonstrates the Camel Walk as it was done at that time. Using a hip thrust to propel him forward, spine in a flexed position with one leg straight and the other bent, the bent-knee leg is on the ball of the foot (it is important to note the foot is in a relaxed position) and the straight-leg foot is flat and lands solidly.

In 1924, the Camel Walk was a favorite step to do whenever Ma Rainey's song "See, See Rider" was played. By this time, the step looked identical to that displayed in the Edison footage, except that now it took on a smoother transition of the heel and toe. During the 1930s–1940s, the Camel Walk had introduced the side Camel Step, which can be seen in the short clips of Earl "Snake-Hips" Tucker performing in the 1943 Olsen and Johnson film *Crazy House.*[10] Mura Dehn filmed the three-part documentary *The Spirit Moves,*[11] initially released in 1987 at Harlem's famous Savoy Ballroom, located at 596 Lenox Avenue in 1950, before it closed its doors for good on July 10, 1958. Dehn was a Russian ballet and modern dancer trained in the style of Isadora

FIGURE 4.1. Camel Walk, Eurocentric aesthetic. Sidney Ramsey (*left*) and Londyn Anderson, USC Glorya Kaufman School of Dance, October 2020.

Duncan. The excitement and fervor that Dehn felt after witnessing a performance by Josephine Baker led her to eventually document this amazing dance in 1950. In *Part 2: Savoy Ballroom of Harlem 1950s*, Savoy Ballroom dancer and Whitey's Lindy Hopper Leon James performed the side Camel Walk.

In 1957, Singer Chuck Willis remade Ma Rainey's song "See, See Rider," changing the title's spelling to "C.C. Rider." Amazingly, the young Black teenagers' dance of choice to Willis's version was the Camel Walk, only this time they called it the Camel Walk Stroll. They added sustained movement by dragging a leg and crossing it slightly behind the other leg, just as in the Adowa. In this version of the Camel Walk Stroll, all the women stood on one side and the men on the other; they met up with their partners in the middle and strolled down the line. Dick Clark, American radio and television personality, commodified the dance when he recognized that this dance was a favorite step to do when "C.C. Rider" was played, but the song didn't mention the dance by name. Clark decided to capitalize on this latest fad, reaching out to songwriters Clyde Otis and Nancy Lee to write a song by the same name to be recorded by the Canadian group the Diamonds. They called the song "The Stroll," and its associated dance was captured on a local teen show in Idaho in 1958.[12]

In 1969, on March 15 at 9:30 p.m., the sixth season of *The Hollywood Palace* aired its twenty-third episode on the ABC network, hosted by the amazing Sammy Davis Jr. with a special appearance of the James Brown Revue. After a medley of some of Brown's biggest hits, James indulges in light banter with Davis before jumping into another hit, "There Was a Time." This song is Brown's adaptation of the song "Land of a Thousand Dances," originally written by Chris Kenner in 1962. The original mentions sixteen dances: the

FIGURE 4.2. Camel Walk, Africanist aesthetic. Sidney Chuckas and Aurora Vaughn, USC Glorya Kaufman School of Dance, October 2020.

Pony, the Chicken, the Mashed Potato, the Alligator, the Watusi, the Twist, the Fly, the Jerk, the Tango, the Yo-Yo, the Sweet Pea, the Hand-Jive, the Slop, the Bop, the Fish, and the Popeye. Wilson Pickett recorded the most recognized version of the song in 1966. Brown's version mentions only five dances: the Mashed Potato (which is just a variation of the Charleston), the Jerk, the Camel Walk, the Boogaloo, and the James Brown, which is made up primarily of the jazz steps the Apple Jack, the Corkscrew, and Brown's footwork, which was inspired by tap dance. Nine minutes into his performance, he starts singing "There Was a Time," then he asks Davis, "Do you remember that old soulful dance the Camel Walk?" Davis does the version of the step just described above as the Adowa, and then Brown does a version equal to the 1924 version. In 1971, when thinking of a signature movement for his dancers, Don Cornelius remembered the Camel Walk Stroll from his teenage years and took the formation, renaming it the Soul Train Line. Years later, Janet Jackson does the Camel Walk thirty-seven seconds into the music video for her 1986 song "Pleasure Principle."[13]

Today you can find a video on YouTube of three young women titled "Jazz Dance Technique & Syllabus" that teaches the Camel Walk through a Eurocentric lens.[14] The dancers have a vertical orientation and forced arched feet. Deprived of any personal style, the movement appears stiff and lacks the lived experience described in the Camel Walk of Mr. Davis, Mr. Brown, or Ms. Jackson. In contrast to the described lineage of the Camel Walk, this example has not maintained form and does not display individual style. The morphology of the Afro-kinetic memory has effectively been whitewashed.

The Morphology of the Charleston

The Charleston went hand in hand with jazz music, and the Charleston craze enchanted all levels of society from shop girl to debutante, from factory worker to royalty.[15] The Charleston was such a phenomenon that it provoked a shifting in White social decorum. Its movements were accused of violating the appropriate uses of the body.

> Physicians all over the country are warning their female patients against the dance, readers are given the etiology of the most dangerous side effect of the Charleston, peritonitis, an inflammation of the tissue that lines the inner wall of the abdomen cavity. The dance apparently does such violence to the internal organs encased by this membrane that it causes an irritation that, if exacerbated by continued "jars, jolts and shocks," will weaken the body's defenses against "germ poison," leading to inflammation and from there to full-scale infection.[16]

The notion of doing this popular Black dance sent White society into frenzy. Internal injuries believed to have been caused by doing this dance were hernias, strained ankles, and thrown-out backs. The frenzy reached a pinnacle on July 4, 1925, when the Pickwick Club, a Boston dance hall located at 12 Bench Street, collapsed, killing around forty-four people and injuring others. The Charleston was to blame, with the *New York Times*, *American Weekly*, and other publications writing articles with titles such as "Ill, Charleston Dance Blamed," "Charleston Causes Death," and "Girl Dead from Charleston."[17] There was no mention of the recent fire that weakened the structure. Despite these attempts to thwart the Charleston, it grew into a myriad of variations like Squat Charleston, Sailor Kick Charleston, Drop Charleston, Scarecrow Charleston, Jump Charleston, Flying Charleston, Kansas City Charleston, Around the World Charleston, Precision Charleston, Collegiate Charleston, and many others. Dance historians suggest that the Charleston can be traced back to African traditional dances.

In the book *Jazz Dance*, authors Marshall Stearns and Jean Stearns make some comparisons to Obolo dance of the Ibo Tribe.[18] Other similarities are found among the Ashanti and Bari-speaking people as well as the King Sailor dance of Trinidad, which looks more like the Camel Walk than the Charleston. Dance scholar Dr. S. Ama Wray mentioned to me that during a trip to Africa, she witnessed the dance being done in Guinea and that it was part of a large dance called the Yankadi.[19] When I performed in Boston for the

Racine Black Dance Festival, I had the opportunity to speak with some dancers from Guinea, who confirmed that what we call the Charleston was part of the Yankadi.[20] The Gullah Islands, where rice was cultivated, are thought to have been a point of entry for enslaved African people from Guinea. The Gullah Islands lie off the Charleston Harbor; the city of Charleston is where the dance got its name.

In 1891, Baptist minister Reverend Daniel Jenkins came in contact with a number of homeless boys in Charleston, South Carolina. Born a slave, Jenkins had been orphaned at a young age. He took in the young boys and started an orphanage; within the first year there were more than three hundred young boys. Jenkins raised money for the orphanage by assembling a band using donations of old musical instruments. At one point the band was earning $75,000 to $100,000 a year.[21] Jazz pianist Willie "the Lion" Smith recalled in his memoir, "One musician [from the Jenkins Orphanage Band] Russell Brown, used to do a strange little dance step and the people in Harlem used to shout out to him as he passed by 'Hey Charleston, do your Geechie dance.'"[22] The dance was born on King Street in Charleston by the kids of the Jenkins Orphanage Band. You can see them playing and dancing the Charleston and other Geechie dances in the *Fox Movietone News Story*, dated November 22, 1928.[23] At 5:24, one young man dressed in high socks and knickers sporting a button-down shirt with a necktie, vest, and a backward Apple Jack hat begins doing some Charleston steps with a few lock turns and the Charleston step the Bees Knees. At 6:32, two girls start dancing the Charleston, and they add some knee drops. Then they do the Mess Around, a few lock turns, Shimmy, Strut, and Camel Walks. The number of variations of the Charleston almost guaranteed its longevity.

THE INFLUENCERS

Born in 1933, James Joseph Brown would be influenced by solo jazz steps and tap that he pulled from those two forms throughout his career. He never truly learned how to tap, but Conrad "Little Buck" Buckner was a huge influence on Brown, who imitated Buckner's falls, knee drops, and slips; even Brown's footwork was his interpretation of fast tap steps. If you watch the 1955 performance of Little Buck on the TV show *Chance of a Lifetime*[24] and then watch the 1964 *T.A.M.I* show (*Teenage Award Music International*),[25] Brown's performance was clearly inspired by Buckner. Brown went on to remix a lot of solo jazz steps like the Apple Jack, the Corkscrew Twist, and the Charleston, and influenced the next generations who copied his movement. He also helped to popularize the Mashed Potato (1960s), which came directly from the Charleston.

In the 1950s, tap dancer Charles "Cholly" Atkins begin working with Do-Wop groups like the Cadillacs, Shirelles, Little Anthony, and Frankie Lymon and the Teenagers, teaching them jazz steps from the 1930s and 1940s in what he coined as vocal choreography. In 1962, Cholly was hired by Berry Gordy to train his groups. He did not work with kid groups, so Jackie Jackson from the Jackson Five would sit on the rehearsal studio steps and put their routines together based on what he saw Cholly teach the Temptations and other vocal acts. In 1969, just eleven seconds into their performance of "I Want You Back" on *The Ed Sullivan Show*, the Jackson Five go into the Drop Charleston. In B-boying, aka breakdance, this step is called the Cholly Rock; in fact, when I spoke to old school New York Rockers (rocking was a prelude to Breaking), Enoch Torres and Frank Rojas told me that it was possible that the Jackson Five performance was an influence for the step. They couldn't say with absolute certainty, just that it was possible. The "Kid n Play Kickstep" (1988) created for rap duo Kid n' Play was originally called the "Funky Charleston," credited to one of their dancers, Nadine "Hi-Hat" Ruffin. Today the Charleston can be found in the Harlem dance called LiteFeet in the steps known as the Tone-Wop and the Rev-up (2003–4).

In the 1934 British film *Evergreen,* directed by Clarence (Buddy) Bradley, there is a Charleston dance sequence featuring all White dancers.[26] While the customary eighth-note bounce is present, what is missing is the aesthetic of the cool and a basic groove. The movement is upright, restrictive, and rhythmically stinted. Ironically, at the end of the dance sequence, Bradley, a Black man, performs the Charleston in its authentic form. Clearly visible in Bradley is the Afro-kinetic memory.

African Americans may not be in control of financial or political policies. We're often not even in control of our cultural products like dance or music. Many of the things that make America hip and are some of the world's greatest influences come from the morphology of Afro-kinetic memory, namely our musical sensibility of time and rhythm, our expressive dances, colorful language, stylish fashion, southern cuisine, even hairstyles. European monarchs scented the minds of the people with their hegemonic ideals, which considered Africans and African Americans as beasts, vulgar, and savages, an ideology that author, professor, and social activist bell hooks so poignantly makes in her book *Belonging: A Culture of Place*: "Whatever African Americans created in music, dance, poetry, painting, etc. it was regarded as testimony, bearing witness, challenging racist thinking which suggested that Black folks were not fully human, were uncivilized, and that the measure of this was our collective failure to create 'great' art. White supremacist ideology insisted that Black people, being more animal than human, lacked the capacity to feel and therefore could not engage the finer sensibilities that were the breeding ground for art."[27] Whiteness made room for styles of dance that eradicated the morphology of Afro-kinesthetic memory. Since this is a necessary ingredient to make jazz, all styles that follow are, at best, merely jazz-influenced.

CONCLUSION

African Americans have been navigating structural racism and its ability to adapt to cultural shifts over the centuries. The evidence of how Black folk have navigated this arduous terrain can be witnessed in the corporeal rhetoric of each dancer and through their unique expression of how these systems have been imposed upon their lives. This is the very essence of jazz music and dance.

The colonizing mind-set continues to approximate, deconstruct, inject its ideologies, package and claim ownership, and then teaches people to preserve the legacy of White jazz dance "paragons." I have been challenged by the disciples of these "jazz greats," and from my position as a Black dancer I know there exist impalpable elements that lie beyond physical movement. They are intangibles that tether jazz dance to an African American experience and hold a deep structural cellular memory of African aesthetics, traditions, and rituals. This historical, philosophical, ethnographic, and anthropological knowledge is found in work by Robert Farris Thompson in *Flash of the Spirit*, Joseph E. Holloway in *Africanisms in American Culture*, Michael Ventura in *Shadow Dancing in the USA*, and Yvonne Daniels in *Dancing Wisdom*.[28] These writings provide a sense of cultural memory that helps the reader to examine the lavish heritage of peoples of African origins, which is not only an attestation to their evergreen lived practice, but it also brings to the light that which was presumed lost to the dark. Decentering Whiteness involves proactive changes in dismantling the anti-Blackness narrative that attributes leadership in jazz dance to White practitioners without context for the appropriation that occurred.

So, what can we do to move things forward as choreographers, performers, dance educators, and tradition-bearers? First, speak truth to power and recognize that the original form has been subtracted from the jazz dance canon. Jazz dance is rooted in the vernacular expression of tap, eccentric dance, Lindy Hop, and solo dances such as the Charleston and the Mooch. Contrary to popular belief, ballet is not the foundation of all dance; there are a plethora of dance forms centuries older than ballet. It is crucial that educators teach their students about the Black pioneers and the origins of jazz dance; they need to abrogate the written White narrative of jazz dance and engage in *sankofa*, which means go back and get it. Teach the original African American jazz dance. Teach Lindy Hop and eccentric dances (Leg-o-mania, Rubberneck, Rubber Legs). Teach the routines, and combinations like Norma Miller's Trickeration, the Pepsi Bethel routine, Earl Tucker's Snake Hips, Mama Lou Parks's the Stops routine, the Little Apple, Frankie Manning's Big Apple, Leonard Reed and Willie Bryant's Shim Sham, the chorus girl routines and solo jazz steps, and the fluid isolations of burlesque dancers like Madeline "Sahiji" Jackson. Learning these movements teaches polyrhythmic flow, asymmetry, grounded weight, and other Africanist aesthetics. These are the Black aesthetics that are paramount to the morphology of Afro-kinetic memory and should be primary and clearly definable. Otherwise, jazz dance created by White choreographers and teachers will continue with prominence and without reparations to Black pioneers of jazz dance.

NOTES

1. Joe Nash, "The Real Thing," *Dance Magazine*, March 1994.

2. Robert White, "Al Minns & Leon James 'The Playboy Clip,'" YouTube, Playboy's Penthouse, October 10, 2012, YouTube video, https://youtu.be/LA-u7rp-SrU.

3. Patricia Cohen, "Jazz Dance as a Continuum," in *Jazz Dance: A History of the Roots and Branches*, ed. Lindsay Guarino and Wendy Oliver (Gainesville: University Press of Florida, 2014), 4.

4. Mark Knowles, *The Wicked Waltz and Other Scandalous Dances* (Jefferson, NC: McFarland, 2009), 161, 237.

5. Ibid., 168.

6. Anne Shaw Faulkner, Head of Music Department of the General Federation of Women's Clubs, *Ladies' Home Journal*, August 1921, 16–34.

7. Daniel J. Levitin, *This Is Your Brain on Music: The Science of a Human Obsession* (New York: Plume/Penguin, 2007), 106.

8. 2nacheki, "Top 10 Best Traditional African Dances," October 12, 2017, YouTube video, https://youtu.be/gDPdBiR5aoQ.

9. Constance Valis Hill, *Tap Dancing America: A Cultural History* (New York: Oxford University Press, 2010).

10. Vintage Swing Dance, "Earl 'Snake Hips' Tucker 1930," *Crazy House,* June 15, 2016, YouTube video, https://youtu.be/zVrwDOQ6jSE.

11. *The Spirit Moves*, dir. Mura Dehn (1987; New York: Dancetime, 2009), DVD.

12. MrMemories, "The Original Stroll—February 1958," *Seventeen TV*, February 4, 2011, YouTube video, https://youtu.be/UrGLNtZorEg.

13. Janet Jackson, "Janet Jackson—The Pleasure Principle (official music video)," A&M Records, December 13, 2009, YouTube video, https://youtu.be/Q-gu1KETjVY.

14. James W. Robey, "Jazz Dance Webcast Episode 7: Camel Walk," Jazz Dance Technique & Syllabus™, September 24, 2011, YouTube video, https://youtu.be/kqu KFyoQQ6Q.

15. Knowles, *The Wicked Waltz*, 166.

16. Amy Koritz, *Culture Makers: Urban Performance and Literature in the 1920s* (Champaign: University of Illinois Press, 2008), 81.

17. Ibid.

18. Marshall Stearns and Jean Stearns, *Jazz Dance: The Story of American Vernacular Dance* (New York: Macmillan, 1968), 12.

19. Several years ago, I was visiting my friend Ama Wray, a professor at the University of California, Irvine. She had recently returned from Africa and shared her experience with me, mentioning the connection of the Yankadi and the Charleston.

20. In another conversation during the Racine Black Dance Festival in Boston, I had the opportunity to speak with some dancers from Guinea, Africa, who also confirmed their belief that the Charleston is related to their cultural dance the Yankadi.

21. "Music: Jenkins Bands," *Time Magazine*, August 26, 1935, http://content.time. com/time/subscriber/article/0,33009,748914,00.html.

22. Willie "The Lion" Smith and George Hoefer, *Music on my Mind* (New York: Da Capo, 1964), 66.

23. Kibble White, "Jenkins Orphanage Band—Outtakes—Moving Image Research Collections," July 12, 2013, YouTube video, https://youtu.be/ZZFoGXZ_NuY.

24. FXBLUES, "Little Buck Tap Dancing 1955 TV Appearance," *Chance of a Lifetime* TV show, 1955, May 20, 2011, YouTube video, https://youtu.be/DpV2Xl4e4YQ.

25. Afra Bass, "James Brown & The Famous Flames, live on the T.A.M.I show 1964," Teenage Award Music International (Santa Monica, 1964), May 5, 2016, YouTube video, https://www.youtube.com/watch?v=6-EoX2JxCs4.

26. Vintage Swing Dance, "A British Charleston 1934 (Jessie Matthews)," *Evergreen,* November 13, 2015, YouTube video, https://youtu.be/K6ou3QmWs3E.

27. bell hooks, *Belonging: A Culture of Place* (New York: Routledge, 2009), 123.

28. Joseph E Holloway, *Africanisms in American Culture* (Bloomington: Indiana University Press, 2005); Michael Ventura, *Shadow Dancing in the USA* (Los Angeles: Tarcher, 1985); Yvonne Daniel, *Dancing Wisdom* (Champaign: University of Illinois Press, 2005).

Madisen Nielsen, Tiara Saddler, Savanna Blocker, Destiney Lockhart, and Cerena Chaney (*left to right*) perform Brandi Coleman's *And One More Thing . . .* , April 2016. BD Pruitt @ East Market Studios.

II

Analyzing Aesthetics

The second part of this book includes chapters by three authors who discuss aesthetics and technique. With collective intent, Julie Kerr-Berry, Carlos R. A. Jones, and Lindsay Guarino forge a pathway for identifying and discussing the elements at the heart of rooted jazz dance.

Kerr-Berry's illuminative discussion on the Africanist elements intrinsic to the roots of jazz dance carves the pathway opening. Her discourse walks us through each element with illustrative definitions and visceral examples of dance where Africanist elements are prominent. Jones continues mining the pathway with a dive into the definition of "technique" and a deconstruction of the dominant practice of absconding with its meaning and ascribing it to the aesthetics and skills of Eurocentric concert dance forms. Using the Africanist elements, he offers explanation on how technique operates in jazz dance, thus laying the groundwork for reclamation of the definition. Guarino completes the pathway and sets the coordinates for new destinations by unveiling a process for identifying rooted jazz dance, moving the conversation forward. Giving space for essence that is specifically and unapologetically African American, that being the Africanist aesthetics, which are steeped in the roots of African ancestry yet nourished in the blended American soil, she outlines a step-by-step approach by asking, "Where's the jazz?" All three authors help provide the tools to better understand jazz dance aesthetics in connection to the West African roots and African American core of the jazz continuum.

5

Africanist Elements in American Jazz Dance

JULIE KERR-BERRY

Tracing the authentic roots of American jazz dance requires a close examination of its Africanist origins. Such focus reveals how this art form carries with it aesthetic elements derived from "the trafficking of African peoples" through the transatlantic slave trade.[1] Once transplanted to the North American continent, their bodies retained these aesthetic elements despite the brutality of slavery. Encoded in the cultural memory of Black bodies lies the origins of jazz dance and how it evolved through the centuries.

While Africanist elements are recognizable in most forms of American dance, this chapter will focus on the pathway they took in the jazz-dancing body. Cultural historian Brenda Dixon Gottschild used the term "signposts of the Africanist aesthetic" as a way to identify their remarkable impact.[2] Due to the potency of the African diaspora, like a large alluvial fan that spanned the Atlantic Ocean, these elements were deposited throughout the Americas. The formation of jazz dance in the United States is one example of the pathways this flow of movement took.

African art historian Robert Farris Thompson formulated what he termed "canons of fine form" as a way to describe what today is referred to as an Africanist aesthetic.[3] He also located these canons, specific to their tribal origins, throughout West and Central Africa.[4] Others have added to or extended Thompson's work, with some more specific to jazz dance than others.[5] For purposes of this discussion, these Africanist aesthetic principles will be referred to as elements. Therefore, this chapter's aim is to make visible the Africanist aesthetic within jazz dance by providing a glossary of these elements. The ultimate purpose of this chapter is to bring into the foreground what has been unrecognized, ignored, minimized, or erased altogether from jazz dance's complex history.

INCUBATION, DILUTION, AND THEFT

Jazz dance developed along a circuitous path and was influenced by other movement elements, namely, European. While its Africanist elements originated in West Africa, they were incubated in the United States early on in plantation dances, minstrelsy, and Vaudeville before they became identifiable as particular to the jazz dance idiom.[6] Dixon Gottschild astutely stated in reference to this contact between Africans and Europeans in North America: "In spite of our denials, opposites intermingle more often than we admit. Cultures borrow from one another, and fusions abound."[7]

Further, due to the unequal power dynamics between Blacks and Whites in the United States, as jazz dance emerged and evolved through the centuries, it was stolen by Whites. It is important to recognize the importance of how oral histories counter common historical accounts. For example, early in his career, Charles Augins danced with Talley Beatty. The dancer/choreographer recounted how Jerome Robbins essentially stole from the work of Talley Beatty.[8] Similarly, Eleo Pomare stated that, "Whites plagiarized the wealth of fertile material that Black Americans produced, material which is glorified only after it has been absorbed and 'whitened,' as in the cases of George Gershwin, Jerome Robbins, and Elvis Presley."[9] As a result of such theft, jazz dance was infused with European influences. Jazz dance's rhythmic density and complexity were flattened, which caused the body to resist its natural weightiness, blurring and/or extinguishing its Africanist origins when appropriated by Whites.

AFRICAN ORIGINS

Tracing Africanist elements of jazz dance to the African continent, Takiyah Nur Amin located the regions, mostly in West Africa, where many Black Americans can trace their roots and, in turn, their tribal ancestry.[10] These dance traditions have lived on as physical and oral practices, and to connect to one's ancestors. Thompson described the metaphorical goal of danced rituals in which the dancing body functions as an intermediator, or crossroads, when this world and the spiritual one converge.[11] For example, he referenced the Yoruba of West Africa: "Ritual contact with divinity underscores the religious aspirations of the Yoruba. To become possessed by the spirit of a Yoruba deity, which is a formal goal of religion, is to 'make the god,' to capture numinous flowing force within one's body."[12] The significance of Thompson's analysis to jazz dance is that centuries later, this spiritual nature or "flowing force" was made manifest in the body in different ways as it responded to emerging jazz rhythms in North America. Thompson's analysis is important to this discussion because it reveals the origins of jazz dance as a secularized offspring of this spiritual force.

Haitian, Cuban, and Brazilian Origins

As the transatlantic slave trade ensued, the alluvial fan spread from West Africa to the Caribbean. Yvonne Daniels described how African-based religious practices were retained in the dancing body of Africans for centuries. Embodied as *orisha*, these practices manifested themselves in response to specific rhythms that were then transformed in the bodies of Haitian, Cuban, and Brazilian devotees.[13] After observing a lengthy ceremony among the Cuban Yoruba, Daniels described herself as feeling "a state of unusual excitement, filled with multiple layers of dance, music, and ritual."[14] Once secularized, these *orisha* were one source of jazz-based isolations. Understanding this complex process is essential to the roots of jazz dance.

Music and Rhythm

Inextricably connected is how movement and rhythm are manifested in the jazz dancing body. The power of the body to articulate Africanist rhythms in the spine, the pelvis, or the shoulders is a fundamental principle of jazz dance. Often these structures were played against one another, musically and through movement. Thompson referred to this as "playing the body."[15] He stated that this "playing" made "the body glitter with multiple response to multiple meter, with playing the body parts as patterns, with wearing design upon, or deep within the flesh, all elements rhythmized with speed and strength."[16] It is worth noting a more recent Africanist perspective from scholar Thomas Talawa Prestø. He conceptualized this complex phenomenon as "Rhythmic Physics," noting that this approach "serves as a way to understand the technical and physical uses of rhythm in movement quality and propulsion."[17]

Tracings

This glossary of Africanist elements appears below, first by definition and then by providing an example in the jazz dance idiom. Essential to this discussion is that in constructing this glossary, there was a risk that the cultural specificity and complexity of this Africanist history might suffer. These elements reflect the tracings of what were once profoundly distinct movement responses, embodied by African dancers from specific ethnic regions, who had unique cosmologies, dances, and traditions and whose homelands were concentrated on the western side of the continent. Nonetheless, it is important to continue such discourse. Jazz dance owes its highly sophisticated artistry and impact on American culture to these Africanist elements. While these elements are addressed independently, they are interconnected in practice.

Glossary

While there are many dimensions of these Africanist elements, for the purposes of this discussion of American jazz dance the most salient include: (1) *asymmetry*; (2) *call-and response*; (3) *coolness*; (4) *ephebism;* (5) *flat-footedness*; (6) *get down*; (7) *improvisation*; (8) *movement initiated from the hips*; (9) *polycentric isolations*; (10) *propulsive rhythm*; and (11) *supple and articulated spine.*[18]

Asymmetry

As much as a design principle in African-based art such as kente cloth or sculpture, *asymmetry* also applies to the dancing body and the musical landscape it inhabits. Thompson's use of the word "staggered" in the following statement captures this element as follows: "Staggered motifs on certain chiefly cloths can be profitably compared with off-beat phrasing in music, dance and decorative structure."[19] This can be applied to the African dancing body that physicalizes asymmetry through *polycentric isolations* when the feet may move to a duple rhythm and the hips, *movement initiated from the hips*, to a triple. It occurs through highly syncopated music, or *propulsive rhythm*. Furthermore, this principle is also manifested in the shape of the body dancing in space.

In the jazz dance idiom, there are countless examples of asymmetrical movement in the body. Drawing from the wellspring of the vintage jazz vernacular, there are several such as the Charleston and the Shorty George. The documentary *The Spirit Moves: A History of Black Social Dance on Film, 1900–1986* offers a treasure trove of the Black jazz dance vernacular like the highly syncopated Charleston performed by Savoy Ballroom greats like Frankie Manning, Al Minns, and Leon James, among others.[20] Asymmetrically, the dancers kick and reach the opposite leg to arm—all facilitated by *get down,* which roots the dancers into the dance floor. The dance called the Shim Sham features the Shorty George.[21] From a *get down* position, the jazz dancer shifts the hips from side to side, causing the knees to swivel in opposition while the upper torso and limbs reach toward the floor. In effect, the Shorty George creates a zigzag shape in the body.

Call-and-Response

This Africanist element describes the relationship between dancer and drummer, soloist and chorus. In effect, it creates an overlap and garners an interconnectivity in which the body responds to a drum or bell rhythm, or a vocalist to an ensemble. According to Thompson, among African peoples south of the Sahara, "solo-and-circle, solo-and-line, solo-and-solo forms of dancing mirror melodic call-and-response."[22] *Improvisation* adds intensity to this element by building upon each iteration as it unfolds.

To the tap dancer, *call-and-response* coupled with *improvisation* also advances the intensity and ingenuity of rhythms created. In the early twentieth century, the Hoofers Club in Harlem was an example of where tap dancers would converge to challenge one another with new steps, employing both elements in the process. Tap legend John W. Bubbles, "Bubbles," recounted that there was "not a dancer who has been in New York—if he was colored—that I haven't watched, and if he thought he could dance, we've had it out."[23] *Call-and-response* is also present in the Big Apple, which is derived from the Ring Shout, a Black-based, sacred step-pattern practiced initially by the enslaved on southern plantations.[24] Due to the Great Migration, the Big Apple traveled from its southern roots to northern dance halls. It consisted of dancers who formed a circle around the caller and responded with dance steps characteristic of the early Black vernacular.[25]

Coolness

As an Africanist element, *coolness* is multilayered and complex due to its pervasiveness across all of the Africanist elements.[26] It is as much a physicality as it is a way one conducts oneself in society. While community creates a collective, *coolness* also supports individualism within this social structure. In her analysis of Thompson's work, Dixon Gottschild described it as "the aesthetic of the cool."[27] She stated: "It is an attitude ... that combines composure and vitality. Its prime components are aesthetic visibility and lucidity (dancing movements with clarity, presenting the self with clarity), luminosity, or brilliance."[28] Yet another layer is that *coolness* embraces "oppositions, asymmetries, and traditional juxtapositions"—or hotness and coolness contained in one moment. Both are present in the dancing body, in music, and in African textiles.

In the jazz dance idiom, to be "cool" signals an authenticity with an ample dose of *les tresors de souplesse* (the treasures of flexibility).[29] A jazz dancer exhibits coolness based on lived experience. It is an attitude, a balance struck between the hot and the cool that the dancer embodies. Dixon Gottschild described the "asymmetrical walk of African American males, which shows an attitude of carelessness cultivated with a calculated aesthetic clarity" that effortlessly translates to a jazz strut.[30] In tap dance, Cheryl Willis described a performance by Jimmy Slyde when "His sliding movement knocks him off balance; but as he gains control his facial gesture reveals a comic surprise which saves the moment and recaptures the 'Cool.'"[31] Alvin Ailey's jazz-influenced work *Night Creatures* (1974), to Duke Ellington's music by the same title, exhibits four Africanist elements: *coolness, get down, movement initiated from the hips*, and *polycentric isolation*.

Ephebism

Thompson described *ephebism* as a quality of youthfulness; and it has several dimensions. To Thompson, African peoples, "regardless of their actual age, return to strong, youthful patterning whenever they move within the streams of energy which flow from drums or other sources of percussion."[32] Here, the "lack of separation between performer and spectator" while present in African forms, is blurred when compared to Western constructs.[33] It is exhibited in the body through "rhythmic speed, sharpness (as in sudden or abrupt changes in dynamics), force, and attack."[34] *Ephebism* is made visible through the *polycentric isolation* of body parts that are played like different instruments.[35]

In hip-hop, Rennie Harris Puremovement embodies the concept of *ephebism*. His dancers fill the stage with speed and a syncopated rhythmicality that is facilitated by hugging and rebounding from the earth as they *get down*. Thompson's description *ephebism* applies to Harris's dancers when "Beauty blazes out of bodies which are most alive and young."[36] His dancers exude a *coolness* when they perform, as their bodies pop and lock through *polycentric isolation* to *propulsive rhythm*. As in African dance contexts, Harris's audiences engage in what Patricia Cohen described as "vocal encouragement" when the separation between them blurs.[37]

Flat-Footedness

As an Africanist element, *flat-footedness* refers to when the full surface of the foot makes continuous contact with the ground and is facilitated by *get down*. The foot is not only flat but is also bare to ensure reverent contact with the earth. According to Stearns and Stearns, "the African style is often flat-footed and favors gliding, dragging, or shuffling steps."[38] Prior to colonization by Europeans, many African belief systems were polytheistic and geocentric because of their belief in multiple gods and links to natural elements like water or thunder. Glass stated that among African peoples like the Dogon dancers, many "dances are performed by lines or circles" and usually counterclockwise in which the feet contact the earth.[39] Moving together in this fashion also helped unify a community and was less about the individual and more about the collective.

To the jazz dancer, the feet retain contact with the ground and require a giving into weight to maintain such connection, or to *get down*. The result is a smooth and flexible style of delivery and an ability to quickly shift in direction, rhythm, and intensity. An early pre-jazz form was the Ring Shout—a sacred dance in which Blacks moved counterclockwise in a circle, connecting their feet to the floor or ground. In the jazz dance context, a circle formation also built a sense of community in a highly participatory, secular context. It also formed the basis of the Big Apple, a staple of the jazz dance vernacular.[40] The execution of flat-footed, step-based movement was common to the repertoire of such Black recording artists as James Brown, Michael Jackson, and dance regulars on the televised show *Soul Train*.[41]

Get Down

This element refers to a giving into weight in which knees act as springs that release into and rebound from the earth. Glass described it as an "Orientation to the Earth": "The African dancer often bends slightly toward the earth, flattens the feet against it in a wide, solid stance, and flexes the knees."[42] *Get down* is also visible in African sculptures where figures' knees are carved into deeply flexed positions. In effect, the body's weight is directed into the earth and does not resist it. Thompson defined it as follows: "the use of 'get down' sequences in the dance, (is) where a performer or group of performers assume a deeply inflected, virtually crouching position, thus moving in proximity to the level of the earth."[43]

One of the most profound markers of an Africanist aesthetic in jazz dance is the ability of the dancer to direct weight into the ground and not away from it. The further a dancer moves from this rootedness, or the ability to *get down,* the more likely the dancer is less rooted in the authenticity of the form. An excellent example of such weightiness is the scene from the 1943 film *Cabin in the Sky* when Lindy dancers enter a dance club from the street. They simultaneously exhibit *coolness* and *movement initiated from the hips* as they prepare for a night of dancing to Duke Ellington's band. Another example of *get down* is embodied in the accompanying photo of Katherine Dunham performing opposite Vanoye Aikens in her 1946 work *Nostalgia*. Dunham drops her pelvis while Aikens lunges deeply forward toward her.

In contrast, Carlos Jones described how racism functioned in jazz dance

FIGURE 5.1. Photograph of Katherine Dunham and Vanoye Aikens in *Nostalgia*, choreographed by Katherine Dunham. Photo by Roger Wood. New York Public Library Digital Collections.

as Whites appropriated jazz dance, infused it with ballet, and repelled the ground, as opposed to giving into it.[44] For example, the weightedness of the Nicholas Brothers' tapping in the 1943 film *Story Weather* contrasts with Frank Sinatra and Gene Kelly's in the 1949 film *Take Me Out to the Ballgame*.[45]

Improvisation

As an Africanist element, *improvisation* promotes individual expression as the dancer responds to various musical stimuli. This element allows for the constant innovation and evolution of an Africanist movement vocabulary.[46] It is both a state of mind as well as a dancer's physical response. Thompson correlated this element to *get down* because it facilitates improvisatory responses from a dancer. Among Surinam dancers, he noted that *get down* helps them to be ready to respond improvisationally, and in effect, "mark time" "until they decide that the psychological moment to improvise has come."[47] Here, Thompson's concept of *les tresors de souplesse* applies because it helps to facilitate such responses.[48] Thus, *improvisation* is connected to the element of having a *supple and articulated spine*.

In the jazz dance idiom, *improvisation* has been the vehicle through which invention occurred and the form evolved. In jazz dance or tap, the ability to improvise promoted creativity on the spot and was a staple of the performance process. It is interesting to consider a statement made by Prestø when he differentiated between dancers who executed "Visual Representation" of polyrhythmic music as in "house dance" and when they engaged in "Rhythmic

Creation."[49] The latter concept involved an improvisatory response, while the former more mimetic. In the twentieth century, consider the role *improvisation* played in the Lindy Hop, or to hoofers like Buster Brown, Bill "Bojangles" Robinson, or Jimmy Slyde, or to the floor shows of Earl "Snake Hips" Tucker. A more contemporary example is the work of S. Ama Wray, who is the artistic director of the JazzXchange. Her group's mission is "to bring jazz music back into alignment with dance" which fuses live music with dance through *improvisation*.[50]

Movement Initiated from the Hips

Stearns and Stearns described this Africanist element when movement "is centrifugal, exploding outward from the hips."[51] In this sense, the pelvis becomes a flexible center from which movement originates and radiates outward from this central core to the body's distal points. Thompson referred to this ability among the "Liberian Dan, Nigerian Tiv, or Zairois Yanzi" to dance "as if she or he had no bones."[52] He referred to this sensibility as a "matter of choreographic law" among the Yoruba in Nigeria and the Luba in Zaire in "that a person must move his hips in as supple a manner as possible."[53] This element is supported by *get down* and a *supple and articulated spine* because both mobilize the pelvis.

During the mid-1920s, Earl "Snake Hips" Tucker emerged in the New York City club scene as part of floor shows at Connie's Inn and the Cotton Club.[54] Within the early jazz dance vernacular, his pelvis was emblematic of such movement initiation. Stearns and Stearns noted that during one such show in which his characteristic silver buckle, which was large and centered at his navel, functioned to throw "rays in larger circles, the fact that the pelvis and the whole torso were becoming increasingly involved in the movement was unavoidably clear."[55] Here, the ability of Tucker to *get down* and maintain a *supple and articulated spine* facilitated his pelvic movement so that it radiated outward, augmented by the shiny silver buckle. Another example is Cleo Parker Robinson's performance of Katherine Dunham's *Barrelhouse Blues* (1938). In the work, she used *get down* opposite her partner, facilitating *movement initiated from the hips*, and a *supple and articulated spine*. As well, Parker Robinson exhibited *coolness* in her body attitude as she moved teasingly about her partner, signifying a youthful and vibrant demeanor in this coupled dance.

Polycentric Isolation

Thompson referred to this Africanist element as "dancing many drums."[56] In effect, the dancer embodies two or more rhythms simultaneously while moving, using a series of movement isolations as in the head, shoulders, or hips. Among the Tiv of Nigeria, Thompson stated that "multi-metric danc- ing restores music to muscular notation in which 'notes' are written in the flesh and can be followed by attention to different body parts."[57] Each 'note' is played in the body as it responds to different rhythms. Use of a *supple and ar- ticulated spine* keeps the torso open and responsive to support such isolations.

Perhaps nothing more vividly denotes jazz dance than body-part isolations. For example, Katherine Dunham and Archie Savage's use of shoulder and hip isolations, or *polycentric isolations,* is particularly evident in her 1941 work *Car- nival of Rhythm*.[58] To Afro-Caribbean rhythms, *get down, movement initiated from the hips* and a *supple and articulated spine* facilitate this rhythmic play and movement dexterity between each other.

Propulsive Rhythm

Its two components, or what Thompson termed an "attack impulse," form the basis of this Africanist element. *Propulsive rhythm* consists of highly syn- copated movement and sound. This sheer rhythmic force created a musical landscape that swings, eliciting multidimensional movement responses in the body.[59] Thompson compared African-based musicality to European: "A classical musician is mindful only of vertical accuracy and pays no heed to propulsive flow nor motion; he does not become involved in the horizontal, rhythmic demands of the music."[60] These elements converge and support *poly- centric isolation* in which individual parts are "played" in the body like separate instruments.

In the jazz dance idiom, the Lindy is an example of how the body swings through time and in space, riding the infectious drive of syncopated rhythms. Responding to music from the Big Band era, dancers dropped their weight, or *get down* using a spring-like response in their knees and hips through *impro- visation*. For example, Stearns and Stearns described this relationship in two well-known swing bands, Chick Webb's Orchestra and Al Cooper's Savoy Sul- tans: "Above all, the two bands were a constant inspiration to dancers, and their propulsive rhythms set the pace at the Savoy."[61] In reality, this was a two- way street in which musicians inspired dancers *and* dancers inspired musicians through the current of energy that flowed between them.

Supple and Articulated Spine

This element allows the body to use multiple planes and connects to *get down* by moving "like your back ain't got no bones."[62] But this element is deeper than that because such suppleness is both attitudinal and embodied. It is what

Thompson referred to as "*les tresors de souplesse*," stating, "Africans are . . . very much aware of the import of flexibility as a sign of youth in life, as demonstration of the bright willingness to respond to change in music and in speech."[63] Thus, to move with an awareness of the spine, to bend, to rotate, to undulate are ways of being, as well as ways of moving.

In the jazz dance idiom, a stilted and erect spine stops the flow of movement energy that is essential to embodying the multirhythm and multitextural aesthetic of this form. In (Katherine) Dunham technique either at the barre or moving across the floor, this causes specific regions of the spine to be articulated independently. Today, the JazzAntiqua Dance & Music Ensemble is a company dedicated to celebrating "the jazz tradition as a vital thread in the cultural fabric of African American history and heritage, and a defining element of the American experience."[64] Under the artistic direction and choreographic vision of Pat Taylor, her work centers on a historical perspective of what she termed "jazz theatre." Taylor draws from the musical wellspring of such jazz greats as Duke Ellington, Miles Davis, Nina Simone, and John Coltrane. Inherent in her work is a convergence of the elements: *coolness, get down, movement initiated from the hips*, along with use of a *supple and articulated spine*. For example, in her 2019 work *Suite Nina,* dancers embody these elements as they move through the musical landscape of Simone's music. The work also resists infusing ballet technique into a concertized form of jazz dance.

THE BEDROCK

These Africanist elements formed the bedrock of jazz dance in the United States. In the early seventeenth century, they were first carried in the bodies of enslaved West Africans through the torturous Middle Passage, and into more than three hundred years of slavery. Colonization engineered and justified slavery to supply a continuous labor force that founded this country. In the process, Africanisms fused with Europeanisms when Blacks and Whites came into intimate contact with one another on southern plantations. Despite the horrors of their sustained captivity, the systematized violence and oppression that continued past the Civil War, through Reconstruction, to the Jim Crow era, and northward through the Great Migration, Black bodies remembered. Encoded in them were dense and overlapping rhythms, a weighted response to the earth, improvisatory structures, and a spine that responded like a central link to its articulated parts. It is the recovery and rewriting of jazz dance history that acknowledges this complex past despite repeated attempts by Whites to confiscate it and call it their own. While born out of a violent past, it was from a people whose hope, tenacity, and artistic brilliance gifted this country with an art form that these Africanist elements so vividly reveal.

Notes

1. Takiyah Nur Amin, "The African Origins of an American Art Form," in *Jazz Dance: A History of the Roots and Branches,* ed. Lindsay Guarino and Wendy Oliver (Gainesville: University Press of Florida, 2014), 35.

2. Brenda Dixon Gottschild, *Digging the Africanist Presence in American Performance* (Westport, CT: Praeger, 1996), 11.

3. Robert Farris Thompson, *African Art in Motion: Icon and Act* (Berkeley: University of California Press, 1974), 5–45.

4. Ibid.; Robert Farris Thompson, *Flash of the Spirit: African and Afro-American Art and Philosophy* (New York: Vintage, 1985), xiii–xvii.

5. Dixon Gottschild, *Digging the Africanist Presence,* 11. Additional pertinent sources include Lynne Fauley Emery, *Black Dance in the United States from 1619 to 1970,* 2nd ed. (Trenton, NJ: Princeton Book Company, 1989); Barbara S. Glass, *African American Dance: An Illustrated History* (Jefferson, NC: McFarland, 2007); Katrina Hazzard-Gordon, *Jookin': The Rise of Social Dance Formations in African-American Culture* (Philadelphia: Temple University Press, 1990); Marshall Winslow Stearns and Jean Stearns, *Jazz Dance: The Story of American Vernacular Dance* (New York: Da Capo, 1994); and Kariamu Welsh Asante, ed., *African Dance: An Artistic, Historical, and Philosophical Inquiry* (Trenton, NJ: Africa World Press, 1998).

6. Nur Amin, "The Africanist Origins"; Tom Ralabate, "Historical Movement Chart," in *Jazz Dance: A History of the Roots and Branches*, ed. Lindsay Guarino and Wendy Oliver (Gainesville: University Press of Florida, 2014), 69–71; Stearns and Stearns, *Jazz Dance*, 18–131.

7. Dixon Gottschild, *Digging the Africanist Presence,* 59.

8. Charles Augins, "Dance History: Then and Now" (panelist, International Association of Blacks in Dance Conference, Philadelphia, January 17, 2020).

9. This quote is from an unpublished article by Eleo Pomare entitled "Racism in America Then and Now," August 1, 2005, 9.

10. Amin, "The Africanist Origins," 39.

11. Thompson, *Flash of the Spirit*, 9.

12. Ibid.

13. It is important to recognize that all *orisha* are not the same. Depending on their country of origin, the word has different spellings. In Cuba it is *orichas*. In Brazil and Nigeria, it is spelled *orixás*. In Haiti, it is spelled *lwas*. Further, each *orisha* is reflected in danced ceremonies unique to its quality and temperament (see Yvonne Daniels, *Dancing Wisdom: Embodied Knowledge in Haitian Vodou, Cuban Yoruba, and Bahian Candomblé* [Urbana: University of Illinois Press, 2005]).

14. Ibid., 5–43.

15. Thompson, *African Art in Motion*, 9.

16. Ibid., 18.

17. From a brochure that was distributed by Thomas Talawa Prestø entitled *Tabanka African & Caribbean Peoples Dance Ensemble* during the 2020 International Association for Blacks in Dance Conference in Philadelphia (January 16, 2020). Prestø is the artistic director of the Tabanka African & Caribbean Peoples Dance Ensemble.

18. Dixon Gottschild, *Digging the Africanist Presence*; Stearns and Stearns, *Jazz Dance*; Thompson, *African Art in Motion*.

19. Thompson, *African Art in Motion*, 11.

20. Mura Dehn and Herbert Matter, *The Spirit Moves: A History of Black Social Dance on Film, 1900–1986* (Dancetime, 2008).

21. In a YouTube clip (www.youtube.com/watch?v=KhnNhr1spoM), Frankie Manning and son Chazz Young perform the Shim Sham, in which several examples of the Shorty George appear. Look for the quick ball-change that occurs on the right foot to signal this step about 2:24 minutes into the clip.

22. Thompson, *African Art in Motion*, 27.

23. Stearns and Stearns, *Jazz Dance*, 218–19.

24. Mark Knowles, *Tap Roots: The Early History of Tap Dancing* (Jefferson, NC: McFarland, 2002), 59–62.

25. Ibid., 62.; Fauley Emery, *Black Dance from 1619 to Today*, 2nd ed., 221; Glass, *African American Dance: An Illustrated History*, 259–64. Some of the steps from the Ring Shout evolved into the Black Bottom, the Shimmy, and later jazz-based vernacular dances like the Lindy Hop, the Shag, the Suzie-Q, and Truckin'.

26. Dixon Gottschild, *Digging the Africanist Presence*; Thompson, *African Art in Motion*; Cheryl Willis, "Tap Dance: Manifestation of the African Aesthetic," in *African Dance: An Artistic, Historical and Philosophical Inquiry*, ed. Kariamu Welsh Asante (Trenton, NJ: African World Press, 1994), 146–49.

27. Thompson, *African Art in Motion*; Dixon Gottschild, *Digging the Africanist Presence*, 16, 17.

28. Dixon Gottschild, *Digging the Africanist Presence,* 16.

29. Thompson, *African Art in Motion*, 10.

30. Ibid., 16.

31. Willis, *African Dance: An Historical and Philosophical Inquiry*, 149.

32. Thompson, *African Art in Motion*, 7.

33. Patricia Cohen, "Jazz Dance as a Continuum," in *Jazz Dance: A History of the Roots and Branches,* ed. Lindsay Guarino and Wendy Oliver (Gainesville: University Press of Florida, 2014), 5.

34. Gottschild, *Digging the Africanist Presence,* 16.

35. Thompson, *African Art in Motion*, 7.

36. Ibid., 5.

37. Cohen, "Jazz Dance as a Continuum," 5.

38. Stearns and Stearns, *Jazz Dance*, 14,15.

39. Glass, *African American Dance: An Illustrated History*, 18.

40. Ibid., 27.

41. Carlos Jones, personal communication, January 1, 2020.

42. Glass, *African American Dance: An Illustrated History*, 16.

43. Thompson, *African Art in Motion*, 13.

44. Carlos Jones, "Jazz Dance and Racism," in *Jazz Dance: A History of the Roots and Branches,* ed. Lindsay Guarino and Wendy Oliver, 231–48 (Gainesville: University Press of Florida, 2014).

45. See the "Jumpin Jive" section *Story Weather*, www.youtube.com/watch?v=Khn NhrıspoM; see the duet "Take Me out to the Ballgame" that Kelly and Sinatra perform in this YouTube clip: www.youtube.com/watch?v=KhnNhrıspoM.

46. Stearns and Stearns, *Jazz Dance,* 15.

47. Thompson, *African Art in Motion*, 14.

48. Ibid., 8–9.

49. Thomas Talawa Prestø stated this during his lecture demonstration entitled "Codifying the Atlantic." It was presented at the International Association of Black in Dance Conference, January 16, 2020.

50. See S. Ama Wray's website for the JazzXchange: http://jazzxchange.org/index.php/about/.

51. Stearns and Stearns, *Jazz Dance,* 15.

52. Thompson, *African Art in Motion*, 9.

53. Ibid.

54. Stearns and Stearns, *Jazz Dance,* 235–38.

55. Ibid., 236.

56. Thompson, *African Art in Motion*, 14.

57. Ibid., 16.

58. Isolations were a part of Dunham Technique, and Dunham's use of them resulted from her ethnographic work conducted in the Caribbean. This said, it is important to note that isolations were already embodied in the jazz dance vernacular as practiced in social settings in the United States.

59. Thompson, *African Art in Motion*, 7.

60. Ibid.

61. Stearns and Stearns, *Jazz Dance,* 317.

62. Ibid., 9.

63. Thompson, *African Art in Motion*, 10.

64. See JazzAntiqua Dance & Music Ensemble's website, www.jazzantiqua.org/companybio.html.

6

Jazz Dance Technique, Aesthetics, and Racial Supremacy

CARLOS R. A. JONES

It would be difficult to find a dance artist who does not have a personal understanding of what it means to use or develop technique. At some level, intentional or not, in depth or minimally, all dance artists work with technique. Transferring dance, teacher to student, mentor to fellow, practitioner to apprentice, or other, is not possible without engaging technique. Yes, there are instances of talented artists who move with natural gifts or are self-taught. Even these dance practitioners work with technique. They rehearse over and over, using skills, organic, invented, or learned, to perfect a set of movements designed for a particular way of dancing. This is technique. If technique is inseparable from dance, why are conversations on technique in jazz dance contentious? Understanding the definition of technique, learning how to identify where technique exists in rooted and vernacular jazz dance, and then clarifying how the concept of technique gets applied along the jazz dance continuum[1] is where we begin to intercede in the contentiousness.

TECHNIQUE AND MEANING

Determining the meaning of technique is quite simple. How it gets interpreted for jazz dance is complex. At a basic level, a dictionary gives a quick, simple answer. *Merriam-Webster's Collegiate Dictionary Online* defines "technique" as:

1. The manner in which technical details are treated (as by a writer) or basic physical movements are used (as by a dancer).
2. A body of technical methods (as in a craft or in scientific research).

The Oxford American Dictionary fleshes out the definition of "technique" a bit more:

1. Method or skill used for carrying out a specific task.
2. A person's level of skill in a particular field.
3. A skillful or efficient way of doing or achieving something.[2]

Dictionary.com offers even more specifics and seems to indicate that technique is particularly attuned to artistic endeavors:

1. The manner and ability with which an artist, writer, dancer, athlete, or the like employs the *technical* skills of a particular art or field of endeavor.
2. The body of specialized procedures and methods used in any specific field, especially in an area of applied science.
3. Method of performance; way of accomplishing.
4. Technical skill; ability to apply procedures or methods so as to effect a desired result.

The definition(s) above identify the arts, and even dance specifically, in outlining the meaning of "technique." Still, there is indication that technique can move beyond the applied sciences and the arts to encompass broad usage. We see this to be true with examples in daily life: memorization techniques, interrogation techniques, meditation techniques. Naturally, this leads one to believe that identifying technique in jazz dance should happen organically and without contention. This is not the case. A century of White-supremacist practices has sent jazz dance spiraling into a fractured existence, plagued with identity crises that do little to solidify what it means to exemplify technique in jazz dance.

TRANSGRESSIONS AGAINST JAZZ TECHNIQUE

Technique, by its very definition, DOES exist in jazz dance. The contentiousness surrounding jazz dance technique has nothing to do with whether or not such technique exists. The culprit for every heated debate sits squarely at the feet of Whiteness, which has perpetuated ideas about the inferiority of all things Black. It was impossible for jazz dance and its technique to escape discrediting. It was born in the middle of Jim Crow America and has never escaped that White-supremacist clutch. As Whites realized jazz dance's massive appeal to society, the pursuit of White economic prosperity fueled one of the most aggressive assaults on Black culture: appropriation. They took jazz dance as their chattel slave and shackled it into submission, beating and subduing it, and stripping it of its African roots. In their racist arrogance, they failed to see, or value, the organic technique already at play in jazz dance. These artists, who were predominantly White men, extracted certain aspects of jazz, repackaged it, and pushed it back out in the world as testaments to their personal genius. They created codified systems infused with European dance forms, such as ballet, that altered the aesthetic trajectory of jazz dance. This practice has continued over the past century, spawning a number of White-centric jazz dance styles that carry little resemblance to the African American origins.

Whiteness has dominated jazz dance for the last nine decades. From choreography to education, Eurocentric aesthetic values (linear bodylines, a lifted and rigid torso, and extended feet) have been passed forward generation after generation as the indicators of technique. The indoctrinating mind-set of Euro-based dance techniques as superior fed the rhetoric that "ballet is the base of jazz dance technique," a sentence that is passionately debated. When challenged, those buying into the rhetoric hold vehemently to their convictions. This is not shocking; it is frustrating to some, but not shocking. The system of devaluing the original Blackness in jazz dance is engrained in the fabric of America. After much discourse and a few clearly presented facts, those who are most staunch in their belief of "ballet as base" cling to reductive statements like, "Well . . . ballet makes jazz technique better." These declarations of ballet as savior are no more than racist claims that are ill-informed, illogical, and ill-advised. Efforts to understand the definition of technique coupled with a bit of investigation of the skills necessary to perform rooted and vernacular jazz dance would illuminate the illogical thought in statements like "ballet is the base of jazz dance." That statement is false because Africanist elements are the origins of jazz and Eurocentric elements are at the origins of ballet. One is not the other. The hierarchy that sets White dance as the savior to Black dance is colonized propaganda. It has been perpetuated widely to ensure the superior status of dance created in Whiteness.

Most dance artists have been indoctrinated with this idea, particularly if they studied dance within a codified system. From my earliest recollection, I was taught that the foundation to any dance was ballet. It was also made clear that when it comes to jazz, following the Eurocentric idea of technique and aesthetics was mandatory for the concert stage, television, film, Broadway, or any other Western-driven art and entertainment venue. All other forms of jazz dance were marked as lacking in technical conception or labeled as simple and fun. It couldn't possibly be "serious, artistic dance." What, then, is jazz dance technique? What does it look like, and which aesthetic values are aligned with technique? You have to head back to the roots to understand how the branches came to life.

Technique at the Roots

If each section of the tree—the roots, the trunk, and the branches—represent a component of the jazz dance continuum, and it is understood that they are specifically and differently shaped by social, political, and cultural agents, it would be reasonable to suggest that operating as practitioner would require a specific set of skills to master any area along the continuum. In addition, with the numerous ways to dance within the Africanist roots, the kindred vernacular, or the influenced branches, it is safe to say that each jazz-influenced dance form (e.g., funk, contemporary, club) carries with it a set of characteristics, conventions, and cognitions required for precise execution. In keeping with the definitions, an argument could be made that there is technique in ALL styles of jazz dance. Scholars speak quite conclusively about the importance of rhythm, social connection, improvisation, and other African elements to jazz dance practice. In her article "Thinking on Our Feet—Improvisation for Individual and Community Expression in Jazz Dance Class," Erinn Liebhard calls jazz dance educators to prioritize improvisation and clearly points to other aesthetics such as rhythm as imperative.[3] In her plea for jazz dance representation in the curriculum of higher education, Lindsey Salfran dives heavily into rhythm, improvisation, and sense of play (ephebism). She concludes these skills are "important benefits that jazz dance provides a student in higher education."[4] These conversations are happening specifically around the advocating for recognition of the African elements and jazz work that is rooted . . . a call to the exiled origins.

Julie Kerr-Berry's chapter in this book goes to great lengths to define the African elements. Her discussion on each aesthetic illustrates how it operates, laying a framework for their collective examination as a technique. Demystifying jazz technique begins with a brief excavation of African elements. As a side note, it bears stating that inquiry into an African element through written form is the antithesis of its original practice. In standing on the shoulders of their ancestors, the original designers of jazz dance participated in oral and visual traditions when transferring jazz dance from one another. While it would be preferable to transfer this information communally via that tradition, the confines of this medium make that mode impossible. Regardless, the conversation is necessary to get to the task of demystifying jazz dance technique.

Double Bounce

Understanding technique at the root of jazz dance requires a mining of the African elements. *Get down* can be summed up as the act of bending the knees in such a manner that the weight hangs close to the earth. This can happen rapidly or gradually. It can be one continuous motion or be completed in a series of movements. *Get down* can be done in conjunction with other Africanist elements. Regardless of the manner in which *get down* occurs, success happens with the mastery of the use of the quadriceps, hamstrings, body core, and pelvic floor. Take the *double bounce* as an example. Catching a "solid swing" (jazz music term) is best realized when expressed with the *double bounce.* This step is one of the most common pathways to *get down* and is comprised of a lowering and rebounding of the weight in a steady tempo that is rhythmic. The weight gets lowered on each beat with the rebound happening on the swung eighth note (the &) in between each beat. The lowering of the weight is accented each time and is slightly faster than the rebound, which carries with it a slight suspension. The result is the dropping of the pelvis with a steady groove. Mastering the *double bounce* requires developing skill at manipulating the quadriceps and hamstrings. The two muscle groups need to work in harmony with the appropriate amount of tension to allow the step to ride the music with ease and at any tempo. Assisting the quads and hamstrings are the pelvic floor and the core. The core, once engaged, makes it possible to set the torso squarely above the pelvis. This centers the body's weight, which facilitates a direct and efficient drop and rebound in the *double bounce.* This is critical. A centimeter in either direction alters the accuracy, which hinders the dancer's ability to trust the earthy and driving power innate in the step. To add, it alters the aesthetic and *get down* just . . . gets. What it "gets" is for another discussion. The core is also active and maintains a surrounding wall of support for the torso in the event the dancer wishes to engage in *polycentric isolations* or other elements. Let us be clear. In this instance, activating the core is not to be confused with the extremely lifted, bound core required in ballet technique. The feeling is different. The muscles are engaged differently. For the *double bounce* the technique is in mastering the core so that it facilitates maximum agility in the entire torso while negotiating tension and rhythmic articulation. Rounding out the technique in the *double bounce* is the pelvic floor. It acts as a regulator, catching the weighted drop at a specific level and capping the rebound at the desired crest. The skill is engaging the pelvic floor at the appropriate moment to stop at a desired spatial coordinate. When held too rigid or

FIGURE 6.1. From the jazz dance work *HOT COLES*, performed by Carlos Jones & Company. Choreographer: Carlos R. A. Jones. *Left to right*: Carlos R. A. Jones, Kristen Wilkinson, Kevin Lee, Beth Benge, Kate Jahnson. Photographer: Rose Eichenbaum.

loose, the quality, timing, and aesthetic are lost. This part of the *double bounce* technique is subtle and difficult to identify. Even so, when mastered, the pelvic floor becomes the final key to locking down the *double bounce*. Often, *get down* is working in collaboration with *propulsive rhythm*. When this happens, as in the case of the *double bounce,* the pelvis works overtime, twisting and turning to press the body rhythmically onward. *Get down* is physical, or kinesthetic, and external. When actualized, you can literally see it in action. There are some elements where the technique does not happen externally. Instead, it occurs internally.

Call-and-Response

Widely respected in African and African American spaces, *call-and-response* is a hallmark of rooted jazz. It is spirited, collaborative, communal, exuberant, and what Pat Cohen refers to as one of the social elements of jazz dance.[5] It is safe to say that all of us have participated in a call-and-response at some point in life—at church, a rock concert, a political rally. At a rudimentary level, a call-and-response is an echoed response of the same. That is, the leader does, and the follower responds doing the same. A call-and-response can also happen where the leader(s) do a predetermined something and the follower(s) respond with something that is also predetermined. Both and any combination of these are valid and used to great purpose.

Call-and-response, as jazz dance technique, can happen at rudimentary levels, but it often doesn't and is more complex than it appears. Not at all physically visible, the technique used in *call-and-response* is not obvious. Highly acute visual and aural skills, lighting-speed analysis, and exceptional connectivity to the entire body are the skills used in *call-and-response.*

In a live *call-and-response,* especially combined with the kinetic element *improvisation,* a dancer or dancers respond to one another in a conversation, very much like everyday conversation and every bit as complex. Reflect on how conversation works. You don't know what the person will say, and depending on which words come out, you have no idea of how you will respond. You listen for vocabulary, which has meaning, and continue to listen for tone, inflection, intonation, emotion, and other qualities. To add, you watch for visual cues. What is their expression? Is there tension in the body? What is the cadence of their speech? All of this occurs quickly, and if your goal is to respond coherently, you must capture everything instantly. Likewise, the jazz dancer in *call-and-response* must see their fellow artist and scan the body for copious amounts of information. What was the *get down*? What *polycentric isolations* occurred? Was the *rhythmic propulsion* duple or triple? All along, the dancer must be acutely attuned to the live or recorded music, listening for nuances, rhythmic structure, tempo, dynamics, etc. There is skill in staying present, being in the moment, especially with the massive amounts of stimuli surrounding the dance space. Keep in mind the dancer must do this while remaining open and engaged and reacting to the larger community/audience. This means physically (an alive and active body) and mentally (awareness of energy in the room.) It is not plausible to stand still and stare, affixed on the action until your turn to move. In a snapshot, the dancer must receive the visual and aural information, and in a nanosecond, analyze, synthesize, and express a movement response. While accomplishing that monumental task, the dancer has to remain connected to every fragment of their physical being. After that nanosecond of calculation, their synapses fire off instructions to be executed by the body. Encoded in the instructions are choices about which body parts to move, when to move them, in what sequence, where in space, and at what rhythmic pattern. Decoding occurs moments before the movement response is released to the dance floor resulting in the intended movement response. A waver in focus or a moment of hesitation at any point of this process yields incoherent movement responses that interrupt the flow and *ephebism* of the dance. As a final nod to technique in *call-and-response*, I would be remiss if I didn't mention the good-natured "one ups-man" that often occurs in rooted and vernacular jazz. In "one ups-man," a dancer sees what another dancer does and returns with same movement only adding a personal flare. The goal is to perform the original phrase with witty embellishment that raises the ante . . . one up.

Unveiling the workings of technique in vernacular jazz dispels the myth of "ballet as the base of jazz." Given that a wide range of jazz styles have been validated through decades of unabridged racial privilege, the remainder of the twenty-first century must reconcile past transgressions and bring equity across the jazz dance continuum.

How Technique Lives on the Continuum

Two seminal texts, Stearns and Stearns's *Jazz Dance: The Story of American Vernacular Dance*[6] and *Jazz Dance: A History of the Roots and Branches*, edited by Guarino and Oliver,[7] are extremely comprehensive in documenting the historical journey of jazz dance over the past century. Chapter after chapter chronicles where and when jazz has happened, but also highlights systems of oppression, glaring instances of appropriation, and unmitigated disregard for the bodies that birthed jazz dance. Social, political, and economic systems, under the auspices of Whiteness, forbade jazz dance from flourishing sans the leadership of Whites. To borrow from Susie Trenka in her writing about jazz dance, race, and Hollywood, "In other words, black culture was appropriated—or colonized—by white people, while black people remained marginalized."[8] As self-appointed White arbiters of this very African American dance charged onward, ways of choreographing and teaching jazz left the Africanist elements (the roots) behind. The fallout was a multitude of styles, each claiming identity as jazz.

Consider, for a moment, the jazz dance tree included in this book, which first appeared in *Jazz Dance: A History of the Roots and Branches*.[9] As illustrated, the roots of jazz dance are African. The trunk, which represents vernacular jazz dance, remains rooted and authentically embodying the African physiognomies. Related dance forms grow as branched extensions to vernacular rooted jazz dance when the trunk is nourished with the nectar of external forces. The branches resemble auxiliary cultures and societies, disassociated and kinship dance genres, or any venue that signifies "place." Let's pause for a few moments to recognize how "place" is being used in this discussion. It is important to mention because much of the labeling around jazz dance is tied to technique by way of venue. In this instance, the term "place" is used to indicate a happening, which includes but may extend past, location, time, agreed consciousness, and negotiated intent. As such, a "place" becomes an entity when it takes on any combination of characteristics that in turn projects an identity that is the sum of those characteristics (for example, Broadway). Voracious consumerism mandates the continued existence of the "place." To remain viable and profitable, the venue (place) must replicate itself or at least not vary greatly from its identity. Jazz dance, or more cleanly, the many forms of dance labeled jazz, have been and continue to own primary positions in art and entertainment venues. These venues as "places," in whole or in part, shape how jazz related dance is created, performed and reproduced. The mandate to re-supply the same kind of jazz for the venue morphs the identity of the place so that it includes the newly self-named dance (that is, Broadway Jazz). As we return to the image of the tree, it is not difficult to see that certain branches are indeed identified by "place." The fractured state of jazz dance is represented in those branches that run a gamut of identities from "place" to social concepts to disassociated dance genres.

Jazz dance as commodity provided, and still provides, economic prosperity for White America. To maintain lucrativeness and to develop dancers for stage shows, methods for training or educating new dancers of jazz were developed. Enter the idea of codification for teaching. The methods that were used to teach and train, quite naturally, looked more like the influences than the roots. The vocabulary, quality, and aesthetics of the Africanist elements were eliminated or so greatly whitewashed they were no longer recognizable. A style such as lyrical jazz occupies a branch on the jazz tree, yet is the antithesis to *get down, asymmetry, propulsive rhythms,* and *supple and articulated spine.* Technical proficiency in lyrical jazz focuses on elevation, symmetry, lyric expression, and a linear, erect spine. Whiteness ensured that rooted forms of jazz dance were excised in favor of White-driven interpretations, forging branch after branch of new jazz styles. The primary technique championed by the new styles continues to be European, codified, and ballet-based. Select branches from the jazz dance tree are named for dances more closely related to the vernacular truck (hip-hop, b-boying, popping, house). These dances have joined jazz in the bowels of subjugation. Being viewed as lacking in technique, they are relegated to the margins by education, trotted out merely as spectacle and to placate the minions (students). Again, racist arrogance impedes many dance leaders' ability to see the technique that is already at play. Similar to their kindred sister jazz, vernacular-rich forms under the umbrella of "Urban Dance" are experiencing the same atrocities perpetrated by White appropriation and erasure. In the spirit of historical repetition, a century later, we continue to see self-appointed White arbiters co-opting, codifying, and commoditizing.

It is long past time to reconcile the debate over technique. It exists in all forms of dance, and this applies to the complex, layered system of jazz-inspired styles. We must move beyond defining jazz by the other. Jazz dance educators and choreographers must turn the tide and reconcile this misstep in their practice. Only then can we ask artists in other genres to respect jazz dance in its entirety. From this point forward, failure to take action is simply irresponsible. Recognize technique along the entire continuum. and when you are using any part, do so with equitable action.

NOTES

1. Patricia Cohen, "Jazz Dance as a Continuum," in *Jazz Dance: A History of the Roots and Branches*, ed. Lindsay Guarino and Wendy Oliver (Gainesville: University Press of Florida, 2014), 3–6.

2. *The Oxford American Dictionary* (Oxford: Oxford University Press, 2008), 854.

3. Erinn Liebhard, "Thinking on Our Feet—Improvising for Individual and Community Expression in Jazz Dance Class," *Dance Education in Practice* 5, no. 4 (November 2019): 6–10.

4. Lindsey Salfran, "Jazz Dance Training: Contributions to a Well-Rounded Dance Education of College Students," *Journal of Dance Education* 19, no. 4 (January 2019): 139–47.

5. Pat Cohen introduces this in "Jazz Dance as a Continuum," 5.

6. Marshall Stearns and Jean Stearns, *Jazz Dance: The Story of American Vernacular Dance* (New York: Macmillan, 1968).

7. Lindsay Guarino and Wendy Oliver, eds. *Jazz Dance: A History of the Roots and Branches* (Gainesville: University Press of Florida, 2014).

8. Susie Trenka, "Vernacular Jazz Dance and Race in Hollywood Cinema," in *Jazz Dance: A History of the Roots and Branches*, ed. Lindsay Guarino and Wendy Oliver (Gainesville: University Press of Florida, 2014), 241.

9. Wendy Oliver, introduction to *Jazz Dance: A History of the Roots and Branches*, ed. Lindsay Guarino and Oliver (Gainesville: University Press of Florida, 2014), xvi.

7

Where's the Jazz?

A Multilayered Approach for Viewing and Discussing Jazz Dance

LINDSAY GUARINO

Viewing jazz dance, or any form of dance, for that matter, can be highly subjective. The lens through which dance is seen is colored by a lifetime of personal experiences, including the embodied information accumulated through the trajectory of one's own dance practices and the implicit biases that shape understanding and action in unintentional ways. In addition to the ways the subconscious informs aesthetic preferences, it also frames what is immediately visible on the surface when viewing dance. There is no way to be free of these biases, even when one attempts to make objective choices.[1]

Over the past decade, I've peeled back the layers of my own training and biases to more clearly see the entire continuum of jazz from its roots, through the vernacular, and into the branches. Upon personal examination I realized that my biases were shaped not only by my experiences as a White female but by the fact that I had spent much of my life training in ballet-based, codified jazz techniques. While editing *Jazz Dance: A History of the Roots and Branches*, I found myself at a crossroads when I realized that the jazz I was teaching and choreographing was too far, in my opinion, from the African American vernacular core. Out of a deep humility and responsibility to the original creators of the jazz language, I shifted my jazz practices to prioritize Africanist aesthetics over Eurocentric posture, cueing, and movement. Through a process of checking my own biases, studying the jazz continuum, and more authentically embodying jazz dance, I now see jazz in a way that was not entirely apparent to me before. Furthermore, I was reignited by the elusive and transformative power of the jazz experience. I needed to *feel* a more rooted connection to jazz so that I could identify it in others.

This chapter offers a guide to seeing jazz. I advise that you begin this process by questioning what has been prioritized in your own training and what is at the forefront of your own aesthetic preferences. I also recommend that you study and physically embody Africanist and African American social and kinetic elements to see and know them in others. For those who have positioned ballet as the foundation of the jazz aesthetic, it will take a certain retraining of the eye to find the jazz. Furthermore, cultural and racial consciousness—or lack thereof—frames the viewing experience. To see jazz dance is to recognize African American ethos and cultural nuances that are often on the periphery of formal jazz training today. Moving these elements into clearer focus makes the jazz aesthetic apparent on both visual and visceral levels.

AFRICANIST, AFRICAN AMERICAN, AND JAZZ ELEMENTS

In *Jazz Dance: A History of the Roots and Branches*, Patricia Cohen asks, "where's the jazz?" Her list of social and kinetic elements derived from West African dance, African American vernacular, and authentic jazz dance (see table 7.1) provides a framework for moving beyond the question "what is jazz?" to enter into a deeper state of inquiry, asking instead, "where's the jazz?" The higher the presence of the social and kinetic elements, the more rooted the jazz is. Cohen identifies jazz that is rooted by its "historical, cultural, social, and kinetic continuity,"[2] which she calls the continuum. When the continuum is interrupted, the jazz moves away from the roots and the African American vernacular trunk of the tree and into the branches.[3]

This chapter utilizes the Africanist aesthetics outlined by Julie Kerr-Berry in her chapter in this volume titled "Africanist Elements in American Jazz Dance," and also Cohen's list of social and kinetic elements from *Jazz Dance* as a method for discussing jazz and evaluating its proximity to the roots. Jazz and jazz-influenced music, groove, and jazz energy are also discussed as essential elements. Because seeing and knowing jazz is not solely a visual experience, I suggest consideration of the following to determine where jazz falls in relationship to the continuum: what can be known; what can be seen; what can be felt; and what can be found.

What Can Be Known

In its origins, jazz was social, improvisational, and reflective of the individual within a community. Jazz was the pulse of African American culture, the spirit moving in conversation with swinging rhythms and soulful sounds resulting

Table 7.1. Social and kinetic elements of West African dance, African American vernacular, and authentic jazz dance

Social elements	Kinetic elements
Community	Use of the flat foot
Individuality within the group (individual creativity)	Bent hip, knee, and ankle joints
Vocal encouragement	Articulated, inclined torso
Lack of separation between performer and spectator	Body-part isolations
Friendly challenges among the dancers	Groundedness (earthiness)
Confrontational attitude ("in your face")	Improvisation
Joyousness	Embellishment and elaboration
Call-and-response	Polyrhythms and syncopation
Conversation between musicians and dancers	Polycentrism
	Angularity and asymmetry
	Personal expression and creativity

Note: Adapted from Patricia Cohen, "Jazz Dance as a Continuum," in *Jazz Dance: A History of the Roots and Branches*, ed. Lindsay Guarino and Wendy Oliver (Gainesville: University Press of Florida, 2014), 5–6.

in a distinct energy known as "jazz." In the Jazz Era, Black musicians "fueled the creative energy that fed the development of new jazz social dances," and the "musicians were creatively influenced by the dancers' movements and rhythms."[4] The symbiotic relationship between jazz music and jazz dancing, once a defining characteristic of the form, fractured when popular social dance music shifted away from jazz and toward rock 'n' roll, rhythm and blues, funk, and Latin music forms in the years during and after World War II.[5] What has remained consistent across jazz dance styles and performance venues from the Jazz Era to today is the way the jazz label is liberally assigned to movement that is connected to rhythm and music. To assess the rootedness, however, requires a consideration of the *type* of music, and of that music's connection to the roots. The presence of jazz music, specifically if it swings and especially if it is live, with dancers visibly in conversation with that music, positions the work in closer proximity to the roots. Just as the African American vernacular trunk of the jazz dance tree can be traced from its African diasporic roots to myriad styles today, the same can be done with the African American trunk of the music tree. Dancing to music of this continuum, including blues, soul, funk, and all contemporary variations of jazz, is inherently more rooted than dancing to music which is not within the African American musical continuum.

To know whether or not this rooted connection exists requires listening and identifying the style of music, which can be supported by some background research about the artist/composer, and also a look at the relationship between the dancers and the music.

Where's the jazz: Connection to music, type of music, and how that music informs the jazz style.

What Can Be Seen

Many of the elements listed in Cohen's social and kinetic list are described in Kerr-Berry's guide. "Seeing" these elements requires a tracing of the jazz continuum through time and place, and a willingness to interpret each element unto itself, separate from Western techniques and aesthetics. For the eye that can see the continuum, from West African traditional dances to the many different expressions of African American vernacular dance (including but not limited to authentic jazz dance), it is fairly straightforward to recognize the elements Kerr-Berry previously outlined: asymmetry, call-and-response, flat-footedness, get down, movement initiated from the hips, polycentric isolations, and a supple and articulated spine. The viewer must keep the entire continuum in mind to be sure that each element is understood in relationship to the roots and not through a generic application of the term. For example, all dancers make contact between the entire foot and the ground at times, regardless of dance genre, but flat-footedness in connection to the diaspora refers to movement that is gliding, shuffling, striking, and simultaneously pressing into and rebounding away from the earth.

Furthermore, Cohen points to vernacular dance as the heart of jazz, the vital piece that keeps the art form "on the cutting edge of responsiveness to the pulse of the people."[6] If vernacular movement is absent, as we see in jazz dance when it is reduced to leaps, turns, and leg extensions, then the jazz is absent. Seeing expressive but unaffected bodies moving authentically with rhythm and style, and without ballet-derived posture or technique, is to find vernacular movement.

Where's the jazz: Social and kinetic elements of West African dance, African American vernacular dance, and authentic jazz dance; vernacular movement.

What Can Be Felt

As previously mentioned, the more elusive aspects of the jazz experience go beyond seeing and knowing, and can be best identified through feeling. Aesthetic of the cool,[7] or coolness, and ephebism, both elements that Kerr-Berry outlines and gives examples of, are multilayered states of being that convey energy and attitude through lived experience. These elements must be felt to be believed. Improvisation is an element that can be known but is also a feeling. When movement is free and spontaneous, and highly individualized, it can feel improvised even if it is, in fact, choreographed. The felt sensation of these elements suggests that the jazz is rooted.

"Groove" is a term that jazz musicians use to describe propulsive rhythms that inspire the musician and listener alike to move, sway, bounce, pat a leg, clap hands, etc. Being "in the groove" is to sit in the pocket of the music, connected to rhythm and musical phrasing, ready to respond through deep listening and play. Groove is evident when the inherent pulse of the music is made visible in the body, and it is also a distinct feeling that connects the viewer to that same pulse. Shared groove, among dancers or between dancers and audience, inspires community—an element on Cohen's list. Community in jazz transcends space and time and manifests as an energy, an atmosphere that supports individuality within a shared groove, uniting music, dance, and genuine human connection.

Jazz energy is not specifically listed in Kerr-Berry's or Cohen's guides, but it is one of the more unique elements since it separates jazz from other dance styles—both Western and diasporic. Jazz energy is distinctly African American with a vitality that moves between dynamic extremes: hot and cool, overt and subtle, percussive and sustained, tense and released. This energy surprises in the moment where a propulsive groove comes to a full stop in the body, only to give back in and ride the rhythms. Playing the full range of dynamic energy makes the humanness of jazz come to life, expressive and responsive in energy and expression.

Where's the jazz: Aesthetic of the cool, ephebism, improvisation, groove, community, jazz energy.

What Can Be Found

An additional step is necessary to assess the proximity of jazz to its roots when taking into account the ways Whiteness shifted jazz away from its African

American origins. The most commonly practiced jazz dance styles today are colonized forms that developed in the mid- to late twentieth century. In order for twenty-first-century jazz to be truly rooted, there should be a respect for the history and culture of African American people made visible through acknowledgment, understanding, and appreciation.

In *Jazz Dance: A History of the Roots and Branches*, Jill Flanders Crosby describes how the question of authenticity was central to her journey into the heart of jazz dance. She unraveled her own complex relationship with jazz dance through field research in Ghana and Cuba, which led her to question, with jazz in mind: "Is one form more authentic than another? Who decides? What does authentic really mean?"[8] In anthropological theory, authenticity presents a conceptual paradox where "parallel authenticities in tension" must be negotiated when evaluating individuals, groups, cultural practices, representation, and authorship.[9] Anthropologist Dimitrios Theodossopoulos argues "for a perspective on the study of authenticity that acknowledges the simultaneous co-existence of more than one parallel manifestation of authenticity in any given negotiation of the authentic."[10] In this case, mining for authenticity within the jazz form collides with the lived experience and singular authenticity of the individual dancing the form. By investigating stories that claim truth, or movement that claims to come from an authentic place, one can attempt to decipher what is real and what is true. The authenticity of jazz "rests in these stories and in the meaning participants find for themselves."[11] A jazz dancer does not have to be Black to connect with the roots, nor is one obligated to work in a specific jazz style, but there must be a "felt aesthetic grounding,"[12] or a known investigation into the roots found through an interplay of inquiry, practice, and lived experience. When asking "where's the jazz?," it is important to question whether or not the dancer and/or choreographer honors the origins and moves from a place of respect. If there is ignorance of or disregard for the African American experience, or if jazz is not understood as the embodiment of cultural knowledge, then the work is not in close proximity to the roots of jazz.

Where's the jazz?: Acknowledgment, understanding, appreciation, lived experience.

DISCUSSION AND ANALYSIS OF TWO CONTEMPORARY
JAZZ COMPANIES

For the remainder of this chapter, I will highlight the works of two concert jazz companies, JazzAntiqua Dance & Music Ensemble and Decidedly Jazz Danceworks, to move the above criteria for knowing, seeing, feeling, and finding jazz into practice. By focusing on which elements are the most salient in these works, with the understanding that both companies are historically informed and aesthetically rooted but each in their own unique way, I hope to illuminate some of the above-mentioned concepts to provide a detailed look at where jazz lives in the twenty-first century.[13]

JazzAntiqua Dance & Music Ensemble: *1960 What?* (2018)

Choreographer: Pat Taylor

What I Know

"1960 What?,"[14] a song of protest by contemporary jazz musician Gregory Porter, is emblematic of the Black experience in America. The bass, then drums, then piano, and finally horns all layer one upon the next in rhythmic play, establishing an irresistible groove. Fighting words in tones that stretch between extremes, a salve and a growl, paint a picture of social unrest, yet the words are in contrast to the catchy and upbeat groove.

> *Young man, coming out of a liquor store*
> *With three pieces of black liquorice, in his hand y'all*
> *Mister police man! Thought it was a gun, thought he was the one*
> *Shot him down y'all that ain't right*

Hearing the full emotional spectrum in Porter's baritone and knowing his reputation as a celebrated jazz musician positions the music right in the African American musical continuum. Taylor's choreography brings to life the intention of the song, while staying in conversation with the rhythm, thus establishing a rooted connection to jazz.

What I See

Most all movement in the piece comes from a vernacular-bodied placement; simple pedestrian walks transform into grounded triplets and quick grapevines with an inclined torso, embodying the propulsive rhythm with raw humanness in posture and presentation. Personal style, often made visible by dancers

FIGURE 7.1. JazzAntiqua Dance & Music Ensemble. Justin Edmonson and Shari Washington Rhone in *1960 What?,* by artistic director Pat Taylor, 2018. Photo by George Simian. Courtesy of JazzAntiqua, Inc.

giving into the funk, drives the walks and vernacular footwork. A deliberate sway of the hips, both weighted and embellished, and a cool casualness in the chest and shoulders, signals a denial of the upright and held placement practiced in Eurocentric techniques.

There are glimpses throughout the piece of arm pathways and body lines derived from ballet and modern training, and also of angular and asymmetrical shapes, isolations, and a lifted chin with an inverted shoulder that draws from codified jazz techniques. Yet, each time a shape emerges as something identifiable from those lexicons, it almost immediately resolves into movement that is wholly within the African American vernacular continuum. From the African roots you see movement characteristic of traditional West African dance: a deep bend at the knees and hips with an inclined torso (get down), arms flung free from the back and body pressing into the earth, sudden releases and undulations in the chest and torso. Farther up the continuum you can see highly stylized and individualized movement that prioritizes rhythm over shape and line. Walking throughout the piece has a propulsive rhythm with a cool restraint, the authority of someone walking in a room knowing they will be the object of stares but remaining decidedly calm, collected, and exuding confidence.

What I Feel

Energy and groove manifest as a rhythmic experience, and I couldn't deny the feeling of rhythmic satisfaction throughout Taylor's work. Each time the groove was punctuated with a stop—making a confrontational statement toward the audience—it created a moment of suspense that softened almost immediately as the groove took back over. Groove, combined with confrontational energy directed outward and the spirit safely moving in dialogue within the group, created a distinct feeling of community. The community feel was only enhanced by the audience, who first erupted into cheers early on in the piece when a dancer does a syncopated traveling step reminiscent of a *Soul Train* solo moment for only a few brief counts—but enough to grab the audience with her style and energy. Their response was audible throughout, but always in celebration of style and individuality.

Individuality takes over in a series of solos to the sound of horns; the music sounds improvised, and it's hard to know whether or not the dancing is as well. Regardless of whether it is improvised or choreographed, the movement and rhythms feel specific and genuine to each dancer, informed by their lived experience and the diverse styles at home in their bodies. One dancer, for example, enters the stage with a flourish, reaching her leg into a high extension followed by a soaring attitude turn. With stylistic nuance dominating the transition from one moment to the next, embellishment, rhythm, and that elusive sense of spirit emanating from the inside-out give the ballet-derived movements a distinct jazz feel. Another dancer uses footwork and torso isolations influenced by hip-hop, grooving while exuding ephebism and cool. With call-and-response propelling one solo into the next, the intensity picks up in the music and the dancers give into it—reaching, throwing, and pushing out of their bodies from deep within their souls—only to come to a complete STOP in a full ensemble moment of both community and confrontation. In that long, propulsive groove followed by that full and complete stop—there's the jazz.

What I Found

As articulated in her chapter in this volume, "The Duality of the Black Experience as Jazz Language," choreographer Pat Taylor *cannot not* embody her own lived experience as a Black woman in America. With that in mind, and seeing the African American vernacular movement at the very core of her style in *1960 What?*, it is apparent that her work is firmly rooted in the jazz continuum. Where other aesthetics arise, they are always supporting and never erasing the vernacular.

1960 What? is in constant flux between tension and release. This tension, however, isn't a stiffness or a placement; it is a resistance in response to the misrepresentation, trauma, and oppression that Black Americans have had to push back against for centuries.[15] In this piece, her company dancers give into the groove, give into themselves, give into the community—but deny the oppressor. There is a push and pull between these worlds that is overwhelmingly evident to me as I contemplate how it might feel to be Black and American. The moments of full release, where the spirit seems to take over but then re-emerges to assess the surroundings suggests that these dancers can't retreat for too long. There is no time or place to be self-indulgent when the atmosphere is one of social unrest, and so there is struggle between these worlds. To see the extremes between resistance and letting go is to recognize the embodied manifestation of the Black experience in the jazz aesthetic.

Decidedly Jazz Danceworks: *Better Get Hit in Your Soul* (2013)

Choreographer: Kimberley Cooper

What I Know

An evening-length work of "dances inspired by the music, life and times of Charles Mingus,"[16] *Better Get Hit in Your Soul*[17] is choreographed and danced to music composed by Mingus, with music direction by Rubim de Toledo. Mingus, considered one of the jazz greats, "shaped and transcended" American music trends of the 1950s, 1960s, and 1970s.[18] The performance weaves together live and recorded music,[19] allowing for the past and present to coexist. This play between worlds allows for all the kinetic energy of the band while also inviting the brilliance of Mingus, through his original recordings, to capture the ear.

Story lines are developed in a way where the choreography not only makes the music visible in the dancers' bodies but also brings to life rich stories about the life of Mingus as imagined and researched by Cooper. The relationship with the music in this work is deep and profound, with the dancers moving in conversation with it so that they embody and play within rhythm and feel, making layers of rhythm and melody become visible in their bodies, yet at other times stepping back and allowing space for the musicians to shine by their own light, honoring the way jazz dancing initially developed socially and performatively to jazz music. The musicians are integrated within the narrative structure, often interacting with the dancers, thus making clear that this connection roots the work within the jazz continuum.

What I See

"Haitian Fight Song," which opens *Better Get Hit*, strikes a balance between elegance and earthiness. The overall presence of the dancers is vernacular-bodied with movement vocabulary that draws from the authentic jazz era of the continuum, including steps such as the Lindy and sugars with swinging kick ball-changes and triplets that get-down in the groove, but also transcends with contemporary innovation. There are moments that reach and extend beyond the extremities, lengthening with a refined sophistication that is undoubtedly Eurocentric, but these moments that lift and sustain are fleeting, always dropping back into gravity with bent hip, knee, and ankle joints.

Through step flicks that reverberate through the body and answer with percussive isolations in the shoulders, hips, and torso, and in accented claps and pivots that make the back beat visible, polyrhythms and syncopation drive the rhythm-generated choreography. The rhythm provides the dancers with a framework for individual creativity and embellishment; it is the style of the choreography, and rhythm, that keeps them "together," so there is less concern for uniformity in shape and line.

The most prominent Africanist element in a later section, a duet to "Cumbia and Jazz Fusion," is a fluid and articulate torso. The two female dancers drop their spines into, lift out of, and move around the edges of their weighted pelvises with torsos responding organically and asymmetrically in rib and shoulder isolations that take turns caressing and punctuating the space. Propulsive rhythm climbs its way through their bodies: subtle step-flicks in the feet, swinging hips, and shoulder isolations around a twisting and turning spine. The symbiotic relationship between groove, weightedness, freedom in the hips and torso, and isolations tether the movement to its West African roots.

What I Feel

With heads cocked to the side, shoulders inverted, and spines oozing into the pelvis, the dancers take on a "cool cat" demeanor in "Haitian Fight Song," aloof but charged, a posture that is a hallmark of the jazz feel. Through both swing-based partnering and solo movement, the dancers move within the groove, and it becomes evident that under the coolness in the head, torso, and shoulders is an articulated rhythmic precision moving the body from the waist down. The propulsive and swinging double bounce roots the choreography,

FIGURE 7.2. Decidedly Jazz Danceworks, Natasha Korney and Sabrina Comanescu with Jonathan McCaslin (drums), Rubim de Toledo (bass), and Carsten Rubeling (trombone) in "Cumbia and Jazz Fusion" from *Better Get Hit in Your Soul* (2019), by artistic director Kimberley Cooper. Photo by Scott Reid. Courtesy of DJD.

keeping the connection to groove alive with momentum that sweeps between tension and release. I could *feel* a jolt of surprise in the moments where the propulsive rhythm is punctuated with a percussive stop or throw, the dancers stopping both breath and time and then releasing back into the groove.

Mingus once said "music is a language of emotions,"[20] and *Better Get Hit* reaches across the spectrum while bringing his music to life. "Haitian Fight Song" moves the dancers with an outward sense of cool, and with subtle moments of internalized joy. Confrontational, fighting energy is the most prominent emotion and aesthetic feel in a later dance performed to the tune "Tonight at Noon," where a group of five women in white tanks and black slacks simultaneously embody the mercurial Mingus in an impulsive and physical ax chase.[21] In "Cumbia and Jazz Fusion" the two female dancers exude sensuality—hips moving like a pendulum and spines undulating while exchanging knowing glances toward each other. Hearing and feeling countless moods and inflections throughout *Better Get Hit* conveys the many ways jazz reflects the full and complete human experience, with music and internal emotion made external through movement.

What I Found

Kimberley Cooper, in her chapter in this volume titled "A Strange Place to Find Jazz . . . ," positions herself as a double-guest in jazz—as a White person and as a Canadian. Acknowledging her identity implies awareness of what she is not. There are experiences, circumstances, and possibly even ancestral memories encoded in the genetic fibers of African Americans that evoke struggle and resistance she could not understand as a White person. As artistic director of Decidedly Jazz Danceworks, however, she is upholding a commitment to aspects of jazz that have been pushed to the wayside in most non-Black jazz dance practices. By choosing jazz music as inspiration and motivation, drawing from West African movement to connect jazz to its roots, and conducting relevant historical research to support her choreographic processes, she honors the aspects of jazz that are outside her birthright. Furthermore, she has performed and choreographed jazz for her entire adult life, providing her with a wealth of lived experiences which are certain to, in the spirit of jazz, lead to future innovation.

Synopsis

JazzAntiqua Dance & Music Ensemble and Decidedly Jazz Danceworks are two examples of concert jazz dance companies that engage in rooted jazz dance practices. Through discussion and evaluation of Africanist and jazz elements in *1960 What?* by Pat Taylor and *Better Get Hit in Your Soul* by Kimberley Cooper, it is apparent that there is a high presence of elements that can be seen and felt, including all of the kinetic elements on Cohen's list, and also aesthetic of the cool, improvisation, groove, and jazz energy. Both artists were inspired by the music and choreograph within it, which roots the work in theory (jazz dance to jazz music)[22] and in practice (jazz dance in conversation with jazz music). The aesthetic of each choreographer slides up and down the jazz continuum, drawing primarily from rhythm-generated, vernacular-bodied movement. When the movement dips into the branches, harnessing shapes and lines from ballet and/or modern techniques, it remains connected to jazz in energy and style. While these two choreographers are informed by different cultures and lived experiences, they embody jazz in ways real and true, connected to the core and honoring the continuum.

Conclusion

Jazz has evolved into a style complex in cultural and aesthetic influences, often transforming or diluting the African American continuum and moving the form away from its core. Understanding our identities as viewers and how it shapes our lenses allows for a more nuanced view of the continuum, fusing historical, social, and aesthetic contexts in a viewing experience both cerebral and visceral. This method for identifying aspects of jazz that can be known, seen, felt, and found provides a culturally responsive and multilayered approach for answering the question "where's the jazz?," and positions Africanist and jazz elements and African American culture at the center of discussions about jazz choreography and performance.

Notes

1. "How to Fight Your Own Implicit Biases," American Association of University Women (AAUW), www.aauw.org/2016/03/30/fight-your-biases/.

2. Patricia Cohen, "Jazz Dance as a Continuum," in *Jazz Dance: A History of the Roots and Branches*, ed. Lindsay Guarino and Wendy Oliver (Gainesville: University Press of Florida, 2014), 3.

3. Ibid., 5.

4. Jill Flanders Crosby and Michèle Moss, "Jazz Dance from Emancipation to 1970," in *Jazz Dance: A History of the Roots and Branches*, ed. Lindsay Guarino and Wendy Oliver (Gainesville: University Press of Florida, 2014), 49.

5. Ibid., 52.

6. Cohen, "Jazz Dance as a Continuum," 7.

7. The term "aesthetic of the cool" was coined by scholar Robert Farris Thompson.

8. Jill Flanders Crosby, "A Journey into the Heart of Jazz Dance," in *Jazz Dance: A History of the Roots and Branches*, ed. Lindsay Guarino and Wendy Oliver (Gainesville: University Press of Florida, 2014), 281.

9. Dimitrios Theodossopoulos, "Laying Claim to Authenticity: Five Anthropological Dilemmas," *Anthropological Quarterly* 86, no. 2 (2013): 339.

10. Ibid., 337.

11. Crosby, "A Journey into the Heart," 281.

12. Ibid.

13. My discussion of each work is through my own lens, supported by some publicly available information regarding the works. I chose not to interview the choreographers about their works, knowing it would inform my viewing experience. Any information incidentally revealed to me by the choreographers has been noted.

14. "1960 What (2018)," Vimeo, https://vimeo.com/394858327.

15. Pat Taylor, "The Duality of the Black Experience as Jazz Language," in this volume.

16. "DJD's 'Better Get Hit in Your Soul'—On Stage," YouTube, www.youtube.com/watch?v=Xe3yShmWbvE

17. "DJD—Better Get Hit in Your Soul—Haitian Fight Song," YouTube, https://youtu.be/yhnYhhTaY2U.

18. *Encyclopedia Britannica,* s.v. "Charles Mingus," www.britannica.com/biography/Charles-Mingus.

19. Kimberley Cooper, email message to author, July 2, 2020.

20. "Why Mingus Matters: An Intro to the Music and Legacy of Charles Mingus," *Jazz Blog,* www.jazz.org/blog/why-mingus-matters-an-intro-to-the-music-and-legacy-of-charles-mingus/.

21. Kimberley Cooper, email message to author, July 2, 2020.

22. Jazz scholars such as Marshall Stearns and Billy Siegenfeld have asserted that "true" jazz dance must be danced to jazz music (Lindsay Guarino and Wendy Oliver, eds., *Jazz Dance: A History of the Roots and Branches* [Gainesville: University Press of Florida, 2014], xvii, 17–23).

Caleb Teicher & Company in rehearsal, May 15, 2019. Photo by Rachel Papo for Dance Magazine.

Choreography and Performance
of Jazz Dance

The nature of jazz has been altered time and again to adhere to traditions and ideologies outside a jazz philosophy. Western systems for composition and performance, often related to place rather than form, radically alter the genetic makeup of the jazz tree when they take precedence over Africanist aesthetics and African American cultural values. For example, the social characteristics of jazz are displaced when the tree is uprooted and replanted in professional performance venues. Social settings where live jazz music is present allow for jazz dance to emerge spontaneously, positioning its original defining characteristics as central to the form: improvisation, call-and-response, personal style, and individuality. In the twenty-first century, rooted choreography and performance requires effort to realign jazz with its ethos, culture, and foundational elements with a focus on nurturing the aspects that do not clearly align with Western compositional values.

The authors of the chapters in part III all look at jazz in connection to its roots and culture. In the first section, "Personal Artist Statements," four performers and choreographers share their own perspectives on making jazz, describing their creative processes while identifying where Africanist aesthetics live in their work. These artists speak to how their identities and lived experiences define the ways they engage with jazz. In the second section of part III, "Rooted Concepts," three authors evaluate distinctly different aspects of jazz choreography and performance: jazz as a language that reflects the Black American experience; gender as learned style for women in jazz dance performance; the influence of modern dance compositional values on jazz choreography. Together, these jazz artists and scholars embrace the spirit of jazz in a variety of ways, honoring its truth while shifting consciousness to move jazz forward into the future.

Personal Artist Statements

8

Must Be the Music

LATASHA BARNES

I am a conduit. A transmitter. A tradition-bearer of African American Vernacular Dance. My function is to usher greater ways of thinking, doing, and being into this plane for myself and others, both through my words and through my dance. While I am an internationally recognized educator and a multitime, multiform, multiplatform award-winning performer with a master's degree in ethnochoreology, Black studies, and performance studies, my most prized education was provided by my family.

As I was growing up in Richmond, Virginia, many of my family members were professional performers. Those who were not paid professionals were social club stars and prepared equally as hard, and I reaped the benefit of their discipline. My cousins and I were inundated daily with invaluable knowledge of and love for the "good music"; in the 1980s, that was Jazz (Swing & Contemporary), Soul, Gospel, Funk, R&B, Pop and Hip-Hop. They also educated us on the movements that went along with those genres: The Swing (Thanks Great Granny—Elizabeth Harris), Two-Step, Popping, Locking, New Jack (Hip-Hop) and Housin'. Along with the physical embodiment of the movements, we learned the significance of the movements to our culture at the times of their creation. Through their example, I learned how to follow a groove, how to cut a groove (one-upmanship), and most importantly how to allow a groove to take me effortlessly from one form of dance to another. I still teach what and how they taught me today. My family were also my first stage performance educators. They taught me the best ways to present the shape of a song physically through movement, staging, and props, as well as succinctly projecting my, or the music's, emotion of a moment. I acknowledge gratefully that I was born to be a dancer. Had I not, I would have still been well groomed and suited to the challenges of being a dancer and creative thanks to the abundant joy and knowledge my family displays toward Black American art, music,

FIGURE 8.1. LaTasha Barnes at Paris Jazz Roots. Photo by Eric Esquivel.

and dance—the arts in general, really. Oh, and in case you're wondering—yes, they all do still throw down at family functions!

While my family instilled dance knowledge and performance practices in me from a young age, the greatest accumulation of my skills as a performer and choreographer came through the community-born arts organization Urban Artistry Inc. when I resided in the Washington, D.C., Metro Area in 2006. As part of this mentorship experience and core group development I became deeply committed to the traditions of House Dance, Waacking, and Hip-Hop. Desiring to bridge the gap between practicing communities and the concert stage, while elevating the cultural artifacts of the Black community and their creators, we were guided and required to see our dance, and ourselves, as equally skillful, dynamic and worthy as more *celebrated* dance forms. Whether creating for the stage, sharing in the cypher at a battle or club, or even representing that sacred space onstage, we did so within performance *standards* but with regard for our cultural values. It is because of that experience that I expanded my repertoire to include (Vernacular) Jazz and Lindy Hop in 2014 as a Frankie Manning Foundation Ambassador Scholar. Receiving this

transgenerational educational experience from those who created and innovated the dance forms, the African American elders, served to shore up the
tenuous connections of the current movement I carried to their inherent Jazz
aesthetics and purpose.

When I prepare to create and share in Jazz, I recenter myself on the purpose
and intent of the elders as they themselves graciously communicated to me.
The elders' seemingly limitless and effortless translations of music to dance
appear so because of their deeply embodied (practiced) swing rhythms and
individual synthesis of the playing nuances of the various bands, intertwined
with their image of their most empowered and evocative selves. This merging
of energies seemed to perpetually fuel their creativity and ability to share and
perform. Through this lens (alignment), it is the acknowledgment of their/my
root, their/my origin, them/my*self*—our collective purpose—that I believe
brings forth authentic (truthful) movement through music.

Like my elders before me, I have cultivated a mental catalogue of shapes,
positions, movement, textures, rhythms, etc. that correspond to particular
sounds, rhythms, or absences thereof. These "knowledge stores" are a direct result of repeatedly moving through traditional steps (Fall off the Log, Suzy Q,
Squat Charleston, etc.) or the breakdown of those moves into kinesthetic mo-
dalities (e.g., squatting, bounding, balancing, tempo variations) to traditional
swing jazz music (e.g., Chick Webb, Count Basie, Catherine Russell) and associated genres (e.g., Roy Hargrove, Rebirth Brass Band). As a result, my body
has developed to instinctively respond to the visceral call of the music with
consideration of traditions as well as the *seemingly* ingenious possibilities that
manifest within me. In doing this, I convey my truth through movement in
the moment. I emphasize "seemingly" because not every applied movement
idea is a winner. However, in the effort to make the music visible, which is my
(our) job as dancers, and to share its rich context as artfully as possible, we step
into our ideas boldly hoping that they will fulfill the purpose of ingenuity. The
sharing/presenting one's perspective or understanding of truth, particularly
through dance, offers the opportunity to witness the physical manifestation
of the dancer's acknowledgment of their lived and carried experiences, their
reality, and many times their struggle to assert that truth. Be it through improvisation, choreography, or improvography, I believe our dance should always
be a reflection of reality through truthful movement.

The most honest place I know this truth to occur is in the social dance
settings of the jam circle and the cypher. When I am in the circle, I am in a
deliciously hyperreflexive state of being—just praying for a moment or melody

to align. While soaking in the music, the space, and the people around me, including my partner or fellow dancers, I listen intently with my ears and eyes. You hear the band quote *The Flintstones* theme song within a phrase of a classic swing tune and hear the roar of laughter from those who are also attuned. Being attuned yourselves, your partner calls out "Carry" in the midst of a Send Out. You verbalize consentingly—"Carry!"—and then find yourself flung over their shoulder while they cart you out of the circle similar to historical images of cave-dwellers, at the same time stirring the circle into a frenzy of surprise and laughter. Or, individually having such an overwhelming visceral reaction to the sound of a baritone sax melody that it actually extracts movement from another dance form you carry and associate more readily with that particular tone. You end up recasting House Dance movement to traditional swing music, aided by the vigorously agreeing head nods of the band members, themselves facilitating personal truth overlaid by musical truth (for example my House Dance movement manifesting in a Lindy Hop dance thanks to "Pickin' the Cabbage" by Cab Calloway—too much sauce!). Bottling and transferring this overwhelming reaction and feeling synchronously to an audience through movement is my choreographic aim.

Choreographers and improvisers alike often look to the footage of the past as sources of inspiration to both learn and compose dance moments that highlight the ebullient, polyrhythmic, polycentric, and relaxed or crazy cool qualities we so readily associate with African American Vernacular Dance. The intent of dance, my dance specifically, is to function as a representation of my feelings in the moment—feelings about a song, situation, setting—as authentically as possible. Fully acknowledging that feelings are not always pretty, or stylish, I err on the side of function to choose movement that speaks true. My catchphrase during creation or rehearsals is, "What is the song doing or saying there?" Does a Lock-Turn more clearly convey eagerness in this moment or does a Shout? Do I need them both? When choreographing our 2019 International Lindy Hop Championship showcase offering, my dance partner and I really gave ourselves over to this process and let the music take the lead. We sat with the music, literally sat and did not dance. We verbalized our feelings about the tone, rhythms, melody, silence, and tempo. Then we got up and danced "full-out" to the song and recorded the explorations and our genuine responses to the music. Between each take we shared our feedback regarding movement choices, lead-follow dynamics, and emotions. We treated our recordings as historical footage and noted the ideas that truly represented and elevated the cultural and our shared values of the art form. By the time we actually mapped the song, counted the bars and breaks, highlighted poignant moments, we had the "steps" selected physically and simply played a game of dance scramble, reorganizing moments to best present our sass and panache as a reflection of the song's theme. Finally taking the presenting space into consideration, an international contest in a grand ballroom with a preferred center-spot for presentation to the viewing audience and judges, we applied elements of travel to available moments and some not so available moments (whew) along with facing and spacing adjustments to optimize the inclusive experience of the piece. What we were able to build together effectively show-cased our talents, acknowledgment of the form, authentic feelings about our partnership and the song (again "Pickin' the Cabbage" by Cab Calloway—the song has taken over my life!). To be completely honest, my process does not differ much when developing solo or company choreographies—the music always leads and movement, per skills and setting, follow.

Holding steadfast to the music, its embodiment: acknowledgment of the form's origin/intent, dancing truthfully, and shaping all that comes forth in accordance with the music are the primary tenets of performing and choreographing that I live by. Circularly, one can see how this process in and of itself becomes a new lived experience which then informs the next dance moment—to produce an even deeper lived knowledge store to draw from when the next dance moment presents itself. This continuum of experience, acknowledgment, truth through/to movement is one of the most beautiful realities that we get to enjoy as dancers, as tradition-bearers. The awareness of this perpetuation is what, more than anything else, keeps me dancing through the music . . . not just to it.

NOTE

While some academic style guides prefer to lowercase dance form and style names, it is the author's preference that the names be capitalized in order to assign appropriate acknowledgment and identification that has not been provided to Black American dance forms and styles.

9

Riding Rhythms and Designing Space

Jazz Dance Composition

CARLOS R. A. JONES

Rhythm. It drives jazz and it drives me. Whether I am creating a work that sits snuggly in a slow tempo caressed by the aesthetic of the cool or I am designing a dance that rides "the pocket" of a fast swing, rhythm, in all its subdivision, accents, syncopations, and propulsion, is the primary source of the octane that fuels my choreography. In my life and in my work, rhythm is the bloodline. Much of it has been intrinsic or passed down. I am from a lineage of jazz and blues drummers, and I am a product of a culture where rhythm wraps itself around even the most mundane activities. I hear it everywhere, and it permeates every choreographic phrase I compose. The rhythm in my work is palpable, inescapable, and at times overpowering, particularly for dancers whose previous experience, albeit rich in its own right, has not required complex rhythmic exploration. Often, during the choreographic process, I find myself training dancers or movers to recognize intricate polyrhythmic layers present in the music I have selected, in the movement I have created, and among the individuals negotiating the rehearsal or performance space. It is, many times, an added step to my process. I hold no malice for including this step. It is necessary. The alternative leaves my compositions flat and lacking in the intrinsic ephebism that is married to rhythmic life. As this discussion continues, you will see the eclectic experience that colors the work I do. Working this way can lead to a composition that wanders and is unfocused. Rhythm is my unifier.

With rhythm as the base layer on my choreographic canvas, I begin to devise phrases constructed out of movement I have been amassing since the age of three and a half—the first time I remember catching a hard groove. The movement is a curated collection of glossaries teeming with dance steps and techniques that are *intrinsic, rooted, colonized,* or *researched.* Let's depart

FIGURE 9.1. Carlos R. A. Jones with Kenzie Tankersley in rehearsal, Teen Dance Company of the Bay Area, Palo Alto, California, 2006. Photo by David Ebersole.

momentarily to decipher the nomenclatures just mentioned. *Intrinsic* refers to the way I have moved since I was young. It has not been taught or influenced; it simply comes out of me. Still, it is deeply connected to my ethos, perhaps genetically encoded. By *rooted*, I am speaking of dances or ways of moving that I inherited as a constituent of the cultural landscape inside the African American lineage. This movement oozes with Africanist aesthetics and navigates between dance forms that are the brainchild of the African American people (e.g., jazz, hip-hop, black social dance). *Colonized* movement encapsulates all dance that I have learned where the goal is obtaining mastery or accreditation. The movement is deemed colonized because the primary focus is on methodologies, theories, ideologies, and systems that position Eurocentric perspectives on quality of movement and proficiency (technical or aesthetic) as authority. Lastly, my glossary of *researched* movement holds dance forms I have actively and purposely investigated with the intention of expanding personal knowledge (i.e., Odissi, Flamenco, Ghanaian). I do not own them, nor are they a part of my personal cultural heritage. Still, extensive study has added these techniques to my muscular memory and has developed layers to the style, quality, and content of my movement. Denying any portion of my lived experience would be denying myself. I am the sum of my experience. Naturally, movement from a lifetime of exploration in dance forms and techniques seeps into my choreographic design. To suggest otherwise is false and futile. As such, I embrace the amalgamated experience that is my truth, and I use everything in my movement arsenal when crafting a movement language for new choreographic works. I do this, however, taking care to name what I am using while making space for historical and cultural dialogue. Recognition and crediting are a must. Let's now return to the choreographic process. I was discussing phrases crafted from several dance techniques and forms.

The phrases are meticulously arranged so that the operative portion of the phrase aligns with the rhythmic groove. By operative, I mean the driving section or step that delivers the main essence or truth of the phrase, very much like the operative word in a sentence. I work liberally between the dance genres embedded within me. In one moment I am working in Africanist aesthetics. In the next, I am decidedly Eurocentric. It is highly probable that my choreography will nab a South Asian (Indian) motif, roll into a swing Lindy, drop down into an African-flavored undulation, only to rebound into an elongated spiral turn. Regardless of where I land, I am consciously crafting a flow that maintains, to the best of my ability, the integrity of the original step. I am purposeful in selecting tools to manipulate the individual steps so that their uniqueness blends at their point of commonality. Asymmetry, polycentrism, juxtaposition, multilayered isolations, and "get down" are the primary tools I use to weave steps into phrases. When melded with the rhythmic structure I have selected, the heart of the dance work is completed, and what remains is the design of the performance space.

Bringing complexity to my jazz dance composition is vitally important. Jazz music is unapologetically sophisticated. It requires cognition, contemplation, interpretation, and translation. It is active. I hold this to be true for jazz dance as well, and I am bound by cultural heritage to develop the complexity of my jazz dance works. How is this achieved? I sculpt the space through the manipulation of the choreography, adding levels of height, floor patterns, depth, and varied pathways. In addition, I use theme and variation, retrograde, inversion, canon, repetition, and other compositional tools to generate tension, rhythmic propulsion, shading, and dynamics. I arrive at the completion of my process, and it is apparent that the product that lies before me is very much jazz dance. The African American ethos is, in total, an amalgamation of beings. It is unapologetically African, unintentionally European, proudly American, and bravely progressive . . . As is jazz dance . . . As am I.

Jazz Is a Feeling . . .

ADRIENNE HAWKINS

I see my work in jazz as a myopic focus on an artistic goal. I use all elements of music, poetry, sound, and movement to inform, transform, enlighten, and entertain the general public about spirituality, identity, and issues that pertain to the social conditions in America. Age has enabled me to look back with a different understanding of my experiences, and to reflect. These reflections have epiphanies that accompany them.

My work is inspired by the environment that I grew up in. I, a Black woman, lived through the civil rights era and had to go through the predominantly White educational and social system, which did not give value or show positive images related to the history of my race in the fabric and building of this country. Seeing few positive representations of Black people and culture on TV, in the papers, and in the media skewed my own views of the contributions made by my race, not to mention the views of all Americans. There was no acknowledgment of the exploitation, rape, and complete annihilation of not one but many cultures through forced enslavement and brutality. Unlike the teaching about Europe, where there are names to each country, Americans are educated to believe that Africa is monolithic and not the many individual societies and cultures that were decimated by colonization. I knew this stereotype to be false due to my family and the community I grew up in. This askew image was not my image, but it was projected as a universal truth and affected my perspective as a person, artist, woman, and creator.

My experiences in my home and community forced me to go outside my education, the laws, and even the country to realize that the propaganda fed to me as a child and as a citizen of this country were untrue. With that being said, I did not choose jazz. I'm not sure if it was because I was the only Black person taking dance classes in my college of more than thirty thousand people, and I didn't know the difference. I only know that my college did not offer a

FIGURE 10.1. Adrienne Hawkins.
Photo by @MoroccoFlowers/
MoroccoFlowersImages.

jazz class, nor jazz teachers, and yet my teachers told me I was doing jazz dance despite all of my formal training in ballet and Graham. Jazz was assigned to me.

I began choreographing at the same time I started taking formal dance classes. My point of reference for movement was social dance, and I considered formal dance training a technique to be used in composition, but not as an exclusive vocabulary for creating dances and works. When I created my dances for composition class, I used movement that would be expanded by technique that was learned, not limited to it. The creation of my vocabulary for dances was based in communication, fun, circles, grounded-ness, action, current events, and my social experience. I had a working vocabulary of movement that I knew communicated certain feelings and understanding in social settings, but due to almost complete segregation, the experience was not shared by the White community at my college.

In graduate school, I met and assisted Daniel Nagrin for years at various summer festivals. He taught a variety of jazz styles and dances such as the Cakewalk, Charleston, Lindy, and Blues in addition to composition and improvisation, which were taught absent of stylistic designation. This experience provided me with a groundwork for social dances and enabled me to get my first teaching job at Boston University. Daniel was a master in creating theatrical characters for the stage and moving stories and people along, but most of his works were solos. I worked with groups, which I found gave me more flexibility to produce works of various themes.

My creative process involves the development of a vocabulary symbolic of the feeling of the subject of the work. When I choreograph, I begin with feelings, which come from my interactions with people in my community, including my relatives and friends, and how my perception shapes my experiences, how we share mutual experiences, and how thorough research and investigation relates back to the feeling itself. There are universal feelings and emotions in response to situations. Collectively we may feel similarly, but not for the same reasons. Some of the basic ones are sad, happy, angry, or fearful; there are many ways to express these feelings, and many reactions to the emotions, but they manifest themselves for different reasons and in different situations. When putting together ideas for works, I try to start by peeling away the layers of situations to get to the essence of "A" feeling, and how that manifests itself in movement qualities that define or communicate the emotion itself.

The same basic principles are utilized throughout college-level composition classes, but lived experience of the elements at hand can cause them to be interpreted as jazz. In using bodies, placement onstage, and qualities that are consistent with an idea, such as tension, release, hard, fast, slow, smooth, continuous motion, I can find ways for the group to connect or disconnect to foster an idea. I waver quite a bit between "line and design" and "communication" pieces; sometimes I just want you to groove with the sounds, and sometimes the sounds drive the movement. I still consider that jazz, because it's feeling driven with the sound. Using sounds that put the audience in a particular place, moment in time, or situation, I connect them with my understanding of the world. I try to draw people into the feelings of a time and space by utilizing production elements including sound, and also the stage, people, lights, and costumes.

If people see my work and question my use of the word "jazz," then I ask them to expand their definition of what jazz is. Since jazz was assigned to me, it is my experience that is driving the vocabulary, sound, and feeling.

A Strange Place to Find Jazz . . .

KIMBERLEY COOPER

Jazz seduced me at a very young age. I have been dancing for as long as I can remember, but when I saw the inaugural 1984 Decidedly Jazz Danceworks (DJD) performance *Body and Sole* in Calgary, Alberta, Canada, my path became clear. I have a long history with the company, first as a student in the DJD school, then company dancer, resident choreographer, artistic associate, and, since 2013, artistic director. Perhaps Calgary seems a strange place to find jazz, but it is thriving here, and by a mixture of hard work and destiny, I have been working as a full-time jazz dance artist for my entire adult life.

Jazz dance and music are uniquely American art forms born out of the transatlantic slave trade. Jazz is perhaps the most beautiful thing to come out of the worst of circumstances. The history of jazz is rich, and inspiring, and horrifying. I'm well aware that I am a double guest in this form, as a Canadian and as a White person. There is a lot of responsibility that comes with working in jazz, and even more as a guest. Studying the history of the form has been paramount in DJD's work since its inception. *Do the research, go to the source whenever possible* has been our internal mantra since day one, and I continue to have an ongoing compulsion to dig deeper. Centuries of people, movement, sounds, rhythms, cultures, and fusions inform our work; it is a form that owes so much to the bodies and minds of those who have shaped it. You have to go back before you can go forward.

My body contains a wealth of information from countless dancers I've learned from, danced beside, and watched. Through those dancers and their movement, I make my own concoctions, inspired by the history and traditions of this path of jazz I have found myself on, and in the spirit of jazz that has survived by invention and evolution. My research in Cuban dance and music began in 1996 and has had a profound impact on me and how I move, and when I feel I need inspiration, I go to West African class. It grounds me and

FIGURE 11.1. Decidedly Jazz Danceworks' Kimberley Cooper (2011). Photo by Trudie Lee Photography. Courtesy of DJD.

inspires my spine. It clears the noisy clutter in my head and body. My movement is musical, rhythmic, and torso-driven.

The root forms of jazz and groove are essential to my work and have always been essential to the DJD mission. Our work is African-rooted and swing-based, with jazz music at its heart. Because of this, DJD dancers are chosen for their uniqueness and sense of groove. Groove is about feel and connection to music; it is personal even when it is communal. It is easier to teach a dancer how to point their feet and make lines than it is to teach them how to groove.

I'm endlessly inspired by the music of jazz and its family. In my next life I want to be a jazz musician, with access to a time machine that would allow me to hang with the jazz greats throughout the decades. I often work with live music that is being composed for the piece that I haven't created because the music hasn't been invented yet. Chicken and egg. Over time I've learned to invent, trust, and articulate seed ideas that can often be very vague. In the beginning, these ideas are like fireflies buzzing around my head that I can't quite catch. They come at random times and are inspired by myriad things: a conversation, an image, a curious character in the street, or in history . . .

Then, I try to solidify some of these ideas so I can speak about them with the composer: "What does that idea sound like? When does that idea sound like?" We may shoot some examples back and forth: "Something with this vibe? Inspired by that artist?" Sometimes the composer may have recordings or music they've been working on that we can jump off from. Or perhaps I've been to one of their recent gigs and might say, "Please, can we use that?!" or, "I love the feel of the bridge in that tune."

The composer chooses the band based on these conversations. The band then makes rough recordings, sometimes entire tunes—standards, original compositions, perhaps sketches of ideas, or improvisations that the composer or I suggest in that moment, or a combination of all of those things. Sometimes I will simply play them a few bars of a tune I like and ask them to respond. I love these sessions.

This music becomes my soundtrack. I listen to it endlessly. Headphones, studio, home. I listen to it while I walk, exercise, sit with a notebook and pen in hand, and of course in the studio where I work on developing the seeds of the movement vocabulary. This is when the movement generation begins. Again, fireflies. Glimpses of grooves, shapes, feels.

Time to catch the fireflies. I improvise and record myself, and then choose phrases or series of grooves to start playing with. If the music immediately seems like a duet, I may ask another dancer to join me so I can make both parts at once. Sometimes when I have a lot of movement in my head, I invite a dancer in so that I can just spit the movement out on a body quickly. Then I take this movement into the company rehearsal and we play with it, shift it, change it, improvise on it, break it up and rearrange it. At times I'm very specific, "enter from stage left doing exactly this," sometimes more ambiguous, "improvise on this theme responding to the bass line . . ."

The process continues for the next fourteen to sixteen weeks. The band then joins us eight to ten days before opening night. This is when the real magic happens. Things come together; transitions are created. Pieces often can't be resolved until all of the artists are in the room; sometimes the band is still composing music in these last few days, and I wait for the music so I can create the dance to go with it. Although these sections can sometimes be created with high amounts of adrenaline in a feverish few hours, they can be some of the best work and most fun to create.

The conversation between this new live music and dance is tricky. Jazz musicians train to never play the same thing in the same way twice. The musicians we work with need to be open to working in a more structured way than usual. I try to give them as much freedom as possible while maintaining the same form, tempo, and feel (within reason). They need to learn the music so they can get their heads out of their charts and watch and respond to the dancers. Sometimes, something unexpected and very cool happens that opens a whole new door. Recently, while on tour in a technical rehearsal for the balcony scene from *Juliet and Romeo* (my version of *Romeo and Juliet*), the band swung a tune that they never had before, and it was incredible. After rehearsal I asked the band to keep that feel for the performance that night and asked the dancers to open their ears and embrace the feel without changing the choreography, to just be the jazz dancers they are, and respond to the music. From that night on, the piece transformed and just got more interesting with each performance. That kind of aliveness, that sense of response and improvisation, that conversation with the music—that is jazz! That deep connection to the music and the ability to listen and improvise, even subtly and with set choreography, is integral to being a jazz dancer.

Someone recently asked me if, when I am choreographing, I have "jazz boxes" to check to make sure I am making jazz. I never thought of it in that way; my process is instinctual and visceral. I trust the movement archives in my body, and I trust how I've learned to listen and connect to jazz music. When teaching a new group of students, I start each class by talking about jazz history, and in my own words, the defining elements of jazz:

- the beautiful, sacred, and profound relationship between dance and jazz music
- the old Kongo proverb, "dance on bended knee lest you be mistaken for a corpse"
- the essential act of embracing the African roots of jazz, of getting down and digging gravity

- the torso that is expressive and responsive, not held and stiff
- rhythm, syncopation and polyrhythm, and more rhythm on top of that
- improvisation that can be free or structured, but is inherently there to embrace and challenge
- the celebration of the individual within the group—Who are you? How do you relate to this community that you are moving with?
- subtlety and nuance; an example of this would be the concept of "cool"

I create visual music, in the form of jazz, with dignity, reverence, and innovation. I'm proud to be a part of this lineage and recognize that I am in an incredible place of privilege. I am beyond grateful to live this life. At this moment I'm about to begin the second day of my rehearsal process for a new piece I'm creating called *Beautiful Noise*. A few fireflies are in the net; the composer and I have been talking; the band has not yet made demos, so I'm working with music that bends my ear and body, a little Don Cherry, a little Abdullah Ibrahim. It's that magical time when anything is possible.

I step into the studio to prepare for this afternoon's rehearsal, thinking of a quote by a bebop player called Hambone: "Relax your body, tighten your mind and be cool," and I thank jazz for showing me the way in art and life.

Rooted Concepts

Decidedly Jazz Danceworks' Dezjuan Thomas (2016). Photo by Trudie Lee Photography. Courtesy of DJD.

The Duality of the Black Experience
as Jazz Language

PAT TAYLOR

The song and the people is the same.

Amiri Baraka

Walking a thin line between shadow and light . . . one step swallowed by darkness, the next struggling to plant itself firmly on visible ground. The tautness of an imagined tightrope that seems all too real . . . balance, counterbalance, pressed down, head held high, doubt, restriction, strength, perseverance. Faith. The exhale into full-bodied movement that first challenges, then threatens the presumed certainty of the line between . . . balance, counterbalance, opposition, tension, resistance, release. Freedom? The navigation of two worlds through movement that is bold in its uncertainty and layered in contradictions.

So unfolds the solo dance section for *Slippin' into Darkness*, a large group concert work I choreographed in 2016 to explore a story of internal and external struggle and the uneasy truce of living between two realities. The music, performed live, riffed on the 1971 classic of the same name by the group War. This feeling of slipping in and out of darkness has always felt like a natural storytelling choice to me, particularly in my explorations of jazz dance and music, and the jazz aesthetic across artistic disciplines. Creating a sense of being there yet not there, appearing-disappearing-gone-but not really, present and absent at the same time—maybe even differing levels of presence, being fully seen or not—has often captivated my imagination. This shadowy metaphor for the experiences of African Americans, indeed the experiences of any marginalized group, is powerful.

Ralph Ellison's seminal novel *Invisible Man* is rich with jazz and blues refer-ences, inspirations, motifs, structures, and aesthetic qualities.[1] The story's un-named protagonist states as a matter of course, "I am invisible, understand, simply because people refuse to see me."[2] A Black man in a White world, he navigates through life as a shadow, trying on and discarding personas while blues and jazz music shadow his journey. He listens to a recording of Louis Armstrong singing "What Did I Do to Be So Black and Blue?" He recognizes his invisibility as "a peculiar disposition of the eyes of those with whom I come in contact."[3] Others see him as they desire to, and he is not allowed to define himself within that gaze. In 1903, W. E. B. Du Bois called this inability of Blacks to see ourselves directly a *double-consciousness* wherein "one ever feels his two-ness—an American, a Negro; two souls, two thoughts, two unrecon-ciled strivings, two warring ideals in one dark body, whose dogged strength alone keeps it from being torn asunder."[4] It is a constant awareness of how we view ourselves and how the world sees us.

The resulting sense of tension and resistance, interpreted through the use of contradiction, juxtaposition, and the layered coexistence of disparate dy-namic qualities is inherent in jazz music. It is paramount in the instigation of its birth (following in the tradition of sorrow songs, spirituals, and the blues) as a distinct language and self-determined means of responding to the distinct existence and experiences of a marginalized and oppressed people. It is a coun-terbalance to restriction and a language of freedom.

The great Frederick Douglass presages Du Bois's articulation of a double-consciousness in his 1845 book *Narrative of the Life of Frederick Douglass: An American Slave Written by Himself.* His early remembrances of the paradoxical nature of free-form songs that "revealed at once the highest joy and the deep-est sadness" and "breathed the prayer and complaint of souls boiling over" shed light on the genesis of a particular aesthetic of duality.[5] Rooted within that singular means of giving voice to shared lived experiences are "the value of improvisation, which allows reshaping of set forms; the ability to represent in art the idea of paradox as a condition of life; song as a means of recording one's life experiences; and fragmentation and doubleness as artistic techniques."[6] These elements exist across the African American music continuum, creating a tradition that has informed Black creative expression from its earliest days.

Jazz's historical relationship to the African American experience is still of great significance today. Many of the characteristics we embody in jazz dance originated from this relationship. At its birth, jazz was dismissed as low art and lower-class, the music considered noise, the dance deemed unrefined and offensive, and its rhythm-driven African roots much too prominent. But for

FIGURE 12.1. JazzAntiqua Dance & Music Ensemble's James MahKween, 2018. Photo by George Simian. Courtesy of JazzAntiqua, Inc.

its initiators, practitioners, and community, "jazz music and dance displayed African-American culture live and in living color; it functioned as an unapologetic and undeniable cultural survival social phenomenon."[7] Its impetus was life. Its motif a juxtaposition and layering of dynamics that reflected the oppositional forces and realities of daily Black life—the paradox. It "reinforced the need for and right to be self-determining beings."[8]

As a jazz choreographer I seek out this *movement in the music*—the physical embodiment of the stories within jazz music as I see, hear, and feel them; and the historical, social, cultural, and political implications therein. It is the "paradox and contradictions that make up African American life" that A. Yemisi Jimoh explores in *Spiritual, Blues and Jazz People in African American Fiction: Living in Paradox*, and that are felt throughout the very core of jazz.[9] These contrastive elements as I am inspired to explore them in dance are realized as a driving forward motion/risk-taking urgency (the dogged strength articulated by Du Bois)[10] overlaid with the laid-back assurance, elegance, and demeanor of cool; a shaping of energy that is taut yet expansive; the spaciousness of joy in the midst of tears; the virtuosity of the individual voice within the community of the ensemble effort; the past embraced in the present with a keen eye to the future; and an embodiment of what I have coined as melodic-syncopation and accented-flow, imagery I use with dancers to deepen awareness of duality within the movement as a reflection of the music. We pay close attention to the rhythm and percussiveness of the footwork as it melds with a fluid expressiveness throughout the torso, as well as the punctuation of movement that is never stagnant or flung away, but continues to breathe within the shape and energy of it.

My interdisciplinary explorations of the jazz aesthetic and how it manifests in jazz-imbued literature, visual art, spoken word, and theater broadens my understanding of the ways in which the Black experience is interpreted through jazz language. This in turn informs my jazz dance practice and fuels my ongoing inquiry. It is in the subtle awareness of the fragmentation of our reality that I find that there is also a very pointed use of silence that in turn guides my storytelling, along with the resiliency that is a hallmark of Black existence and triumph *in spite of* and reflected in the spirit of improvisation.

In his 1999 essay "In Praise of Silence," John Edgar Wideman contemplates the enslaved African in America: "In order to save your life, when you attempt to utter the first word of a new tongue, are you also violating your identity and dignity? When you break your silence, are you surrendering, acknowledging the strangers' power to own you, rule you? Are you forfeiting your chance to tell your story in your own words some day?"[11]

It is a small wonder that the American story is permeated by Black creative expression (what we've often had in place of a fully felt sense of freedom) that pulses with style, panache, and an audacity that is "so vibrant," as author Walter Mosley writes, "because they are barely veiled codes that express the pain we've experienced for so many years."[12] Certainly we often feel this in a jazz musician's playing, especially when we find present a balance and freedom achieved through a sense of tension, resistance, and ultimately release. And it resonates metaphorically when the energy of subverting restriction is viewed as what Wideman describes as characterizing "the practices African-descended people have employed to keep their distance from imposed tongues, imposed disciplines."[13]

When voice was found within a self-determined expressive form of our own creation as a means of self-preservation, birth was given to spirituals, the blues, jazz, and the music forms that preceded them and those that have come after. These are distinctive languages growing out of the powerful need to express a distinctive existence.

Wideman writes: "Silence marks time, saturates and shapes African-American art. Silences structure our music, fill the spaces—point, counterpoint—of rhythm, cadence, phrasing. Think of the eloquent silences of Thelonious Monk, sometimes comic, sometimes manic and threatening."[14]

Silence in jazz dance can literally be felt in the quiet moments of contrast. In the working of syncopation. Choreographer S. Ama Wray notes that "rhythm calls for stillness to make itself clear."[15] Space is vital. I also find it in sustained sound and movement, and in the breath before and in between. It is in the active listening, seeing, and feeling of a jazz dialogue, and in *the break*.[16] Silence can release tension as it follows a phrase of music or movement, or build it as a precursor to the same. Conversely, I also use a lack of silence/stillness in works of nonstop movement to illuminate assertion of the communal self as a never ceasing journey, and a reclamation of spaciousness that all too often is still restricted.

Jazz improvisation (both music and dance) highlights individual virtuosity within the ensemble effort and requires being fully in the moment and deep within the conversation in order to maintain the equilibrium needed in order to not only share one's own truth but also achieve the outcome of the greatest good for the group or community. It allows for multiple, simultaneous interpretations of a single idea, and celebrates how each voice aids in fostering freedom for many. Wray notes jazz as a music form that "arose directly out of African-American communities, and like music of African origin, it has a significant improvised and individually defined component . . . [T]here are creative spaces for individual expression to shape the content of performance while maintaining a close engagement with the aesthetic intention of the whole."[17]

Researcher and writer Alfonso W. Hawkins Jr. relates jazz improvisation to the nonlinear, bumpy road of progress for African Americans, "a personal evaluation and contemplation of conditions."[18] Self-taught visual artist Sam Middleton speaks of feeling like an improvising soloist as he describes filling the space of his canvas "with what you are, what you know, what you think." Harlem born and raised, Middleton found himself surrounded by music, and it was the colors, shapes, textures, rhythm, lyricism, fluidity, and sense of space that jazz in particular evoked for him that helped to shape elements of his creative process: "Monk taught me not to be afraid to take a chance, not to be afraid of making a mistake."[19]

The freedom represented in jazz music can be realized in jazz dance through an expansiveness of movement, and in energy that is strong and directed, yet not cast away. I find it in the ways in which elements of contradiction, what Paul Rinzler, a professor in jazz and music theory, calls *dynamic tension*,[20] ground us for an astonishing range of expressiveness and physicality. As counterintuitive as it might sound, this dynamic tension allows us to move with abandon, with a freedom that is framed by self-determination and realization. It is the result of a deeply rooted awareness of how the use of oppositional energy provides the balance and assurance within which one can fully release. In teaching and choreographing, I often reference a tautness in jazz music and jazz movement—an uninhibited fluidity that breathes within a punctuation of energy and ideas, that nevertheless heightens our sense of spaciousness. Equally as important, there is freedom in the stories we are compelled to tell.

In spite of the precarious act of duality honed to a state of being and survival mechanism, there also exist characteristics and qualities within jazz that help to quell feelings of dislocation and provide a powerfully rooted way of moving. The low notes on the bass provide the bottom in the music, creating the stability of a foundation from which everything else can *jump off*. In the dance we purposefully stay low to the ground, maintaining a spiritual connection to the earth and working within and against the pull of gravity to achieve balance, to keep our *cool*, and to empower our explosive moments of release. The double bounce, felt as the groove, also anchors movement to the music. The drums propel us, yet we ride the rhythm, ever striving to be *in the pocket* and dancing deep within that groove. There is safety and assurance there, along with an awareness of community. The melodies allow us to soar and tell our stories from the deepest places in our souls.

Jazz dance can remain steeped in roots and heritage at the same time that it presses forward. It can be part of the long history of expression that gives birth to what theologian, activist, and author Cornel West describes as *jazz freedom fighters*.[21] Ultimately, for me, the dynamic tension of jazz as languaging the duality of the Black experience, however it might manifest in the dancing body, is about how my dancers and I use the imagery of this conviction; that we are dutifully and inspirationally aware and conscious of it, and that we seek it out as an expressive ideal.[22]

The jazz aesthetic permeates across artistic disciplines, and within jazz-imbued art the often contrastive conditions of African American life are examined, challenged, embraced, wrestled with, expressed, and reconceived in a variety of ways. From the collage art of Romare Bearden to the theatrical jazz work of Omi Osun Joni L. Jones, Laura Carlos, Sharon Bridgforth, and

Daniel Alexander Jones, to the gritty and life-affirming writing of poet Kamau Daáood, jazz shapes energy. In describing how she relates *the break* of a soloing jazz musician to characteristics of theatrical jazz, Omi Osun Joni L. Jones writes:

> This idea of opening a "spot" in the work often happens in a theatrical jazz aesthetic when an individual performer releases into the work with courage, abandon, and mastery . . . An inner hidden dynamic is brought forward to an outward expression; something palpable yet almost indescribable is brought into the room. There is a powerful fusion between the degree of risk-taking and honesty in the performer's personal life and the degree of idiosyncratic creativity the performer unleashes in the performance. Performance then becomes a place of freedom.[23]

Uncompromising in its presentation, the paintings of Kerry James Marshall are counternarratives, stories that defy the invisibility of Blacks in America. The visual representation of Blackness in Marshall's work is much more than skin deep. He also captures symbols of Black culture, and the amplified way in which African Americans navigate through the shadow and light. He draws "upon the rich layering of language, music and art characteristic of black expression. Like a jazz composer superimposing multiple rhythms and harmonies."[24]

Pioneering pianist-composer Mary Lou Williams once said: "Jazz is love. You have to lay into it and let it flow." This is one way in which the jazz-rooted artist moves—releasing into the process, the conversation, the legacy, the forward motion, the tension and resistance . . . the contradictions. It is not without its challenges, yet it can lead to awakening, catharsis, revelation, liberation, connection, and survival.

The continual self-defining by African Americans through creative modes of expression are acts of self-preservation. And self-preservation is an act of resistance. Jazz at heart is a stand for freedom. I continue to be drawn to examining the nature of this brand of opposition throughout the African diasporic journey, and for my specific focus its manifestation through jazz dance. My growing sensitivity as a choreographer in conversation with jazz spurs me toward uncovering ways in which duality and paradox are embodied in its very essence. It is an ongoing series of personal discoveries around my practice as it lives on the concert stage, in the classroom and studio, and within the community.

NOTES

1. Recognized with the National Book Award in 1953, and with many other honors through the years, Ralph Ellison's *Invisible Man* is told in the first person by an African American character who remains nameless and believes that he invisibly moves through society. Invisibility is not a physical condition but rather the belief that others refuse to really see him. Jazz and blues music, imagery, and symbolism weave throughout the story. Ellison, also widely known and highly regarded as an essayist and cultural critic, uses jazz techniques in the telling of the story and is often referenced in discussions of jazz aesthetics.

2. Ralph Ellison, *Invisible Man* (New York: Vintage International, 1995), 3.

3. Ibid.

4. W. E. B. Du Bois, *The Souls of Black Folks* (New York: Dover, 1994), 2.

5. Frederick Douglass, *Narrative of the Life of Frederick Douglass: An American Slave, Written by Himself* (digitized copy of book, originally published Boston: Anti-Slavery Office, 1845), 13–14.

6. A. Yemisi Jimoh, *Spiritual, Blues and Jazz People in African American Fiction: Living in Paradox* (Knoxville: University of Tennessee Press, 2002), 7.

7. Tamara Thomas, "Making the Case for True Engagement with Jazz Dance: Decolonizing Higher Education," *Journal of Dance Education* 19, no. 3 (July–September 2019): 99.

8. Ibid.

9. Jimoh, *Spiritual, Blues and Jazz,* 36.

10. Du Bois, *The Souls of Black Folks,* 2.

11. John Edgar Wideman, "In Praise of Silence," in "The Best of Callaloo Prose," special issue, *Callaloo* 24. no. 2 (2001): 641–43, www.jstor.org/stable/3300543.

12. Walter Mosley, *Workin' on the Chain Gang: Shaking off the Dead Hand of History* (New York: Ballantine, 2000), 13.

13. Wideman, "In Praise of Silence."

14. Ibid.

15. S. Ama Wray (Sheron Wray), "A Twenty-First-Century Jazz Dance Manifesto," in *Jazz Dance: A History of the Roots and Branches,* ed. Lindsay Guarino and Wendy Oliver (Gainesville: University Press of Florida, 2014), 13.

16. A break in jazz music is when a soloist plays for a short period of time without the accompaniment of any other instruments.

17. Wray, "A Twenty-First-Century Jazz Dance Manifesto," 14.

18. Alfonso W. Hawkins Jr., "A Jazz Schematic," in *The Jazz Trope: A Theory of African American Literary and Vernacular Culture* (Lanham, MD: Scarecrow, 2008), 201.

19. Sam Middleton, interview by Graham Lock, "Sam Middleton: The Painter as Improvising Soloist," in *The Hearing Eye: Jazz & Blues Influences in African American Visual Art* (New York: Oxford University Press, 2009), 120–33.

20. Paul Rinzler, *The Contradictions of Jazz* (Lanham, MD: Scarecrow, 2008), 8. Rinzler explores the opposites that he finds present in jazz: individualism and inter-connectedness, assertion and openness, freedom and responsibility, and creativity and tradition.

21. Cornel West, *Race Matters* (Boston: Beacon, 1993), 105.

22. I cofounded my company JazzAntiqua Dance & Music Ensemble with jazz composer-bassist Marcus Shelby in 1993 to celebrate jazz as a vital thread in the cultural fabric of African American history and heritage and a defining element of the American experience. The ensemble is comprised of dancers and musicians, actor-singers, spoken-word artists, educators, culture-bearers, mentors, and artist-activists. Our credo is jazz arts education/preservation/creation.

23. Omi Osun Joni L. Jones, *Theatrical Jazz: Performance, Ase, and the Power of the Present Moment* (Columbus: Ohio State University Press, 2015), 167. Omi Osun Joni L. Jones is an artist/scholar and professor emerita of African and African Diaspora Studies at the University of Texas at Austin. Her work focuses on performance eth-nography, theatrical jazz, Yoruba-based aesthetics, and areas of social activism through theater.

24. Lorie Mertes, *Kerry James Marshall: One True Thing: Meditations on Black Aesthetics,* exhibit brochure, February 6–April 25, 2004, Miami Art Museum Publication.

13

Performing Gender

*Disrupting Performance Norms for Women in Jazz Dance
through Gender-Inclusive, Human-Centric Choreography*

BRANDI COLEMAN

> Identity categories tend to be instruments of regulatory regimes, whether as the
> normalizing categories of oppressive structures or as the rallying points for liberatory
> contestation of that very oppression.
>
> Judith Butler

The dance industry often functions culturally and structurally along binary
lines through language, environmental factors, class structures, teaching philosophies, movement aesthetics, and choreographic narratives that are positioned as either male or female.[1] Hypermasculine and hyperfeminine ideals
and attitudes, determined and implemented according to cultural influences
both in and outside of dance, are endorsed through some forms—primarily
those that uphold Eurocentric aesthetics—of jazz dance pedagogy, choreography, and performance.

As a woman in jazz dance, I have deep memories of navigating signals from
teachers and choreographers in positions of power about how I should look
and move in order to get a job. My first professional commercial dance job
required that I perform highly seductive and hypersexualized movement in
fishnets and heels, conflating confidence and attitude with overt sexuality. At
twenty-three, I did not understand the complex issues at play but instead was
ecstatic and grateful for the generous salary, benefits, and the opportunity to
develop and hone my skills as a performing artist during twelve shows a week.
For the first time in my young career, I was financially stable, contributing to
a savings account, and gaining invaluable performing experience while being

praised and rewarded for dancing movements that put my body and perceived availability onstage under the guise of sassy, energetic, upbeat, fun dancing.

In this example, commercial jazz dance, defined as jazz dance that is associated with selling a product,[2] could be seen as a vehicle for feminism and empowerment—a way to reclaim the narrative of how and when I presented myself in this context. What I didn't know then was that my privilege as a White woman in jazz dance afforded me the ability to frame the hypersexualized movement-for-profit through a feminist lens of self-empowerment and advancement that ignored the intersectionality of race and gender presentation for women in jazz. There are examples of Black women in jazz dance who access an internally felt and externally presented sensuality with agency and ownership of their personal narrative. This can be seen in African diasporic movement that utilizes the pelvis as a democratic part of the entire moving body, employing it in rituals of fertility, birth, and life. It can also be seen in the performance of a prominent pop-artist such as Beyoncé who, through her platform and celebrity status, frames her sexualized movement through a feminist lens. However, in her book *The Black Dancing Body: A Geography from Coon to Cool*, Brenda Dixon Gottschild notes that, "by Europeanist standards, the Africanist dancing body—articulating the trunk that houses primary and secondary sexual characteristics—is vulgar, lewd. The *presumption of promiscuity* leads to the lubricious stereotypes attributed to black dancing bodies."[3] In contrast, the privilege I experience as a White woman allows me to transition between jazz dance forms, from commercial jazz to vernacular-based jazz, and perform these particular movement aesthetics seamlessly and without judgement or bias. Sexualized movement centered around the pelvis was acceptable for me; it was determined to be offensive and unrefined for Black women.

Becoming a member of Jump Rhythm® Jazz Project[4] and learning Jump Rhythm® Technique (JRT) was a pivotal moment in understanding myself as a performing artist and woman in jazz dance because the technique and choreography disrupted the stereotypes often assigned to the female dancing body. Created by Billy Siegenfeld, JRT prioritizes rhythmic clarity, movement efficiency, and emotional and personal authenticity, none of which rely on gender-specific movement initiatives. At no point was I asked to be sassy or have "attitude," words that can subconsciously cue one to jut out a hip, lift the chin, stick out the chest, and adhere to stereotypical body postures primarily, but not exclusively, used by women who wish to emotionally as well as physically display confidence, ownership of self, and command of the narrative. Instead, JRT uses "gravity-directed body mechanics, singing as well as dancing the rhythms of movement, and improvising in rhythmic community with others"[5] to inform and determine the movement aesthetics. It calls upon the Africanist aesthetics in the social and kinetic framework of pedagogy and choreography by prioritizing concepts such as embracing the conflict, polycentrism/polyrhythm, high-affect juxtaposition, and the "aesthetic of the cool"[6] over Eurocentric-driven body postures that position the body in uplifted, presentational alignments.

Additionally, JRT utilizes characteristics of feminist pedagogy in its underlying philosophy that inform the learning process in class and during the choreographic and rehearsal process that include "collaborative learning, democratic orientation, inclusivity, and critical reflection."[7] This is important to note because the work is counter to commercial jazz dance perspectives that uphold the patriarchal and hegemonic view seen in the work of artists such as Jack Cole[8] and Bob Fosse, who were credited with a deep understanding of how a woman should move and were known specifically for promoting and enhancing the onstage and onscreen sexuality of the women they worked with. JRT did not determine how I should look or ask me to rearrange my posture or body shape to conform to idealized notions of beauty, but instead asked me to move in the pedestrian-body that I walked in the room with. I was enough.

With my first introduction to JRT, I discovered that I could "be myself so that what comes out is truthful"[9] and that I could rely on my autonomous sense of self to determine how I was seen in performance and in the studio. Additionally, through my work with Jump Rhythm® Jazz Project, I found employment in the field that did not capitalize off of my gender presentation but instead provided a path of long-term work as a performer, teaching artist, rehearsal director, associate artistic director, and now assistant professor in higher education, all based on the foundational requirement that I move, and most importantly, that I *be* myself.

Considering jazz dance's social ethos of communal inclusivity, individuality, and personal expression along with its propensity to respond to, as well as subvert, sociopolitical and cultural norms, the field is ripe for discussion and change with regard to gender expression and representation. Where do we, as educators, choreographers, performers, directors, innovators, and scholars, stand regarding gender roles, gender expression, and representation, specifically of women in jazz dance? Considering the heteronormative, highly gendered stylizations that are hallmarks of various forms of jazz dance, can we imagine a way in which we might be more gender expansive in our pedagogy and choreography? Can we identify pedagogical and choreographic approaches that offer alternative ways for female-identified persons to move?

FIGURE 13.1. Jordan Batta and Brandi Coleman perform *And One More Thing . . .* at Rhythmically Speaking in Minneapolis, MN 2018. Photo by Bill Cameron Photography.

Can we disrupt the notion that jazz dance, especially commercial jazz dance, is automatically or inherently synonymous with hyperfeminine, pelvis-centric, sexually inviting and seemingly available, presentational-style dancing?

There is a breadth of scholarship that focuses on gender politics (inequality, identity, expression, and representation) in American modern dance and contemporary ballet as seen in texts by Wendy Oliver, Doug Risner, and articles from Susan Leigh Foster. Other scholars such as Carolyn Hebert and Karen Schupp have specifically addressed gender as it relates to competition culture and boys in dance.[10] This chapter will focus on the performative nature of gender, specifically in the female moving body as it relates to jazz dance in a heteronormative dance culture that reinforces binary gender expression and gender roles. The research aims to identify the physical and cultural tropes that often define women in jazz dance and will present gender-inclusive, human-centric examples of choreography that disrupt the binary or heteronormative, societally induced constructs pertaining to gendered movement. I am writing from a perspective informed by Whiteness but have attempted to quote and learn from Black historians, authors, and artists, and I acknowledge the privileged space from which I write.

Performing Gender/Gender Expression

American philosopher and gender theorist Judith Butler states that the "performativity of gender is a stylized repetition of acts, an imitation or miming of the dominant conventions of gender."[11] She establishes gender as a stylization of the body that is separate from the female sex. Additionally, in her article "In the Margins: Dance Studies, Feminist Theories, and the Public Performance of Identity," Julia Zdrojewski states: "I was born with female sex organs, but I choose to perform womanhood through specific movements or 'acts' that align themselves with a female gender. I style my hair, walk a specific way, wear a certain style of clothing that all read as female-gendered to a societal audience."[12] When applied to the overt stylizations of some forms of jazz dance, this theory shows that specific movements, particularly those with an intense focus on the pelvis and outwardly thrust chest as an adopted posture, are learned stylizations of how a woman should move in jazz dance rather than an inherent, naturally assumed movement aesthetic. Women are not born with the innate knowledge of how to execute a highly stylized and gendered jazz walk; they learn to *perform* the movement as an expression of gender, with an added air of sass and attitude.

Butler emphasizes that performing gender is not as simple as changing one's outward appearance to reflect a stylistic choice and has worked to "refute the reduction of gender performance to something like style. Performativity has to do with repetition, very often with the repetition of oppressive and painful gender norms to force them to resignify."[13] This is a crucial clarification when considering the ways gender is learned, practiced, and embedded in the attitudes and behaviors of young girls, teens, and women in jazz dance. Feminine-identified movement aesthetics are often instituted at an early age, thereby creating a years-long study in how to be a woman through the repetition of movement and the affirmation of aesthetic ideals that are then reinforced by years of applause and positive affirmation.[14] This dynamic creates a standard by which some forms of commercial, presentational-style jazz dance are then upheld. Sexy becomes synonymous with jazz.

This was ever-so-evident in a recent jazz dance master class in which I taught a class combination that included a simple half-time walk with a slight double-bounce feel to the song "C Jam Blues" performed by the Lincoln Center Jazz Orchestra with Wynton Marsalis. The only prompts I gave the students for how to execute the walk related to timing (what beat to step on) and musical feel (light, swinging, triple-rhythm feel with directed, engaged energy through the body). Inevitably, every single student in the class, regardless of their gender expression, adopted a hip-swinging, chest-protruding, slithering walk that communicated "look at me," "look at this." I reminded the students that personal expression and individuality are two philosophies inherent to jazz dance and encouraged them to acknowledge and respond to their inside-felt, emotional impulse in response to the music while moving within the framework of the rhythm and musical feel of the walk. If anything changed, the students now felt empowered to double-down on their highly charged and hypersexualized walk.

I'm sharing this anecdote not because I propose there is anything inherently "wrong" about performing a walk this way; I'm sharing this because the entire class *instinctually* performed the walk this way. The jazz walk they embodied is so synonymous with jazz dance that it was automatic for the students to choose this walk as a default. The qualities of motion and movement aesthetics traditionally associated with jazz dance, especially for women, have been repeated for so long that they are now inherent to jazz dance culture in a way that is like a well-known brand but without any acknowledgment of its deep ties to the commodification of sex and racism in its origins.

REPRESENTATION OF WOMEN IN JAZZ DANCE

Origins of the traditional hip-centric jazz walk can be traced to Storyville,[15] the infamous New Orleans red-light district in the late 1800s and early 1900s.[16] The Storyville District, often considered the home of jazz music, was, by city ordinance, an area of the city segregated by race and industry that was relegated to prostitutes[17] working in high-end brothels and smaller one-room shacks called cribs.[18] The creation of Storyville happened on the heels of the Supreme Court's 1896 decision in *Plessy v. Ferguson*, which made racial segregation in public places legal: "For nearly twenty years, Storyville flouted the segregationist order by aggressively advertising the availability of mixed-race women for the sexual pleasure of white men. Where *Plessy v. Ferguson* mandated racial separation, Storyville promoted interracial intimacy, as the district openly offered nonwhite prostitutes for its white customers."[19] In establishing the Storyville district, the local government attempted to address the long history of corruption embedded in the DNA of New Orleans but instead "offered a stage for acting out cultural fantasies of white supremacy, patriarchal power, and a renewed version of American manhood for the twentieth century."[20]

The brothels and cribs operated in close quarters with dance halls, concert saloons, and cabarets. Jazz musicians played at the brothels, and, in turn, many of the prostitutes, madams, and pimps frequented the music halls after work. The music, dance, and sexual commerce were interchangeable in the district as prostitutes used hip-centric, pelvis-articulated movements as a means to attract customers; this inspired chorus girls to evolve the movements into the vernacular jazz dance known as the Boogie Walks (or the Boogie Forward or the solo jazz dance, the Boogie Woogie).[21] Through evolution and reinvention, these walks became synonymous with jazz dance, performed with variations and individual stylizations. The through line, however, is the use of the pelvis as a device for attracting attention in a presentational and commercialized situation.

The use of the pelvis in hypersexualized movements in the Storyville district complicates the significance of the pelvis and hip-centric movements in some Western and Central African dances that praise fertility and celebrate birth. *Ikoku* dancing, one of the dances specific to the Punu people of Congo-Brazzaville, contains hip thrusts used at specific, structurally dictated moments to signal an invitation for an individual to join in the dance, and uses hip rotations that are "connected to the fecundating sexual encounter and to the action of collective pool fishing, linking the dance universe to the maternal life-bearing universe of the water spirits."[22] *Ikoku* dancing also serves as a form of self-affirmation, pride, and collective joy amongst the participants.[23] The difference is the female moving body as a site for presentation and commerce as seen in Storyville versus the moving body as a site for honoring life-affirming rituals in African dances.[24] In other words, presentational, commercial dancing versus social and cultural-driven dancing; this could also be distinguished as Eurocentric-informed dancing in relation to Africanist-based dancing.

Jazz dance forms that are hypersexualized and gender conforming according to heteronormative gender roles are heavily influenced by Eurocentric ideas of aesthetics and beauty. Gottschild states that "the social dances that originated in African diasporan communities had to be controlled and straightened up to a vertical, Europeanist standard before they could be considered acceptable for white consumption."[25] By infusing social jazz dance forms with ballet-based alignment principles, the formerly flexible and mobile spine, which includes the responsive pelvis, became upheld and rigid so that the body was in a presentational stance.

THE PRESENTATIONAL BODY AS A SITE FOR COMMERCIALISM

One would be hard-pressed to find jazz dance choreography in music videos, music tours, and popular television shows where the dancing and subject narrative did not include some form of overt sexualization of the body. The eyes, tilt of the head, outwardly thrust chest, and leading pelvis signify a person who presents as in control, commanding of the self as well as others, and posits an invitation to availability. Why is this particular genre of jazz dance so closely associated with hypersexualization of the dancers? In her article "Two Ways a Woman Can Get Hurt," author and educator Jean Kilbourne examines ads and advertising practices that showcase the rampant exploitation of women through sexism, racism, and a system of patriarchy that upholds highly gendered stereotypes. Commercial jazz dance is playing out these same social constructs, some of which are determined by the power of White male privilege and the male gaze. Similar to the Storyville District of New Orleans, contemporary commercial jazz dance forms rely upon the commodification of women, and specifically sex, to sell products from clothing, music, fashion, to a myriad of other products—in the Storyville District, it was actual sex; in music videos, concert tours, and televised dance shows, it's a product sold on the *idea* of sex.

GENDER-INCLUSIVE, HUMAN-CENTRIC CHOREOGRAPHY

> Why do we not choose what and how we teach based upon what will make us more fully human?
> Susan Stinson

My experience as a performer and teaching artist with Jump Rhythm® Jazz Project and Billy Siegenfeld has greatly influenced my perspective as a choreographer. At the heart of each piece of my choreography is Jump Rhythm® Technique—an egalitarian technique that does not have any gender-specific movement aesthetics, but rather calls upon functional alignment and emotion-driven instincts as its foundation. JRT does not rely on outward, physical movement identifiers to signify gender but instead relies on the internally driven, externally realized execution of emotion-driven rhythm supported by an alignment principle called Standing Down Straight® (SDS). SDS asks one to reconsider the body-posture needed to execute the foundational elements of rhythm-generated movement[26] and shifts the conversation away from the society-informed and culturally accepted posture of "standing up straight," which in and of itself aligns women in a chest-out postural position.

I made a piece, *And One More Thing . . .*, set to Stevie Wonder's popular tune "Tell Me Something Good,"[27] which explored the idea of women taking up/reclaiming physical and emotional space without adhering to prescribed notions of what women should look, feel, move, or sound like. The women begin the piece by standing still for several measures of music, only moving to slightly shift their weight from one foot to the other. They are resisting the irresistible funk intro of the music, controlling space and time until they are ready to move (referencing the idea of women being interrupted, spoken over, or not allowed time to speak and say what they mean). The choreography does not hold the body to physical norms that are Eurocentric or have any notion of "good" or "proper" or "beautiful." The movement vocabulary is purposefully human-centric, action-driven, emotion-focused, and anatomically informed as opposed to gender-descriptive or gender-assuming.

The choreography purposefully strips away the stereotypical physical markers of acceptable dancing for women by eliminating fluid, slinky, and hyperflexible movement designed for long and lean bodies.[28] Instead, the dancers' energy-driven body shapes toggle back and forth between smooth, calm, "cool"[29] walks and raw, disjointed, angular outbursts. Their focus is unwavering, supported by movement vocabulary that is unabashedly hard-hitting and unapologetic. During the creative process, outside of functional alignment and movement efficiency, the body was never discussed in terms of aesthetics or positions but instead, each performer was addressed as an emotional, feeling, responsive being moving in musically articulate jazz-rhythms. True ensemble dancing was dictated by the embodiment of the rhythmic score and expressiveness of each person as they interacted and related to each other. There are no gendered movements that suggest male or female. The movement vocabulary for the choreography is built on social and kinetic elements drawn from West African dance and African American vernacular dance: energy, propulsive rhythm, percussiveness, improvisation, asymmetrical movements, vocalizations, individuality within the community, joyousness, and groundedness[30] and are less concerned with showcasing societally and culturally determined gendered aesthetics.

When I first began working with Jump Rhythm®, I had a lot of "unlearning" to do to unravel years of physical and emotional attachments of what it meant to be a woman in jazz. Physically and functionally, I had to undo many years of ballet training, of lifting my weight away from the earth and organizing my body into shapes determined by other people and deemed to be

FIGURE 13.2. Madisen Nielsen, Tiara Saddler, Savanna Blocker, Destiney Lockhart, and Cerena Chaney (*left to right*) perform Brandi Coleman's *And One More Thing*... April 2016. BD Pruitt @ East Market Studios.

right and necessary for jazz dance. Emotionally, I had to navigate the feelings of what this meant: to realize that I didn't *have* to reorganize my body into Eurocentric-informed positions to determine my worth or financial wellness in jazz dance. Similarly, when creating *And One More Thing*... with the group of young college-aged women, I realized they were navigating the complicated feelings that came with being allowed to stand in a neutral, physically unaffected stance and putting their humanity, their personhood at the forefront of the narrative. I kept reminding them, in the words of master vocalist Barbara Cook, "you are enough."[31] While this may seem obvious, these are fairly revolutionary sentiments to hear as a woman who has spent years conforming to socially-prescribed gender-norms that uphold conventions of commercialism and self-worth.

Conclusion

Despite the prominent images on television dance shows, music videos, commercial endeavors, and musicals, feminine-identified movements are not necessary in making jazz dance works. To disrupt a performed gender, such as the hyperfeminine jazz walk, takes a conscious and sustained refocusing of pedagogy and choreographic practice.

In all, jazz dance's embedded ethos of personal expression and inclusivity, along with its constant evolution of movement and philosophy that is closely aligned with popular culture, make it prime for a conversation about performed gender and the recognition and adoption of nonbinary artistic expression. Jazz dance is subversive; jazz music is subversive. The challenge moving forward as twenty-first-century dancemakers and educators in jazz is to subvert the default of sexualized jazz dance aesthetics, movement stereotypes, and narrative tropes. It is now necessary to create a gender-inclusive jazz dance experience that is reflective of the human-centric voices present in jazz dance—a true "of-the-people-ness" that includes *all* people without asking *some* of the people to conform to societal gender expectations.

NOTES

1. Carolyn Hebert, "Boys Only! Gender-Based Pedagogical Practices in a Commercial Dance Studio," in *Dance and Gender: An Evidence-Based Approach*, ed. Wendy Oliver and Doug Risner (Gainesville: University of Florida Press, 2017), 97–114; Wendy Oliver and Doug Risner, "An Introduction to Dance and Gender," ibid., 1–19; Karen Schupp, "Sassy Girls and Hard-Hitting Boys: Dance Competition and Culture," ibid., 76–96.

2. Lindsay Guarino and Wendy Oliver, "Jazz Dance Styles," in *Jazz Dance: A History of the Roots and Branches*, ed. Guarino and Oliver (Gainesville: University Press of Florida, 2014), 24–31.

3. Brenda Dixon Gottschild, *The Black Dancing Body: A Geography from Coon to Cool* (New York: Palgrave Macmillan, 2003), 147, emphasis added.

4. In 2018, Jump Rhythm® Jazz Project was rebranded as Jump Rhythm®. More information at jumprhythm.org.

5. Billy Siegenfeld, "Standing Down Straight: Jump Rhythm Technique's Rhythm-Driven, Community-Directed Approach to Dance Education," *Journal of Dance Education* 9, no. 4 (2009): 110–19.

6. Brenda Dixon Gottschild, *Digging the Africanist Presence in American Performance: Dancing and Other Contexts* (Westport, CT: Praeger, 1996), 11–19. The term "aesthetic of the cool" was coined by scholar and teacher Robert Farris Thompson (see Robert Farris Thompson, "An Aesthetic of the Cool," *African Arts* 7, no. 1 [1973]: 41–91, doi:10.2307/3334749).

7. Sherrie Barr and Wendy Oliver, "Feminist Pedagogy, Body Image, and the Dance Technique Class," *Research in Dance Education* 17, no. 2 (2016): 97–112, doi: 10.1080/14647893.2016.1177008.

8. Debra Levine, "Jack Cole Made Marilyn Monroe Move," *Los Angeles Times*, August 9, 2009, www.latimes.com/entertainment/arts/la-ca-marilyn-monroe9-2009aug09

-story.html. Jack Cole positioned as the man who made the woman move: "Jack Cole took a gorgeous woman at the height of her physical beauty and gave her the ability to communicate with her body, a means of expression beyond cinema's main instruments of face and voice."

9. Quote from Billy Siegenfeld.

10. As evidenced in Barr and Oliver, "Feminist Pedagogy, Body Image, and the Dance Technique Class"; Susan Leigh Foster, "Choreographies of Gender," *University of Chicago Press Journals* 24, no. 1 (1998): 1–33; Doug Risner, "Rehearsing Heterosexuality: 'Unspoken' Truths in Dance Education," *Dance Research Journal* 34, no. 2 (2002): 63–78; Hebert, "Boys Only!," 97–114; Oliver and Risner, "An Introduction to Dance and Gender," 1–19; Schupp, "Sassy Girls and Hard-Hitting Boys," 76–96.

11. Liz Kotz, "The Body You Want: An Interview with Judith Butler," *Artforum* 31, no. 3 (1992), www.artforum.com/print/previews/199209/the-body-you-want-an-inteview -with-judith-butler-33505.

12. Julia Zdrojewski, "In the Margins: Dance Studies, Feminist Theories, and the Public Performance of Identity" (dance master's thesis, The College at Brockport, State University of New York, 2014), 30.

13. Kotz, "The Body You Want."

14. Schupp, "Sassy Girls and Hard-Hitting Boys," 76–96. In her chapter, Schupp covers appearance norms, movement expectations, affirmation for young female dancers.

15. Moncell Durden, private message conversation with author, December 5, 2019.

16. Emily Epstein Landau, *Spectacular Wickedness: Sex, Race, and Memory in New Orleans* (Baton Rouge: Louisiana State Press, 2013), 1.

17. Ibid. Regarding my use of the term "prostitute" in this context over the preferred term "sex worker," I am following the lead of author Emily Epstein Landau, whom I reference in this section. She uses the term "prostitute" rather than "sex worker" because "the latter term connotes a kind of autonomous existence that many of these women did not enjoy. This is not to say that all prostitutes were, or conceived of themselves as, 'victims,' with no agency. Prostitutes were not a monolithic subset of women, inherently different from other women; nor were they recognizable unless they chose to be. Some were victims, some agents, some rebels, some a combination of all, or none of the above" (Landau, *Spectacular Wickedness*, 10).

18. Ibid., 20.

19. Ibid., 5.

20. Ibid., 1.

21. Moncell Durden, private message conversation with author, December 5, 2019.

22. Carine Plancke, "On Dancing and Fishing: Joy and the Celebration of Fertility among the Puno of Congo-Brazzaville," *Africa: Journal of the International African Institute* 80, no. 4 (2010): 620–41.

23. Ibid., 626.

24. Jacqui Malone, *Steppin' on the Blues: The Visible Rhythms of African American Dance* (Urbana: University of Illinois Press, 1996), 9. The use of the plural "dances" is meant to acknowledge the many cultural differences in musical and movement styles throughout the continent of Africa.

25. Gottschild, *The Black Dancing Body,* 148.

26. In SDS, one directs the three principal weights of the body, the head, torso, and pelvis, downward into the earth through the arches of the feet; to allow the body to release into a downward-pulsing motion, working efficiently by releasing excess muscle tension; and directing one's emotional attention and intention to others in the group.

27. Performed by Rufus and Chaka Khan.

28. Oliver and Risner, "An Introduction to Dance and Gender," 1–19; Schupp, "Sassy Girls and Hard-Hitting Boys," 76–96.

29. "Cool" in reference to the Africanist "aesthetic of the cool," a term coined by Robert Farris Thompson, see note 6.

30. Pat Cohen, "Jazz Dance as a Continuum," in *Jazz Dance: A History of the Roots and Branches,* ed. Lindsay Guarino and Wendy Oliver (Gainesville: University Press of Florida, 2014), 3–7.

31. Charles Isherwood, "Take off Your Emotional Clothes and Sing," *New York Times,* December 11, 2005, www.nytimes.com/2005/12/11/theater/newsandfeatures/take-off-your-emotional-clothes-and-sing.html.

14

Considering Jazz Choreography

MELANIE GEORGE

Jazz choreography has a unique set of values and elements that have not been examined thoroughly. While there has been consideration of the pedagogical aspects of technical training, this has not translated into the production of a new generation of jazz choreographers. What are the conditions that contribute to the limited visibility of jazz choreography in the twenty-first century? Why are there fewer jazz choreographers than in years past? What are the shared characteristics of jazz choreography among the many jazz dance styles? By examining these questions, we gain insight into the key component of what makes jazz wholly unique and separate from ballet and modern dance, forms it is too often measured against.

This examination of jazz choreography is distinct from studying the work of individual jazz choreographers. There is existing scholarship on the aesthetics of Cholly Atkins, Bob Fosse, Katherine Dunham, and their peers in the field across generations. While that is necessary content for our understanding of jazz dance history, examining the individual work of specific choreographers speaks to the idiosyncrasies of their compositions, not the overarching characteristics of what comprises jazz choreography. Where Dunham zigs, Atkins may zag, making for a rich, but not necessarily cohesive palette. The framing of these artists in discussions about choreography often aids in keeping jazz adjunct to discourse about creative process and vision. In the cases of Dunham and Fosse, they are often the lone jazz choreographers considered on par with their ballet and modern peers. Their works are identified as outliers to the conventions of well-crafted choreography, successful in spite of themes, movement vocabularies, arrangements, and casts not conforming to conventions widely accepted within ballet and modern dance. The iconoclasm of their work is both a bug and feature to contextualizing their success, rather than an indictment of the stranglehold that modern and ballet choreography

FIGURE 14.1. Katherine Dunham pointing during dance rehearsal in Hamburg, Germany. Photograph by Nicolaus Gorrissen, 1954. Missouri Historical Society, St. Louis.

have on favorability in dance criticism. Additionally, the characteristics of jazz composition are separate from assessments of what is deemed "good" or "bad" choreography. Discussions on the perceived success of individual jazz works is highly subjective, and both "good" and "bad" dances can share elements that define the compositional form.

This essay is concerned with conditions for producing jazz choreography— its support, volume, and literacy. If jazz is our uniquely American art form, the study of its compositional values is long overdue, and necessary to its survival in the twenty-first century.

CHOREOGRAPHIC OBSTACLES

Embedded in twentieth-century dance composition models are distinctions between high and low art, equating process oriented-abstract modern works with high art (read as Eurocentric or Euro-American) and concrete product-based work with low art (read as non-Eurocentric or nonwhite). Vernacular dance choreography and works of entertainment are commonly associated with the latter. Art historian Jody Sperling writes of this divide:

> The development of the conceptual differentiation between high and low art remains embedded in the fractious intellectual debates over immigration, ethnicity, class and race in mid- to late nineteenth century America, when an insecure economic and political elite sought to preserve and defend the status quo, particularly the privileged position of those self-same elites. Since then, the wholesale defense of high art and culture has been conjoined to the wholesale denigration of popular art and culture; elites describe high art in terms of "significant form"; "artistic autonomy"; "absolute form"; and "antitheatricality."[1]

Sperling's identification of high art being associated with antitheatrical presentation firmly excludes much of jazz, past and present. Though the development of composition instruction has evolved, notably after the postmodern movement of the 1960s and 1970s, the implications of race and class are embedded in the conversations and criticism of contemporary choreography of all dance forms. In the book *Dance Composition and Production*, published in 1993, Elizabeth R. Hayes asserts that the role of improvisation in jazz music means "jazz choreographers cannot study a score as ballet choreographers do . . . the jazz dance depends a great deal upon his own kinesthetically felt response to the music, which is seldom intellectually determined."[2] Jazz choreography, as developed by Black Americans, has suffered from a stigma that it is guided by instinct in lieu of craft, and "primitive" rather than skilled. Primitive is one of many coded words used to imply that Africanist art is "childlike" and "lowest on the evolutionary ladder."[3] Brenda Dixon Gottschild dissects the racist implications of this perspective, noting: "A criticism of African and African American Dance has been that it is not 'real choreography' (which seems to mean choreography based on European concert dance principles) but simply steps strung together. It is interesting to note what happens, however, when the 'steps-strung-together' approach is given a Europeanist pedigree. Then it is quite likely to garner critical praise as a plotless avant-garde experiment in 'pure movement.'"4

One of the more challenging issues is the identification of jazz choreography through so-called masterworks. These pieces are usually associated with concert dance presentations, a venue where jazz, tap, and related dances of the African diaspora have been largely absent proportionally to modern dance and ballet. Though iconic jazz choreography does appear on the concert stage, it is just as likely to appear in film, nightclubs, and social environments. It has been noted many times that some of the best work of theatrical jazz dance greats Buddy Bradley and Jack Cole is lost to history because it was performed in nightclubs long before video cameras and smart phones could capture every performance.5 Great works of concert jazz obviously exist. Katherine Dunham's *Barrelhouse Blues*, Talley Beatty's *The Stack-Up*, and Hubbard Street Dance Chicago's *The 40s* are three examples. Longevity is another indicator of a masterwork; the aforementioned works have been performed over decades and restaged on other companies, further propelling their lifespan in the public consciousness. However, consider Whitey's Lindy Hoppers' performance in the film *Hellzapoppin'*. This performance showed clear indication of choreographic and technical mastery but, to my knowledge, has never been restaged on new performers in recent history. This piece is cited as excellent, arguably, more than any other performance of its era. When masterworks are looked at through this lens, the concern becomes less about the works included and more pointed about what has been left out.

When considering the criteria of what constitutes jazz choreography, we must examine the range of media and venues in which jazz appears, and identify conditions that produce jazz masterworks, specifically those derived from African diasporic traditions, as these pieces are more likely to have been overlooked in the pantheon of important choreography. Too often, the assessment of jazz dance choreography is based on criteria not germane to the dance form, affecting its accessibility and popularity in all areas outside of the communities from which it developed. The association of jazz dance with the venues in which it is presented contributes greatly to the designation of high or low art. Though it is not often discussed in these terms, masterful choreography is occurring in informal, social settings regularly. Vacillating from improvisational scores to set choreography, or the mix of the two known colloquially as improvography, masterpieces are being made in the moment, in most cases, never to be captured or replicated again. The limitations of what is and is not considered jazz choreography has never been appropriate for jazz dance-makers. If these are the conditions in which some of the most adventurous work is being developed, then the boundaries of the definition need to be stretched.

Where Are the Emerging Jazz Choreographers?

When considering the dearth of jazz choreography in preprofessional settings, one might argue none of what is authentic about jazz developed in these environments, so why should we expect the academy to produce jazz choreographers? But jazz is being studied to varying degrees in conservatories, higher education programs, and professional intensives. In my own undergraduate training, two courses were devoted to teaching students the values and tools of modern dance choreography (though it was never expressed in those terms), and half of a third course involved musical theater choreography. Sadly, this mirrors my students' experience in the college programs I taught in during my time as a college professor, ten to twenty years later. Even when preprofessional dance students receive ongoing training in jazz technique over four-year periods, and have opportunities to perform jazz repertory, they are left to their own devices to determine what jazz choreography is and how to make it. Moreover, novice jazz choreography is often scrutinized as lacking sophistication or growth on behalf of the student; it is easily dismissed as a product of precollege training. Herein lies the Catch-22 for students interested in jazz choreography. The work may be perceived as representing stagnation in the development of the choreographic aesthetic, but there is no mechanism for deepening the study of jazz choreography. Thus, there is no room for the jazz aesthetic to develop. When layered with the knowledge that grades may be awarded for this work, jazz choreography becomes less and less appealing.

The institutions I was affiliated with are not unique. They reflect the traditions of choreography studies in postsecondary education: traditions that promote the principles of modern dance choreography as neutral and applicable to all forms. The lack of study devoted to the craft of jazz choreography is grounded in the manner in which jazz is taught in the academy, for it is in the academy that formal choreography classes largely take place and promulgate what is deemed valuable. To be sure, not all choreographers come out of the academy, but it is in the academy where most formalized choreography training lives. Simply stated, there are fewer jazz choreographers because the training not only discourages jazz choreography, it impedes it. The history of choreography study in higher education bears this out.

Degree-granting dance programs in academia developed through the introduction of modern dance artists to the curriculum. Modern dance found a home in colleges and universities early in its lifespan through the work of Margaret H'Doubler at the University of Wisconsin in the 1920s, Charles Williams at Hampton Institute in the 1930s, Merce Cunningham's work at Black Mountain College in the 1950s, and Martha Hill's tenures at New York University, Bennington College, Connecticut College, The American Dance Festival and The Juilliard School throughout the twentieth century. These artist-educators, along with the founding of organizations such as the Council of Dance Administrators and the American College Dance Festival (now American College Dance Association) in the 1970s, formed the bedrock of dance curricula in postsecondary education, a decidedly modern dance-centered curricula. As dance programs emerged from physical education departments to align with other performing arts programs, the continued emphasis on modern dance as the form most aligned with advanced studies and critical thinking persisted. Reflective of the demographics and racial politics at predominantly white institutions, most programs were led by white women. Educator-historian Thomas K. Hagood notes, "This was a decidedly Euro-centric argument about modernist ideas played out in a homogeneous educational milieu. For decades dance in the American university was a white woman's world."[6] The 1960s brought a shift toward postmodernist aesthetics as reflective of the artists of Judson Church collective. The 1970s had a boom in the growing number of university dance programs. The 1980s saw a move toward multicultural dance education.[7] Throughout all of this, modern dance, in its many guises, maintained dominance in the aesthetic training of preprofessional dance-makers.

A literature review of widely circulated dance composition books presents a number of examples pointing to a lack of regard for jazz as composition worthy in the academy. Chiefly, the near complete lack of discussion of jazz in most of the books, and when mentioned it is often pejorative. Of note is Daniel Nagrin's 2001 book *Choreography and the Specific Image*, which includes a chapter titled "Modern Dance Choreography—Ballet Choreography."[8] The title and contents of this chapter establish a binary for the serious consideration of choreographic principles in Western concert dance to the exclusion of all other forms. It is all the more curious because Nagrin was a jazz choreographer. In addition to his long career as a modern dancer, he presented lecture-demonstrations on the history of the Cakewalk, Charleston, Lindy Hop, and blues dances throughout his career.[9] Nagrin's approach to choreography, which centers on intent and motivation, does not discuss jazz at all with the exception of brief mentions of character motivation and audience response to his solo *Jazz: Three Ways*. This solo, set to the music of Jimmy

Yancey, Count Basie, and Nat "King" Cole, is categorized as a jazz work by Nagrin, who included it in self-produced video compilation of his jazz work titled *Jazz Changes*.[10] Why is jazz worthy enough for use as source material in creative work and helpful in the marketing on creative product, but dispensable when the time comes for serious academic discussions about the choreographic process?

These texts and their corresponding college courses focus almost exclusively on developing the individual compositional voice, regardless of solo or group performers. This is reflective of a primary value in modern dance in the twentieth century, and, indeed, Euro-American identity: the championing of the individual voice and personal statement. Techniques are named for their founders. Masterpieces are conceived by lone architects. But what of the sociocultural group dynamic found in Black American dance forms from which jazz choreography frequently results? Nonhierarchical, cooperative dance-making is celebrated as progressive in postmodern and contemporary dance circles. Can the same not be said of the interactive play in vernacular-based jazz dance?

Perhaps the most problematic constraint for burgeoning jazz choreographers is the absence of music in these classes. The various authors of the choreography texts actively advocate for compositional studies made in silence, and, in my experience, most college choreography classes use this method. As many second generation, postmodern dance-makers explored staging dances in non-conventional spaces, so too went many other conventions in relation to sound, lighting, props, and costumes. To be sure, postmodernism benefited greatly from these explorations, but where does this leave jazz if the tenets upon which the experimentations are based do not apply? Additionally, there is sometimes active disdain for the use of the popular music that is customary in jazz works. A passage in Lynne Anne Blom and L. Tarin Chaplin's *The Intimate Act of Choreography* reads: "in using vocal music people often end up either miming the words or having no relationship to them whatsoever . . . Broadway musical hits or movie theme songs can be difficult . . . So, unless it's a conscious attempt at satire, unusual juxtaposition or period playfulness, these musical compositions can harm rather than help your piece."[11] I am not proud to admit I regurgitated these sentiments in my early teaching career. The sentiment was so pervasive that I was fully indoctrinated. The deemphasis on music in choreography pedagogy is not simply devaluing of the role of music in the creative process. It is a profound misunderstanding of the fundamental and multilayered relationship between movement, rhythm, and music in jazz. How are jazz choreographers to discover and develop sophisticated relationship to the music, if it is relegated to the margins of the course? Or worse, not considered at all.

In his book *Dancers Talking Dance*, Larry Lavender cautions against implicitly biased choreography training models as universal to all of dance, noting that "they state as facts the assumptions governing their particular theories. These assumptions in turn imply or lead explicitly to a predetermined way of judging dances."[12] This leaves jazz dance-makers with little room for development when the compositional values are not reflected in the postmodern leanings of the objectives and assessments in these courses. Of course, there are no jazz choreographers coming from higher education; we have not created the conditions for them to develop.

While jazz choreographers might find exploration of the postmodern tools of development useful, absent the jazz elements, they will likely not produce jazz choreography. Given that colleges and universities are the primary venue for formal choreographic instruction, the hidden curriculum within these dance programs is training students to be modern dance choreographers. These methods, which are further reinforced in the dance field at large through funding and presenting rosters, fail to teach students how to create jazz choreography, thus, failing to produce new jazz choreographers in the field. As a result, the assessment of jazz dance choreography is based on criteria not germane to the dance form, effecting the volume, stature, and visibility of jazz dance.

RHYTHM AND MUSICALITY ARE THE FOUNDATION OF JAZZ CHOREOGRAPHY

Though there is a lack of scholarship on jazz choreography, it is not completely nonexistent. Scholars reference it toward presenting a greater understanding of jazz aesthetics, Black dance history, the evolution of vernacular dance, and theatrical dance history. As in Larry Billman's encyclopedia on theatrical dance, *Film Choreographers and Dance Directors,*[13] the specificities of choreographic characteristics are used to chronicle change in the dance form over time, and place important figures in their proper era. The pervasive view is our knowledge of jazz as a choreographic form comes by way of its movement vocabulary, social characteristics, and performance qualities. However, this line of thinking presents problems when considering the many established styles of jazz along the continuum from authentic to contemporary jazz, where uses of the body can vary dramatically. Choreography is the arrangement of bodies and movement in space and time and the devising of relationships to

FIGURE 14.2. Caleb Teicher & Company in rehearsal, May 15, 2019. Photo by Rachel Papo for *Dance Magazine*.

performers, audience and environment. So, the question becomes: What do the many styles of jazz have in common choreographically when movement aesthetics diverge?

In jazz dance, content, form, and function are interrelated. While it is difficult to align all the choreographic principles of the many styles within the family tree, there are salient elements that appear from style to style that are subservient in other dance forms. In an unpublished paper from the mid-twentieth century titled "Thoughts about the Special Character of Jazz Choreography," Mura Dehn asserts: "Choreography of jazz is essentially different. It is clear in the attitude of dancers towards stage presentation. The main respected steps are the rhythm steps."[14] Here, Dehn highlights one of the key characteristics that sets jazz choreography apart from other forms, the organization of rhythm as foundational to the composition. Where ballet prioritizes space as a design principle, in jazz choreography spatial arrangement resulting from the attention to rhythm is a feature, reflecting its West African roots. It is from rhythm that steps are generated, either propelling jazz dancers through space or keeping them stationary. Peggy Harper emphasizes this point in her discussion of dances from Nigeria noting, "In European dance the emphasis is on the performer moving from one distinct spatial position to the next, whereas dancers in Africa often move through a subtle complex of spatial gradings with the emphasis on the rhythmo-dynamic aspects of the movement."[15]

The connection of rhythmic choreographic choices to musical accompaniment cannot be understated here. While all dance forms have relationships to musical accompaniment, a universal attribute in jazz choreography, irrespective of style, is the use of music as a guide to the composition in macro (theme, structure, style) and micro (accent, duration, quality) ways. Jacqui Malone expands on this point in her discussion of dances from African cultures, "The rhythm of melodic and non-melodic instruments and song rhythms defined for dance movement determine which movement sequences are chosen and how they are grouped."[16] Musicality in jazz movement is felt, and it is arranged rhythmically.

In this context, rhythm in jazz is distinct from the larger category of "Time" as framed in many dance composition texts. In discussions of time, theorists offer rhythm as an option, not a rule. When rhythm, and by extension musicality, are tenets of the compositional form, there must be a reconsideration of the other elements. Conventional books on choreography assert time as equal to space and energy, and consider each of these elements discrete from the others. In jazz, this is neither true nor helpful, and contributes to a watering down of jazz choreography by lessening the distinction between jazz and modern dance. This emphasis on musicality as critical to the creative process is referenced by notable choreographers of earlier and contemporary eras repeatedly.

> "In order for me to choreograph a jazz dance, it is necessary that I listen to a passage of music any number of times before I can structure a step."—Pepsi Bethel[17]
>
> "Ultimately a marriage must occur between the music and movement. You can't have the music on one planet and the movement on another."—Frank Hatchett[18]
>
> "[I listen] carefully to the accenting of improvised solos . . . I had to get a picture in my mind of how the dance should look, and those accents always gave me new ideas."—Buddy Bradley[19]
>
> "The choreography should have its own rhythmic trajectory that interlaces with the music . . . The movements of jazz dance convey the nuances of rhythm including the color and tone that musicians produce."—S. Ama Wray[20]

It is from the relationship to rhythm and music that additional choreographic characteristics spring forth. These include:

- repetition as tool for emphasis, building momentum, and structural form (as in the classic shim sham or blues structure);
- improvisation or improvography (a blend of improvisation and choreography);[21]
- retention, interpretation and manipulation of shared (often vernacular) vocabulary by the performers;
- the performance of social relationships manifested within the choreography; and
- acknowledgment of the audience through front-facing staging and/or direct engagement.

There are additional choreographic elements specific to individual jazz styles that are not found in others (e.g., the use of partnering in Lindy Hop or Latin jazz). Additionally, there are characteristics found in some jazz styles with origins from other dance forms (e.g., mass group symmetrical spatial formations in contemporary jazz or repetitive ballet-based turn sequences in commercial jazz). The breadth of jazz styles contributes greatly to the brevity of this list because the list of styles is so vast and can diverge significantly from style to style. The above characteristics can be present in choreography without the rhythm-music dynamic, but in aggregate they will not add up to jazz. Moreover, because rhythm and music are foundational to movement invention and arrangement, their absence is usually replaced with composition principles from another dance form. When emphasis on space is added in place of rhythm, we are more in the land of contemporary dance without jazz as qualifier. Consider rhythm and musicality to be the roux of the gumbo that is jazz dance, it both thickens and flavors the composition.

A WAY FORWARD

Jazz choreography is not in peril, but it is underrepresented, undervalued, and underserved. By outlining a framework for investigating jazz choreography, we identify conditions under which the form can thrive, absent the rubric of ballet and modern dance criteria. Dance programs must realign curricula so the choreography syllabi reflect the techniques being offered in the program. Possible options include offering units within composition courses or full courses on choreographic tools of African diasporic dance forms, as part of a larger decolonization approach to dance pedagogy. The elements of jazz choreography are worthy of being studied because they are valued and employed artistically by the culture from which they originate.

It is incumbent on curators, presenting organizations, and critics to educate themselves on the values of jazz choreography and its related forms as their programming and assessment are a critical part of the ecosystem that contributes to the health and visibility of choreographic works of these genres. In the words of Brenda Dixon Gottschild, "One of the easiest ways to disempower others is to measure them by a standard that ignores their aesthetic frame of reference and its particular criteria."[22] Our educational institutions, scholarship, criticism, and performances are not discrete from each other. They are in an active dialogue from which, too often, jazz works are excluded. Our path forward must be inclusive of the many jazz choreographers ignored by our dominant historical narratives, address the generational abyss in the development of new jazz choreography voices in the academy, and seek out and actively support innovative voices operating outside of it.

NOTES

1. Joy Sperling, "Artists Taking the High Road and Low," in *Popular Culture Values and the Arts: Essays on Elitism Versus Democratization*, ed. Ray B. Browne and Lawrence A. Kreiser Jr. (Jefferson, NC: McFarland, 2009), 416.

2. Elizabeth R. Hayes, *Dance Composition & Production* (Pennington, NJ: Princeton Book Company, 1993), 222.

3. Brenda Dixon Gottschild, *Digging the Africanist Presence in American Performance: Dance and Other Contexts* (Westport, CT: Praeger, 1998), 35.

4. Gottschild, *Digging the Africanist Presence,* 53.

5. Marshall Stearns and Jean Stearns, *Jazz Dance: The Story of American Vernacular Dance* (New York: Da Capo, 1994), 161; Glenn Loney, *Unsung Genius: The Passion of Dancer-Choreographer Jack Cole* (New York: Watts, 1984), 69–100.

6. Thomas K. Hagood, *Legacy in Dance Education: Essays and Interviews on Values, Practices and People: An Anthology* (New York: Cambria, 2008), 512, Kindle.

7. Kim Chandler Vaccaro, "Jazz Dance in Higher Education," in *Jazz Dance: A History of the Roots and Branches*, ed. Lindsay Guarino and Wendy Oliver (Gainesville: University Press of Florida, 2014), 210–11.

8. Daniel Nagrin, *Choreography and the Specific Image: Nineteen Essays and a Workbook* (Pittsburgh: University of Pittsburgh, 2001), 90–98.

9. Don McDonagh, "Nagrin Jazz Dances a Relaxed Program," *New York Times*, January 5, 1975.

10. Daniel Nagrin, *Jazz Changes: A Jazz Retrospective* (The Daniel Nagrin Theatre, Film & Dance Foundation, Inc., 1974), VHS.

11. Lynne Anne Blom and L. Tarin. Chaplin, *The Intimate Act of Choreography* (Pittsburgh: University of Pittsburgh Press, 1994), 166.

12. Larry Lavender, *Dancers Talking Dance: Critical Evaluation in the Choreography Class* (Champaign, IL: Human Kinetics, 1996), 35.

13. Larry Billman, *Film Choreographers and Dance Directors: An Illustrated Biographical Encyclopedia, with a History and Filmographies, 1893 through 1995* (Jefferson, NC: McFarland, 1997).

14. Mura Dehn, "Thoughts about the Special Character of Jazz Choreography," manuscript, New York Public Library, n.d.

15. Peggy Harper, "Dance in Nigeria," *Ethnomusicology* 13, no. 2 (May 1969): 293.

16. Jacqui Malone, *Steppin' on the Blues: The Visible Rhythms of African American Dance* (Urbana: University of Illinois Press, 2006), 13.

17. Pepsi Bethel, *Authentic Jazz Dance: A Retrospective* (New York: American Authentic Jazz Dance Theatre, 1990), 41.

18. Nancy Myers Gitlin and Frank Hatchett, *Frank Hatchett's Jazz Dance* (Champaign, IL: Human Kinetics, 2000), 11

19. Stearns and Stearns, *Jazz Dance*, 166.

20. Sheron Wray, "A Twenty-First-Century Jazz Dance Manifesto," in *Jazz Dance: A History of the Roots and Branches*, ed. Lindsay Guarino and Wendy Oliver (Gainesville: University Press of Florida, 2014), 12–16.

21. Lucia Mauro, "Improvised or Planned Tap, It's about Groove to Glover," *Chicago Tribune*, April 22, 2005.

22. Gottschild, *Digging the Africanist Presence*, 140.

Hayley Robichaud and Marissa Masson improvising in jazz warm-up exercise, Salve Regina University. Photo by Kim Fuller Photography.

IV

Teaching Jazz Dance

We are at a pivotal moment in dance education. The Black Lives Matter movement has sparked widespread conversation and revelation, challenging dance educators to reconsider the systems and ideals that have historically marginalized Black American people and culture. This lens brings into focus all the reasons why jazz has never earned its rightful place in the academy. Equity for jazz dance and its related forms demands a cultural shift in the field of dance education, positioning the form as an African American cultural treasure with roots, values, and aesthetics separate from its ballet and modern counterpoints.

At this critical juncture, jazz dance educators today are called to investigate rooted jazz movement, music, and pedagogical practices while questioning previously accepted norms in jazz dance training. In jazz, a form that celebrates individuality, educators must be acutely aware of their own identities. A historically and culturally rooted jazz class requires self-reflection, efforts at decolonization, and respect for Black American people and culture.

The authors in part IV of this book lay out the methods they have developed to preserve and protect jazz and carry it into the future through responsible pedagogy. Each author presents the tools, exercises, and considerations they have found to be transformative. While each author has a unique approach, they are united through a shared philosophy that connects jazz to its African diasporic roots and to Black American history and culture. Furthermore, these authors exemplify how jazz itself acts as a teacher, revealing itself through movement and music while evoking empathy and heightened awareness through its community-oriented properties. By turning to jazz for the wisdom to generate highly individualized rooted jazz practices, they have found ways for it to flourish in its own right.

.... *15*

Valuing Cultural Context and Style

Strategies for Teaching Traditional Jazz Dance from the Inside Out

KAREN W. HUBBARD

The course described in this chapter is a model for providing experiential learning in authentic jazz dance, also known as traditional jazz dance.[1] Concurrently, the course addresses what Brenda Dixon Gottschild, Temple University dance faculty emerita who has lectured and written extensively on African American vernacular dance as a folk form, describes as "mainstream Eurocentric historical erasure of African-based influences in our culture.[2]

In the course, students are given opportunities to learn about jazz dance from the perspective of African American culture: the source of origin of the major jazz dance crazes. In addition to practicing the rhythmic expression and bodily actions of traditional jazz dance, students learn the history of the form. The primary outcomes are increased historical awareness of Black culture in the United States and enhanced possibilities for expressiveness in terms of form and rhythm when it comes to performing the variety of forms referred to as jazz today (lyrical jazz, Broadway jazz, funk, and so forth). In addition to providing an overview of course content and methodology, a resource list is available at the end of this chapter.

BACKGROUND

I was introduced to authentic jazz dance by Pepsi Bethel, former Savoy Lindy Hopper and artistic director of the American Authentic Jazz Dance Theatre in New York. Pepsi was one of the instructors with whom I studied as a scholarship student at Clark Center in New York City. I also performed with his fledgling company during the early part of 1970. However, it was not until 1985, as a graduate student at Ohio State University that I realized the historical

FIGURE 15.1. Karen Hubbard teaching authentic jazz dance at Salve Regina University for NDEO's "Jazz Dance: Hybrids, Fusions, Connections, Community" conference, August 2019. Photo by Kim Fuller Photography.

significance of the material I had learned from Pepsi Bethel. My graduate project entitled "Ethnic Dance: The Origins of Jazz" integrated research involving the history of jazz dance with stylistic concepts and vocabulary learned from Pepsi Bethel. The project is outlined in an article by the same title published by the *Journal of Health Physical Education Recreation and Dance*.[3]

The studio course described in this essay is an expanded version of the curriculum I began to develop in the mid-1980s. As when the course was initially conceived, the material focuses on authentic jazz dance as a form evolved primarily from Africans held captive in the United States. These vernacular dances, which originated on the plantation and would later become known as jazz dance, were practiced among Blacks in social settings like house parties, dives, honky-tonks, and jook joints during the first half of the twentieth century. Simultaneously, the dances were theatricalized and performed in staged floor shows in nightclubs like the Cotton Club in New York City as well as in staged musicals, beginning in 1921 with *Shuffle Along* (Sissle/Blake) and *Runnin' Wild* (Sissle/Blake).

COURSE DESCRIPTION

The two-credit-hour course entitled "Traditional Jazz Dance" meets twice weekly for seventy-five minutes over the span of one semester. Enrollment is capped at twenty students. As the only jazz class required for dance majors and minors that is also open to elective students without special permission, the course serves a diverse student population in terms of previous dance training and experience. However, since the movement material focuses on style and rhythm instead of technique, all students have the possibility of completing the course successfully.

Historical, traditional jazz dance vocabulary from the first half of the twentieth century is taught through demonstration and description. Practice and repetition are the primary means of learning this material. Related readings on reserve in the campus library and observation of films, videos, and performances are followed by electronic and classroom discussions.

On the first day of class, students are asked to keep an open mind. Next they are informed they will learn a style of dance that will no doubt be new to them, their "great-grandparents' jazz dance." In order to develop an awareness of subtle syncopated weight-shifts, students are asked to take class barefoot. However, they are encouraged to wear attire reminiscent of Jazz Age fashions including hats, feather boas, pleated trousers, skirts, shorts, and dresses.

COURSE OBJECTIVES

The stated objectives for the course are: (1) to allow students to experience jazz as an indigenous U.S. dance form, preparing them to become part of an educated audience that enjoys, supports, and possibly participates in dance or a related field; and (2) to explore the history and stylizations characteristic of authentic jazz dance.

AUTHENTIC JAZZ DANCE

According to Pepsi Bethel, in authentic jazz dance "each individual imbues the dance with a quality of uniqueness, . . . no two authentic jazz dancers do the same step the same way, . . . one's virtuosity is revealed through one's feet and knees, . . . [and] the entire body is fully engaged into the movement at each and every moment."[4] Therefore, lessons are planned with emphasis placed on "style" rather than "technique." For the duration of the course, ballet vocabulary is neither practiced nor spoken, and students are encouraged to become engaged stylistically regardless of their perceived or actual level of technical competence in ballet or modern dance.

THE WEST AFRICAN CONNECTION

As is consistent with traditional jazz dance, the stylistic characteristics of material closely reflect the movement elements of West African dance. Specifically, the center of gravity is lowered; therefore, most actions taught in the course are executed with bent support leg(s). The torso is inclined forward, the spine remains mobile, and the limbs are articulated as the entire body is engaged, resulting in movement that is initiated almost entirely through syncopated foot actions. As is evidenced in West African dance, in traditional jazz dance, the limbs, torso, and head work in contrasting rhythms, described by Kariamu Welsh Asante as "polyrhythm in motion,"[5] and there is often vocalization with the movement.

The quality "swing" is another essential element of West African music and dance. Marshall Stearns and Jean Stearns believed, as with jazz music, that the identifying characteristic of American vernacular dance, also called jazz dance, is "*swing* which can be heard, felt, and seen, but defined only with great difficulty."[6] I concur with the Stearnses, and I am also in agreement with Margaret Batiuchok, who writes, "swing is not a body upswing as in the arc of a circle."[7] Rather, weight is dropped into the ground and retrieved with a rhythmic response described by Ray Walker in *Let's Talk Jitterbug* as a "peculiar lilting syncopation."[8] Jazz hoofer Jimmy Slyde called swinging "a state in which the dancer performs with ease and finds a common denominator with the music, the musicians and the audience."[9]

Swing is also a prominent aspect of course design because I believe that in order for all of the bodily actions and rhythmic nuances to come together as jazz dance, the quality *swing* must be a consistent element in the movement. That is, the dancer must swing the movement (on the vertical plane) by engaging the pelvis in a duet with gravity where energy is released into and retrieved from the ground, producing a weighty quality. In the absence of swing, the dancing appears brittle and very unlike jazz. Swing allows the dancer to "get down" and "push the rhythm." When this happens, the dancer is "in the rhythm" or "in the pocket" rather than "on the beat." Jazz musician Fats Waller once described swing as two-thirds rhythm and one-third soul. Remember, when it comes to jazz, "It Don't Mean a Thing (If It Ain't Got That Swing)."[10]

Although improvisation is a distinguishing aspect of West African dance, it is a misperception that rituals in traditional culture are improvised.[11] In West African culture, improvisation occurs when the participant asserts individual style by embellishing rather than inventing movement within the context of traditional rituals. The material in the course I developed connects with the improvisational aspect of the West African aesthetic in that historic vocabulary and traditional jazz style provide a context for expressing individual flair.

The West African quality referred to by art historian Robert Farris Thompson as "aesthetic of the cool" best describes how the dancer must approach movement with a "jazz state of mind."[12] Brenda Dixon Gottschild refers to "high-affect juxtaposition" to cover what I believe both scholars portray as a way of moving that is simultaneously energized and laid back.[13] For example, when executing a syncopated sequence in quick time, the dancer must project a cool appearance. If the jazz attitude is missing, the "jazz" in the dance is lost.

Especially relevant to the "jazz state of mind" are comments by deceased foremost archivist of African American dance and noted Black dance historian Joe Nash, who believed that "you can't teach jazz because jazz is an attitude and you can't teach attitude. To dance jazz you have to think of yourself as being bluesy or jazzy." According to Nash, the point of reference for being "jazzy" is the brothel, where "women used their individual walks to attract customers." He goes on to describe how the women "moved with a sense of freedom, or contempt for everything, of relaxation."[14]

In addition to citing the jazz attitude, Nash implies that in order to fully connect with and effectively express the nuances of the jazz aesthetic, one must experience the culture from the inside out. While this may or may not be the case, there is a huge difference between learning jazz in the studio and actually experiencing the style as it is expressed in Black culture. For example, teachers who are unfamiliar with the aesthetics of Black culture often spread the misperceptions that Africans dance entirely to "celebrate" or to "have a good time" and that African slaves in America danced only to "relieve the monotony and burden of work and/or for the purpose of entertainment."[15] The implication is that the energy observed in the dancing of Black people happens because they are excited solely about dancing rather than the significance of the dancing to culture. These references are intended to encourage students to bring more "energy" and "excitement" to their dancing. Unfortunately, this approach reinforces stereotypes about Black people and bypasses the jazz attitude completely.

In order to discover the jazz attitude so that traditional jazz dancing can happen in an authentic manner, students are introduced to the concept of West African dance as an integral, functional, and participatory aspect of traditional culture. They learn, for example, how dancing actions in religious rituals are intended to connect the worshipper with deified ancestors. Dance may also be used to value work. When this happens, the movements in the dance mimic actions like washing garments, gathering berries, chopping wood, hunting, and preparing meals. Dance is also present during rites of passage like coming-of-age ceremonies and matrimony. Whenever or wherever dance appears in West African culture, it validates cultural heritage and affirms one's allegiance to the group.

An awareness of the ways in which dance serves specific purposes within the cultural context, along with an understanding of the meaning of cultural validation as it relates to dance, at the very least gives students a clue that tapping into the energy, attitude, and spontaneity of traditional jazz dance involves more than wearing a pasted-on smile and being propelled by the music while performing manic maneuvers and manipulations.

ACCOMPANIMENT

In keeping with the West African tradition in which the dancers and musicians experience an exchange of energy, I prefer live rather than recorded music for the course I teach in traditional jazz dance. In the past, I worked with a young man who was familiar with jazz music history and aesthetics who had the following skills: West African traditional drumming and dance, improvised vocal melodic and rhythmic scatting, and improvised body percussion. Many of the strategies developed for my course are the result of our teacher-musician collaborations. I also worked with a musician who was an accomplished jazz pianist and vocalist. My current musician is a percussionist who works in a variety of styles including swing rhythms. When a musician is unavailable, I use recorded selections by jazz greats like King Oliver, Louis Armstrong, Jelly Roll Morton, J. P. Johnson, Fats Waller, Cab Calloway, and Count Basie.

INTERACTIVE WARM-UP

Class begins with an interactive warm-up, the structure of which is solidified over several lessons. In addition to preparing the body to move safely through the rest of the class, the interactive warm-up provides opportunities for students to practice the characteristics of traditional jazz dance. They also express individual style through the manipulation of a series of stylized walks, freezes, call-response scatting-patting, a stylized sequence of limb and upper-spine isolations, and historical jazz dance vocabulary. Interaction takes place as the students acknowledge and respond to one another through movement and vocals as they improvise structured material. The interactive warm-up sets the participatory tone for the entire lesson. Therefore, students who arrive late must observe the entire class. In order to receive half credit for the period, latecomers are asked to comment in writing on what they "discovered" while observing class.

Stylized Walks and Freezes, Vocal Scats, and Body Rhythms

The interactive warm-up is initiated when one student begins to execute walks around the room in the style of traditional jazz dance: the center of gravity is lowered, the torso is inclined forward, the spine and limbs articulate, and the quality swing is engaged. At this point, the only accompaniment is a swing rhythm riff vocalized by that student. As the other students feed into the action, the dancers accumulate, the vocal riffs grow louder, and the percussionist begins to play a swing riff. During the stylized walks, students may experiment with time (sustain, quick, freeze) or they may execute walks that are rhythmically "in the pocket." They also play a call-and-response exchange with vocal scats and rhythmic body percussion led by the musician. At the same time, students must listen for rhythm breaks played by the percussionist because each rhythm break signals a transition to the next section of the interactive warm-up.

Limb and Upper-Spine Isolation Sequence

Following stylized walks, students execute a sequence that allows them to practice the actions called for in traditional jazz dance. I learned this sequence from Pepsi Bethel, and it has been reconstructed to my best recollection. The actions are intended to isolate and articulate the limbs and upper back through a series of shoulder-socket, thigh-socket, and upper-spine initiations. With the exception of a step called "Flippin' It to the Wings," a reference to how performers acknowledged, with a flip of the hand and leg, observers watching the performance from the wings of the stage, all actions are performed on bent support legs with the torso inclined forward. At the point when students have learned the limb and upper-spine isolation series, they are challenged to change facings throughout the sequence. Again, the musician plays a rhythm break, signaling to students that it is time to begin the next portion of the interactive warm-up.

Historical Jazz Dance Vocabulary, Call-and-Response

In the next segment of the interactive warm-up, students take turns "calling" historical vocabulary. Once a step is "called," dancers respond by executing that particular step until a different historical step is called. After several exchanges, a rhythm break calls for the "individualized" portion of the interactive warm-up where students are free to improvise historical vocabulary on their own. When the musician believes the dancers are ready to move to the final section of the interactive warm-up, the students will hear a rhythm break.

Historical Jazz Dance Sequence

The final component of the interactive warm-up consists of a stylized sequence arranged from historical steps learned in previous classes. As in the previous portions of the interactive warm-up, this sequence provides the basis for improvisation. By the sixth or seventh lesson, students no longer perform the sequence in unison. Instead, they begin the historical jazz dance sequence facing any direction except the mirror, and as with other material in the interactive warm-up, they are encouraged to manipulate the historical vocabulary in terms of time and sequence. As they perform the stylized sequence, students must listen for the musician's next rhythmic break, at which time, no matter where they are in the sequence, they perform a set of eight flaps with a four-count finish in unison facing the mirror. From start to finish, the action in the interactive warm-up never stops. In fact, many students who observe class comment on how it is possible to "see" jazz as dancers move around the studio.

PROGRESSIONS

At the end of the interactive warm-up, as the musician plays softly, the dancers use stylized walks to move to the end of the studio in preparation for progressions. For students, progressions provide the practice and repetition necessary to physicalize the actions, rhythms, and shapes associated with traditional jazz dance vocabulary. Progressions give the instructor an opportunity to observe fewer students at one time and to give feedback while dancers are on the move.

Once students have gathered at the end of the studio, I demonstrate a new historical step or call out a familiar step. Students are encouraged to make their best effort to reproduce the step. If necessary, I will break the actions down into what I refer to as bare-bones movement or unembellished transfer of weight. Rhythm is communicated via melodic or rhythmic vocal scats. I always let the students and musician know how many counts apart each line should begin as this varies depending on vocabulary. Each line begins when the musician calls dancers into the progression with a rhythm break. Once students have become comfortable with a particular step in terms of weight transfer and rhythm, they are given opportunities to improvise within the context of the progression. For example, students may practice a step like Pickin' Cherries several times back and forth across the floor. Next, they will be asked to embellish or improvise on Pickin' Cherries as they move across the studio.

STYLIZED SEQUENCES

During the semester students learn several sequences comprised of historical vocabulary initially introduced as progressions. As students become familiar with new vocabulary, the material is arranged in sequences taught in chronological order from the 1920s through the 1940s. For example, during the initial class sessions, in addition to stylized walks students learn Gaze the Fog, Pickin' Cherries, Eatin' Cherries, Treads, Boogie, Shuffles, Scoot, Pattin' Juba, Rock, Flaps, Sim-Sham, Scronch, and vibratory actions. They will have practiced the vocabulary and actions via progressions. At the end of the fourth or fifth class, I begin to arrange the historical vocabulary into a sequence. This arrangement of traditional jazz dance vocabulary, which is my signature sequence, then becomes the basis for improvisation in the last section of the interactive warmup as described previously.

Charleston

As the historical jazz dance sequence in the interactive warm-up solidifies, historical vocabulary representing the 1920s, including steps like the Long-Legged Charleston, Rubber Legs, Itch, Scarecrow, Screwball, Sugar Foot, Raising the Roof, and Black Bottom. There is also a call-and-response section, as well as a thirty-two-count window for improvisation.

The Big Apple

The next sequence is built on the Big Apple. Originating in the 1930s at the Big Apple Club, which was formerly a Jewish synagogue in Columbia, South Carolina, the dance is a constellation of historical jazz steps executed in a circular formation.[16] A caller in the middle of the circle shouted steps and spatial directions as the dancers provided improvisatory response. Some of the steps that appear in the staged Big Apple performed by Charles White's Savoy Lindy Hoppers in the film *Keep Punchin'* (1939, M.C.P. Pictures, Inc.)

are Shorty George, Scronch, Long Leg Charleston, Boogie, Peckin', Truckin', Rockin', Praise Allah, Spankin' the Baby, and Suzie-Q.

In addition to participating in the Big Apple as a spontaneous "call-and-response" experience, students are given the opportunity to create a Big Apple based on vocabulary they select and arrange from material learned up to this point in the semester.

"Ballin' the Jack"

"Ballin' the Jack" is an instructional song I often teach in this course. Instructional songs were popular because the lyrics are a roadmap for learning dances that were popular. This particular song refers to traveling fast on a locomotive and living the high life.[17] Although bits of the melody, lyrics, and movements resided in childhood memories, I officially learned the song and movement along with my students in a master class taught at UNC Charlotte by tap dance master Buster Brown in 1989. "Ballin' the Jack" provides a structure for singing, as well as expressing individual style.

Shim Sham Shimmy

The next sequence students learn is known as the Shim Sham Shimmy, a dance first performed by professional dancers at the New York City Savoy Ballroom in the mid-1930s. Steps in the Shim Sham Shimmy are related to a solo southern style (Flat Footin', Hoe Downin', and Buck and Wing) practiced by Blacks of African descent and Whites of Irish decent in the southeastern part of the United States.[18] The sequence exemplifies how vernacular and folk dance became embellished for stage performance. Subsequently it was fed back into the context of social dance as Savoy Ballroom patrons enjoyed the dance so much they learned it too. Also known as the tap dance national anthem, the Shim Sham Shimmy emphasizes foot rhythms, but it does not require tap shoes. Individual style is an important aspect of this sequence, so students are encouraged to embellish the movement in the sequence during the rhythm breaks and in the main structure of the sequence.

Class Act

Next, students learn a sequence based on the smooth jazz style of Cholly Atkins of Cole and Atkins, the quintessential jazz dance class act. Atkins became known for his vocal choreography performed by Motown groups like the Temptations. His Broadway credits include *Gentlemen Prefer Blondes* (1949) and *Black and Blue* (1989), for which he won the Tony Award.[19]

This particular sequence was introduced during a master class taught at

UNC Charlotte by now-deceased New York professional dancer Luther Fontaine, whose Broadway credits include *My One and Only, Timbuktu, Eubie,* and *Two Gentlemen of Verona.* When Fontaine taught the master class, students had already learned the Shim Sham Shimmy, so he incorporated it into the sequence; students are challenged to remain "cool" and "smooth" as they execute repetitive actions combined with subtle but tricky rhythmic transitions. The improvisational aspect of the sequence is expressed as students make alterations by substituting vocabulary or making embellishments in timing to suit their individual preferences.

Rock-and-Roll

The remaining three or four lessons are devoted to the point in history when rock-and-roll replaced jazz as the teenager's dance music of choice. Students now experience two different sequences set to a backbeat riff. As they learn vernacular vocabulary from the 1950s and 1960s, they "discover" commonalities between traditional jazz dance vocabulary and rock-and-roll dances. For example, students are quick to point out the similarities in the foot actions of Sugar Foot from the 1920s and the Mashed Potatoes popular in the 1960s, and how the Twist reminds them of the shoulder shakes used to embellish foot sliding actions of the Shim Sham. They seem to take great delight in demonstrating how Dusty-Dusty, a vigorous knee-flipping traditional jazz dance action, transitions into the Tootsie Roll with the addition of pelvic action.

Contemporary Jazz-Influenced Dance with a Faux Hip-Hop Twist

Depending on how a class has moved through material presented during the semester, there may be one or two sessions during which students experience contemporary jazz-influenced movement as taught in studios during the last half of the twentieth century. Students with previous training are more adept at learning and performing contemporary jazz dance because they are already familiar with technical requirements of this style: elongated vertical spine, turned-out legs and feet, and use of ballet vocabulary. All students follow along as I share a contemporary isolation series I learned through study with Fred Benjamin, a New York City jazz dance teacher and the director of the Jazz Department at Alvin Ailey American Dance Center. They also learn a short sequence set in the style of modern dance–influenced jazz dance. If there is time, on the last day of class they experience a "faux hip-hop dance" sequence that reflects contemporary popular entertainment culture. In a recent semester, with the help of a "B-girl" enrolled in the course, this sequence was transformed into a more authentic hip-hop dance experience.

HISTORICAL CONSIDERATIONS

In order for students to gain deeper understanding of jazz dance history, they are given handouts from a variety of sources that reference the cultural context of the form (see resource list). Class discussions are centered on assigned reading that varies from semester to semester. Topics related to jazz dance include the slave trade, dance on the plantation/Congo Square, West African dance/Irish dance connection, blackface minstrelsy/application, patterns of transmission, and dance crazes (Cakewalk, Charleston, Lindy Hop, Big Apple, Twist).

Each semester students are provided guidelines for the purpose of completing an oral history assignment in which they interview someone from their parents', grandparents', or great-grandparents' generation. Their goal is to discover what kind of social dance that person engaged in as a teen. They also ask questions about the context in which the dancing took place. Finally, they are asked to comment on how what was revealed in the interview relates to what they have been learning in class in terms of style and historical context.

While vivid descriptions of the context and style of authentic jazz dance are found in books and periodicals, visual resources provide opportunities for students to observe and identify vocabulary practiced in class. Since 1985, I have collected numerous examples of jazz dance on video from a variety of sources. In some cases, clips culled from a particular video can be as short as thirty seconds. A recent find was the film *Pardon My Sarong* (1942) starring Abbott and Costello, which contains a sequence choreographed by Katherine Dunham. I also have on video Mura Dehn's *The Spirit Moves*, a fifty-minute excerpt of her three-hour film by the same title that captures Blacks performing jazz dance from the first half of the twentieth century. I encourage teachers to find the videos most useful to them.

CONCLUSION

The course outlined allows students to experience authentic jazz dance through methodology that acknowledges and respects the cultural context of the form. This approach educates students regarding the history of jazz dance. Also, students are given opportunities to experience aspects of jazz dance that make the style distinctive. By the end of the course, in addition to a written and visual historical frame of reference, students also develop a body catalogue of authentic jazz dance vocabulary that, in my opinion, better enables them to express jazz aspects of contemporary jazz dance.

NOTES

1. This chapter was previously published as "Valuing Cultural Context and Style: Strategies for Teaching Traditional Jazz Dance from the Inside Out," *Journal for Dance Education* 8 no. 4 (2008): 110–16. Reprinted by permission of The National Dance Education Organization, www.ndeo.org.

2. Brenda Dixon Gottschild, "Cultural Identity and Sociopolitical Oppression: The Afrocentric Basis of American Concert Dance!," *Faculty Herald*, Temple University, February 13, 1990, 4.

3. Karen Hubbard, "Ethnic Dance: The Origins of Jazz," *Journal of Health Physical Education, Recreation and Dance,* May/June 1988, 57–61.

4. Pepsi Bethel, *Authentic Jazz Dance: A Retrospective* (New York: The Authentic Jazz Dance Theatre, Inc., 1990), 43–44.

5. Kariamu Welsh Asante, *African Dance: An Historical, Artistic, and Philosophical Inquiry* (Philadelphia: Chelsea House, 2004), 34.

6. Marshall Stearns and Jean Stearns, *Jazz Dance: The Story of American Vernacular Dance* (New York: Macmillan, 1969), xiv.

7. Margaret Batiuchok, "The Lindy" (master's thesis, New York University, 1988), 2.

8. Ray Walker, *Let's Talk Jitterbug,* information and education release from the US Swing Dance Council, Phoenix, Arizona, 1987, 2.

9. Qtd. in Brenda Dixon Gottschild, *Digging the Africanist Presence in American Performance* (Westport, CT: Greenwood, 1996), 55.

10. Duke Ellington, *It Don't Mean a Thing (If It Ain't Got That Swing)* (Columbia Records, February 2, 1932).

11. Kimberly Chandler-Vaccaro and Lorraine Kriegel, *Jazz Dance Today* (St. Paul, MN: West, 1994), 81.

12. Robert F. Thompson, "An Aesthetic of the Cool," in *West African Dance: The Theatre of Black Americans,* ed. E. Hill (Englewood Cliffs, NJ: Prentice-Hall, 1980), 99–111.

13. Dixon Gottschild, *Digging the Africanist Presence,* 14–15.

14. Joe Nash, "The Real Thing," *Dance Magazine,* March 1994, 66.

15. Chandler-Vacarro and Kriegel, *Jazz Dance Today,* 8.

16. Arthur Murray, "The Big Apple," *Literary Digest,* October 2, 1937, 22–23.

17. Stearns and Stearns, *Jazz Dance,* 98–99.

18. Ruth Pershing and Mike Seeger, *Talking Feet: Solo Southern Dance Flatfoot, Buck and Tap* (El Cerrito, CA: Flower Films, 1989).

19. Stearns and Stearns, *Jazz Dance,* 359.

SELECTED TRADITIONAL JAZZ DANCE RESOURCES

Traditional Jazz Dance on Selected Films and Videos

Baby Laurence: Jazz Hoofer. 1995. Facets Multimedia, Inc.
Black and Blue. 1991. PBS, from Broadway Production.
Cabin in the Sky. 1943. 20th Century Fox.
The Call of the Jitter Bug. 1935. NY Filmmakers Video Library.
Cookie Cook's Scrapbook. 1978. Circuit Theatre, Inc.
Dance Black America. PBS, Original Music Inc., 418 Lasher Rd. Tivoli, NY, 12583–5514.
Dancing through West Africa with Chuck Davis. 1986. Filmmakers Library, Inc.
Duke Is the Tops. 1938. Million Dollar Productions.
Gang of New York. 2002. MiraMax Films.
Gregory Hines, Tommy Tune Tap Special. WNET.
Hallelujah. 1929. Metro-Goldwyn-Mayer.
In a Jazz Way: Portrait of Mura Dehn. 1987. Filmmakers Video Library.
No Maps on My Taps. 1978. George Nierenberg, producer.
Miss Ever's Boys. 1997. Anasazi Productions.
Pardon My Sarong. 1942. With Abbott and Costello. Staging by Katherine Dunham.
Social Dance at the Cotton Club and the Savoy. 1985. Eye on Dance.
Soundies #1/#2. Festival Films, 2841 Irving Ave. S., Minneapolis, MN, 55408.
The Spirit Moves. 1987. Mura Dehn documents Black vernacular dance.
Stormy Weather. 1943. 20th Century Fox.
Sunday Sinners. 1940. Goldberg Productions.
Watch Me Move. 1987, PBS. A. Cromwell, W. E. Baker, procedures.
We Sing, We Dance—Nicolas Brothers. 1992. PBS.

Articles and Books

Baker, Josephine. *Josephine.* New York: Harper and Row, 1977.
Bethel, Pepsi. *Authentic Jazz Dance A Retrospective.* New York: Authentic Jazz Dance Theatre, 1990.
"Popular Dance in Black America." Special issue, *Dance Research Journal* 15, no. 2 (Spring 1983).
Dehn, Mura. "Is Jazz Choreographic?" *Dance Magazine*, February 1982.
———. "Jazz: A Folk Dance." *Dance Magazine*, August 1945.
Dixon Gottschild, Brenda. *Waltzing in the Dark.* New York: St. Martin's, 2000.
Emery, Lynne F. *Black Dance in the United States from 1619–Today.* Pennington, NJ: Princeton Book Company, 1988.
Giordano, Gus. *Anthology of American Jazz Dance.* Evanston, IL: Orion, 1975. Contains articles on historical jazz dance.
Haskins, Jim. *Mr. Bojangles: The Biography of Bill Robinson.* New York: William Morrow, 1988.
Hubbard, Karen. "Curriculum Design for Dance-Ethnic Dance: The Origins of Jazz. *Journal of Physical Education Recreation and Dance,* May/June 1988, 57–61.
———. "Jazz Dance: An Historical Overview." *Artspace* 10, no. 2 (1987): 8–9.

Huet, Michel. *The Dance Art and Ritual of Africa.* New York: Pantheon, 1978.

Kisland, Richard. *Hoofing on Broadway.* New York: Prentice-Hall, 1987.

Malone, Jacqui. *Steppin' on the Blues: The Visual Rhythms of African American Dance.* Urbana: University of Illinois Press, 1996.

Rose, Phyllis. *Jazz Cleopatra.* New York: Vintage, 1991.

Southern, Eileen. *The Music of Black Americans.* New York: Norton, 1971.

Stearns, Marshall. "Is Modern Jazz Hopelessly Square?" *Dance Magazine*, May 1959.

Stearns, Marshall, and Jean Stearns. *Jazz Dance: The Story of American Vernacular Dance.* New York: Macmillan, 1969.

Valis-Hill, Constance. *Brotherhood in Rhythm: The Jazz Tap Dancing of the Nicholas Brothers.* New York: Cooper Square, 2002.

Cultivating African Diasporic Ethos and Cultural Values in Contemporary Jazz Dance

MONIQUE MARIE HALEY

> We begin to understand this dance form as being grounded not only in African-derived
> movement vocabulary but also in an African cultural ethos that continues to inform
> dance today, even if its cultural roots go unacknowledged or are otherwise obscured.
> Takiyah Nur Amin, "The African Origins of an American Art Form"

The efflorescence of African diasporic culture and dance in slave communities gave birth to jazz dance and music in North America. These origins give jazz an innate spirit and flow contrary to the American ethic cultivated in much of today's collegiate jazz instruction. This is driven by jazz dance educators who often detach African perspective and ethos from the root of jazz dance pedagogy. In an effort to remedy this detachment, I have reconceptualized what jazz pedagogy could look like, infusing an Africanist aesthetic through a contemporary jazz lens called the Diasporic Encounter Method (DEM) as the foundation for all of my jazz classes.

Implementing the somatic theories of African educators Kwame Gyekye (1998)[1] and Malidoma Patrice Somé (1999),[2] the DEM emphasizes African Cultural Values (ACV): humanity/brotherhood, communal/individualistic value, and the importance of ritual and kinship. ACV are crucial in shaping the course intention because of the African Soul and lived experience of the people. The DEM is not purely an experience-based methodology; it is a technique that produces visible and significant results, through an awareness of African heritage, cultural values, and aesthetics.

This chapter explores how the integration of African cultural perspectives awakens the African ethos through somatic experiencing within a communal environment. According to Marimba Ani (2004), African culture operates through the concept of *Nommo*.[3] The consistent use of improvisational tactics integrated into a contemporary jazz class structure allows transformative states in the learning process. The ability of *Muntu*[4] conjures the African somatic approach, focusing on an individual's connection to the universe to effect an outcome. In incorporating these tactics, DEM is an intentional mode of practicing jazz technique through a holistic, somatic Africanist perspective.

METHODOLOGIES. AUTHENTIC DEFINITIVE ETHOS: A CONCEPTUAL FRAMEWORK

Using African Cultural Values as the conceptual framework for my contemporary jazz class structure, written discussion posts reflect the student's movement experiences after exploring the *Diasporic Encounter Method* processes. Delivering tasks and practices such as biweekly focus topics derived from ACV (explained in the "Process Development" section below) creates shared intention in the class environment and allows students to individually examine valuable steps toward self-embodiment. This framework highlights the lived experience and collective presence authentically, putting Africanist principles in the forefront of the learning process.

Ritual and Community

Honoring the past, present, and future is essential in both the African American and African cultures. Researching the social and humanistic spirit of the African ethos (definitive spirit) correlates with my jazz dance practice; it is the ethos that drives this purpose. Aligning the inherent African Cultural Values of the ancestors is specific and necessary to guide the Diasporic Encounter Method and jazz pedagogy; there is a lot of play and freedom in this structure.

The student's communal sensitivity is well-defined, focusing on specific elements of ritual and community within the structure of the pedagogy. The use of repetition serves as common knowledge and feeds the connection among the group. Not only is there an intensity in the clarity and intention of their work, but these creative and pedagogical processes also provide a class culture and consciousness that focuses less on internal and external chatter. The outcome fosters a cohesive and shared environment reflected in the type of work the students display physically.

Process Development

By way of narrative analysis—a research process that uses different recounts of shared experiences—I collected data to observe the advanced jazz students at Western Michigan University's Department of Dance (WMU) over two semesters. The perspective of this narrative, the language of jazz dance, is the ethos. Data was obtained through students' written discussion posts assessing their experiences, and following the discoveries they made while integrating the concepts of the African Culture into their daily jazz practice.

The written discussion posts of four students are highlighted in this section, utilizing the following operationally defined characteristics that construct the symbiotic relationship:

1. African Ethos—A Definitive Spirit
2. Community—Collective Experience in Class
3. Embodiment—Transformative Experience in Physicality

DEM encourages open communication and direct cognitive intention through biweekly focus topics and online discussion assignments for the class to build discoveries as a collective. These tools aid in cultivating an environment of trust as students investigate the characteristics that are synonymous with jazz technique: expressive patterns of rhythm, musicality, improvisation, and the intentional focus of the aesthetic of cool. These assignments also allow the teacher to introduce other educators, authors, and specialists who are practicing in the field involving cultural and somatic dance studies. Student-written discussion posts are shared online and explored viscerally in the dance studio. This allows an opportunity for the movement to navigate an authentic way of embodying jazz characteristics and aesthetics through cognitive knowing. The following sections describe the structure and content of my jazz class chronologically. Each heading reflects core African Cultural Values to provide an outline and a sense of flow for the class experience.

Honoring Ritual—the Greeting

An essential value in the African community is to honor the greeting—it is not ethical to allow any person to pass another without saying hello. The concept is celebrated in the Diasporic Encounter Method as students enter the room, greeting the dance space with their presence, lying on the floor in a spot that speaks to them. This ritual prepares and creates connective energy in the dancers' bodies.

The use of "constructive rest" follows,[5] allowing the individual to settle the mind and begin to connect with others in the space of the room. The use of level change, weight-shift, and textures within the construction of the warm-up parallels with vocal prompts, encouraging dancers to use every part of their body. An intentional focus is to investigate a deep appreciation for their surroundings and each other.

African Ethos—A Definitive Spirit in the Class Environment

Improvisation derives from the freedom of self-expression and focuses on a sense of play and intuition. During improvisation, a jazz dancer uses impulse, rhythm, and music simultaneously. Together, they provide energy, the spirit of excitement that evokes a genuine release of authenticity in the body. Improvisation has always been a part of the African diasporic cultures. Structured improvisation is in the music patterning and rhythm of jazz and is in likeness to the drum circle in African communities.

The Diasporic Encounter Method and class structure allows the instructor to use movement cues from the jazz dance aesthetic, aligns them with African Cultural Values, uses vocal prompt/sound cues that reflect motion in the body, and uses spoken affirmations repeated by the students before authentic movement improvisation.

This model uses the pedagogy of "the interrelatedness of speaker and listener" mentioned by psychologists Joseph L. White and Thomas A. Parham in *The Expressive Patterns of Black Folks.*[6] The vocal affirmations often reference an African maxim that reflects African Cultural Values. Take, for example, the Akan maxim, "The clan is like a cluster of trees which, when seen from afar, appear huddled together, but which would be seen to stand individually when closely approached."[7] The instructor would use the maxim to engage vocal affirmations centered around brotherhood, honoring individual expression

Table 16.1. DEM principles

Jazz movement aesthetics	ACV (African Cultural Values)	Vocal prompt/sound cues
Polyrhythm	Brotherhood	Clapping
Musicality	Humanity	Communal breathing
Weight-shift	Kinship	Spoken affirmations
Off-axis movement	Community	Stomping
A sense of groove	Individualism	
Intuitive play	Purpose	

among the group and a sense of agency. The affirmations serve as a mechanism to engage a verbal call-and-response between teacher and student:

> Teacher: I am a strong voice in a community of many. (*students repeat*)
> Teacher: My body moves, and it reflects my strength. (*students repeat*)
> Teacher: Repeat after me 3 times, "I am!"

Communication between teacher and student (with the eyes closed) heightens their senses through a somatic exchange. Music plays as they take in the verbal cues, and students are encouraged to find their groove, sensation, and poly-centered understanding of the melody and rhythmic structure of the music. Students follow the impulse to move, showing individual expression and celebration. Investigating these types of somatic connective methods to inspire ethos is critical. Student One, a sophomore, describes this experience:

> I experience the "trance dance" often during jazz class. This typically happens during the part of the warm-up where we stand with our eyes closed as Monique speaks and has us repeat phrases. This is a very introspective, reflective moment in class. I feel the words we repeat seep into my body and my soul. Each set of words makes me feel slightly different and resonates in a different way. This deep embodiment of the words influences my movement, in a way that I am conscious of. I go into a "trance" where the movement simply flows from my body, driven and inspired by the words we were meditating on.

Student One experienced a rooted connection to profound energy in the body, an example of ethos through positive affirmation and improvisation. The student let the spirit of the moment expand their movement quality, therefore strengthening their fluency in jazz improvisation. Improvisation ignites the soul, reflecting the symbiotic agency that African ethos and jazz dance share. The sensory stimulation used in the warm-up aided the connection between students and teacher, inspiring the characteristics of the six expressive patterns that psychologists White and Parham have provided in their analysis of the Black psychological perspective.[8] Furthermore, jazz music and dance embody all the traits they mention in their study, especially emotional vitality, realness, resilience, interrelatedness, and the true value of direct response.[9] Each value exudes a dominant display of the African diasporic ethos.

Celebration of Community

Paying homage to the popular African belief, "Let the circle be unbroken,"[10] the structure of class then shifts to the dancers and instructor clapping in

FIGURE 16.1. Monique Marie Haley with Cerqua Rivera Dance Theatre. Photo by Leni Manaa-Hoppenworth.

rhythm. Each dancer takes turns dancing in the center of the circle. "In African Culture, the young are still fragile in the world and must be securely held up, that safety comes from the hands of older generations,"[11] and the community. The students explore musicality, intuitive sense, play, and rhythmic dynamics among the support of their peers. The Diasporic Encounter Method invites students to focus on how the jazz aesthetic emboldens communal sentiment, deepens consciousness in their practice as artists, and illuminates how Africanist points of view embrace these elements. Author Kwame Gyekye mentions how communal sentiment is in the fiber and nature of African cultures: "Art in traditional African cultures has both functional and purely aesthetic dimensions. One outstanding feature of artistic performances such as music and dance is their participatory character: music-making and dancing are communal activities, aimed—apart from their purely aesthetic qualities—at deepening communal sentiments and consciousness.[12]

The aesthetic of jazz has rhythm, pause, a through-line of connection, and honors individuality, expressivity, playfulness, and much more. The students took time to consider the aesthetics of jazz that have guided them toward cultivating a more conscious "being" in class and into expressing an intentional communal sentiment in their jazz practices. Student Two, a junior, reveals how the aesthetic of jazz continues to enrich not only the connection to others but also the consciousness they exuded as an artist:

> When viewing my growth as a jazz dancer through an Africanist lens, I start to see a growing correlation between my technique and my understanding of the African aesthetic. When Kwame Gyekye refers to communal sentiment, he directly relates it to the art of dancing in the context of the African aesthetic. Through Monique's class, this sense of communal sentiment is so strong in a lot of our discussion and exercises. For example, I'm always excited to watch others dance in the improvisation circle, but more excited for that moment of togetherness, which follows. Where we all create contact with each other and breathe as a singular entity, just for a moment. Emotionally, I am so regenerated by this no matter how tired or burnt-out I am from the week. There is an excitement and tender sentiment which we all understand. This is what I believe the communal sentiment is about.

The beauty of jazz does not rely only on external experience; it also relies heavily on the nature of a student's conduct and character as an individual. By embracing the holistic approach DEM provides, Student Two has gained an understanding of the jazz aesthetic based on cultural knowledge and an openness to allowing the ethos to strengthen their understanding of what it means to embody jazz technique.

Community—Nurturing the Collective Experience in Class

The Diasporic Encounter Method invests in ways to capture the community by building rituals that inspire trust and growth of an authentic ethos. Student Three, an advanced jazz senior, responds to a biweekly focus topic influenced by a quote from Somé. The focus allows them to become aware of how community development in the class structure inspires one to move toward self-discovery after movement exploration:

> Thinking about the dynamic and ethos of our Jazz II class, I now approach class with sincere intention, opening my awareness to the energy of my peers and the space each day. It has caused me to consider my role as a contributor to our community on a deeper level. What stuck with me was that individuality, not individualism, is the core of community. Before, I did not realize the difference between those two words. By

taking class and thinking about the unique energy in the room and how my contribution feeds the group, I am becoming less individualized and held back by insecurities, becoming invigorated and inspired by sharing my energy and supporting my peers.

It has helped us get to know our classmates' unique movement better and to establish an ethos that pushes each of us to become better versions of ourselves by knowing that we will be supported.

Ethos is vital to fluid interactions between individuals in a shared space. The students' willingness to express themselves complements the nature of the culture and spirit of the community built into the class structure. The movement language that developed during improvisation showcased their attention to the energy (ethos) between others in the room. When students involved the play of improvisation in the thread of the jazz dance technique, the symbiotic relationship between African ethos and the culture of jazz dance was more than apparent. In his article on healing, Somé reveals: "The truth is, that one doesn't lose one's self as a result of being a part of a community. On the contrary, being in the community leads to a healthy sense of belonging, greater generosity, better distribution of resources, and a greater awareness of the needs of the self and the other. In community, the needs of the one are the needs of the many . . . In this way, being a part of a strong community strengthens one's individuality by supporting the expression of one's unique gifts and talents."[13]

Dance educator and creator of the movement practice Embodiology®, Dr. S. Ama Wray, mentions the Yoruba term *Etutu*—serious play, investigation, and improvisation.[14] This word sums up jazz dance in my pedagogy and practice, and both are critical factors in the Diasporic Encounter Method. In class, these tools invite the creative spirit to excel and thrive while dancing. The sense of play must occur seriously so that all the minds are open to a somatic connection during warm-up, across the floor, and technique/phrase-work.

Embodiment—Transformative Experience in Physicality

Wray focuses on the nuances, rhythm, pattern, and feeling found in West African dance. Jazz musicians inspire emotion and expression in the rhythm and melody; their technical skill evokes a feeling and "spirit" inside the dancer. In using DEM, Africanist principles are the foundational pull. Student consciousness exposes possibilities that engage intuitiveness inside the downbeat. In exploring the jazz, they draw toward the freedom in the structure within the rhythm. If the spirit moves by the rhythm, and the cosmic mix of emotions spark an embodied reaction from the body, causing an authentic expression in the dance, is that not the ethos working?

Student Four, a senior, recounts an experience involving African ethos, community, and embodiment. The influences of African Cultural Values had this student delve into the jazz dance culture with pure expression. In researching African ethos and its symbiotic connection to the culture of jazz, impulse, improvisation, intuitiveness, and connection, we discover that all are in sync with embodied action and a somatic understanding. Student Four took time to consider where they began in their process, finding growth they had cultivated within the jazz aesthetic:

> The playful improvisational element of jazz, the emphasis on rhythm, and syncopation have greatly informed my consciousness and jazz dance practice. Throughout this class, woven within the structure and emphasized with Monique's verbal cues, improvisation and interaction with others in the space is always in my thoughts. Which has heightened the awareness of my presence and the energy I am sending to the people around me. Jazz dance cannot be done in isolation.
>
> Exploring the jazz aesthetic through an Africanist lens has shown me the importance of connection—to myself, the floor, the space, the music, and to my peers. Our work in this class demands mindfulness and the ability to respond in the moment, which keeps the work fresh and eliminates rigidity and striving for perfection.
>
> Attending to the communal sentiment of jazz dance enriches the technical aspects of the genre by feeding an ongoing conversation. In becoming more aware of the energy, I contribute to our class; my dancing has expanded in volume. I am less afraid of messing up because I know that even mistakes can help me and my peers grow. I have noticed that gratitude for myself and others makes for a more joyful experience and cultivates greater uniqueness in artistry.

Student Four has begun to experience the essential characteristics of the ethos in the jazz practice. An internal realization has carried the student forward as information is applied to the whole body in movement. The Diasporic Encounter Method shows that an authentic source of an embodiment can happen. A deep connection to the culture created in the jazz dance class community is integrated by what a student feels internally on a personal level. How the individual receives it is strengthened by the synergy in the dance space.

CONCLUSION

Jazz dance is a vessel often used by the African diasporic peoples to spread the glory of the African roots and ethos from which it authentically derives. The art form transfers a profound history, a history that lives within the African American culture. The students' written discussion posts proved this point by highlighting the characteristics that showcase parts of the African essence through the symbiotic relationship—ethos, community, and embodiment. The Diasporic Encounter Method allows students to experience a holistic jazz practice and pedagogy, experiencing ways to deepen a connection to jazz culture, aesthetics, and tradition.

Communal sensitivity resonates deeply in the heart of jazz movement and music. Writer Takiyah Nur Amin said it best: "African people in the West before, during, and after enslavement contributed not only to jazz dance, but to the larger national, global dance landscape through jazz dance [it was a vessel]. By decentering the primacy of non-African cultural contributions, we can understand jazz dance as an amalgamation of cultural influences that remains persistently African at its core."[15] When energy, spirit, connectivity, and emotional outbreak evokes, that is jazz. The essence of the African people is at the core of the rhythm. Their African roots and ethos will forever be invaluable, residing profoundly in the thread of jazz music, dance, and culture.

> A physical body alone cannot have any sort of direction in this life, so it is important to recognize that the body is an extension of the spirit [ethos], and the spirit is an extension of the body, and that the two are inseparable, with a communication that goes both ways.[16]

NOTES

1. Kwame Gyekye, *African Cultural Values: An Introduction* (Accra, Ghana: Sankofa, 1998).

2. Malidoma Patrice Somé, *The Healing Wisdom of Africa* (New York: J. P. Tarcher/ Putnam, 1999).

3. Marimba Ani, *Let the Circle Be Unbroken* (New York: Nkonimfo, 2004), 40.

4. Ibid.

5. Constructive rest—a way of lying down in a comfortable position that promotes a release of tension and stress in the body. It is used to engage openness and clarity in the mind/body in DEM at the start of class.

6. The "six expressive patterns" devised by White and Parham to describe six

psychological reoccurring themes of Black Folk: emotional vitality, realness, resilience, interrelatedness, the true value of direct response, and trust and deception.

7. Gyekye, *African Cultural Values,* 47.

8. Joseph L. White and Thomas A. Parham, "Psychological Themes in Black Language, Oral Literature and Expressive Patterns," in *The Psychology of Blacks: An African-American Perspective* (Englewood Cliffs, NJ: Prentice Hall, 1990), 83.

9. Ibid., 56–83.

10. Ani, *Let the Circle,* 53.

11. Malidoma Patrice Somé, "Elders in the Community," in *The Healing Wisdom of Africa* (New York: J. P. Tarcher/Putnam, 1999), 123.

12. Kwame Gyekye, "Ancestorship and Tradition," in *African Cultural Values: An Introduction,* by Gyekye (Accra, Ghana: Sankofa, 1998), 178.

13. Malidoma Patrice Somé, "Relationships of Healing: The Community," in *The Healing Wisdom of Africa,* by Somé (New York: J. P. Tarcher/Putnam, 1999), 91–92.

14. Sheron Wray, "A Twenty-First-Century Jazz Dance Manifesto," in *Jazz Dance: A History of the Roots and Branches,* ed. Lindsay Guarino and Wendy Oliver (Gainesville: University Press of Florida, 2014).

15. Amin, "The African Origins," 43.

16. Malidoma Patrice Somé, "Healing in the Indigenous World," in *The Healing Wisdom of Africa,* by Somé (New York: J. P. Tarcher/Putnam, 1999), 31.

Jazz Dance Pedagogy

Its Own Thing

PAULA J. PETERS

My journey into dance began at age four in the typical fashion of a White female growing up in suburban America in a solidly middle-class family. Because of this socialization, I trained and performed in two genres: ballet and jazz. My ballet training started at the age of four, and at the age of fifteen, jazz class was introduced to the curriculum as a one-day-a-week class. In the jazz instruction we received, it was never taught as a form with its own history, theory, or practices, but rather as a subset of ballet. Due to these methods of training, by the time jazz dance entered my life, I had only one way of speaking about dance technique: using ballet vocabulary and verbal cueing. However, because it was in my nature to categorize elements in my life, and ballet and jazz felt different in my body, I neatly separated them into two categories, enjoyed the opportunity to study both, and never thought further about their differences.

Once I began my professional performing career with Spectrum Dance Theater in Seattle, we trained in ballet and jazz but performed in many styles of jazz, with a strong focus on concert jazz (1992–2002). During this time, I learned that jazz dance was an art form whose emphasis was based in African diasporic social and kinetic elements[1]—elements that focus on inclusion, individuality, groove, rhythm, and the creation of new ideas. As I began to shift my career from performer to professor, the realization occurred that on anatomical and somatic levels, my body operated differently in each genre. Further, through deeper investigation into the history of jazz dance, it became clear that jazz was uniquely its own thing. This crystalized that despite having one set of verbal instruction methods for both forms, I spoke two languages of dance in my body. I was bilingual.

BILINGUAL MOVEMENT FLUENCY

The Merriam-Webster Collegiate Dictionary defines bilingual as (1) having or expressed in two languages; and (2) using or able to use two languages especially with equal fluency.[2] Because ballet and jazz have such different requirements to communicate their aesthetic values, they each demand physicality in distinctive ways. Further, the movement vocabularies of jazz and ballet are unambiguously different. Every gesture, twist of the spine, flip of the wrist, tip of the shoulders, turn of the head, or articulation of the limbs is distinctly specific to each form. Finally, both use a variety of detailed energetic inflection to convey meaning to the observer. For example, to communicate a sense of restraint and to engage in conformity, ballet requires a vertical spine and neutral pelvis, a restrained torso, exact replication of codified shapes, and a continual act of lifting the body up and away from the ground. On the other hand, jazz communicates groove that is connected to rhythm and makes room for individual expression within the group. Jazz requires the spine to alternate between articulate and bound, shift the torso to different spatial planes, movement improvisation, and getting down into the legs to be closer to the earth. Based on these diverse qualities of form, function, and specific messages, each genre is clearly its own language. Just like any person who is able to use two verbal languages with equal fluency from years of immersion in each, my depth of training, performance, and choreographic experiences in both movement languages enables me to code-switch between ballet and jazz with ease.

CODE-SWITCHING

Language is powerful, and the vocabulary we use verbally and physically inherently communicates what we value. In my own teaching practices, I realized that using terminology such as plié, tendu, chassé, passé, relevé, battement, pirouette, and jeté during jazz dance instruction superimposed ballet, a movement language with different values and meanings, on top of jazz. As a jazz dance historian, it is deeply important to me, both in words and actions, to teach jazz dance in a way that honors its own movement aesthetics and lineage. I began to consider that by not using verbal cues specific to jazz dance, my teaching was inadvertently communicating to my students that jazz was a subset of ballet rather than a form with its own history, and depth of physical nuances. It became clear to me that in order to become fluent bilingual code-switchers, students needed to practice the dialect of jazz dance in relationship to itself.

STRATEGIES FOR DEVELOPING NEW LANGUAGE

In order to speak a new movement language, you have to practice. This requires a shift in the way class content is structured, and how you approach
the fundamentals of jazz dance movement vocabulary. In general, improvisation, syncopation, and call-and-response are important elements to include
in jazz class practices. Another way to approach these shifts is to restructure
the warm-up into interchangeable sections. For example, you might use call-
and-response and improvisation as entry points to frame the class. As Lindsey
Salfran asserts: "The ability to improvise with a sensibility of call and response
requires a sense of play . . . and allows them to communicate to one another. It
lays the groundwork for a communal environment that is necessary for most
vernacular forms."[3] Because improvisation and call-and-response are central
in diasporic movement sensibilities, and thereby to jazz dance, restructuring
the warm-up from this starting point honors this tradition. Below are some

FIGURE 17.1. Hayley Robichaud and Marissa Masson improvising in jazz warm-up
exercise, Salve Regina University. Photo by Kim Fuller Photography.

suggestions for reworking studio practices and assignments to increase student understanding of jazz dance as a distinct dance form.

Cueing

One of the ways to get started is to move away from using codified ballet vocabulary in jazz technique classes and rehearsal processes, and try replacing them with terminology and phrases that refer to the anatomical action of movement. For example, bend or bounce (for plié); half-toe (for relevé); outside turn or inside turn (for pirouette); triple step or triple slide (for chassé); back-side-front (for pas de bourrée); leap or jump (for jeté); and kick (for battement). Other cueing options that are useful to help students embody jazz aesthetics are "get down in the legs," "drop the pelvis behind the knees," and "let the chest be free."

Another approach is to let go of exclusively using counts in jazz class. Try using rhythm-sounds and singing during movement demonstration, verbalizing rhythmic or musical sounds and encouraging students to join the party. This helps students increase their awareness of musicality, and abilities to *feel* rhythm as the verbalization of sound resonates in their chests. Another fun way to get at rhythm and musicality is to have students sing the melody of the song in conjunction with the movement, and/or create words that mirror the quality or rhythmic structure of a step. Some language-sounds that we developed in class are: bam, ba-da, boom-ba, zaaa, be-dop, while we accent more dynamic parts of the movement, and deemphasize the more subtle parts of the movement.

The Circle

Form a circle and choose music that has a clear downbeat to get the body down into the ground and into a groove. One option that works well to engage students in the process of active learning is to have them research and suggest songs from jazz, funk, soul, contemporary jazz, or a specific artist who falls into a jazz-related category. To begin moving, bring the legs into a wide parallel, knees deeply bent in a squat position, with the pelvis behind the knees, a deep crease in the hip joint, and the torso tipped forward leaning into the circle. Start rocking side to side on the downbeat, allowing the torso to be fluid and respond to the reverberation of movement from the legs, perhaps switching to double bounces on each leg, or any rhythmic weight shift that students might want to explore.

After this initial movement exploration, try a call-and-response improvisation where each student will have the opportunity to be the leader within the circle. Whoever is leading the call improvises movement, followed by the rest of the students mimicking the movement in response. Have this travel around the circle, with each student having the chance to be the leader, until each student has had a turn. Some sample "rules" that work well in this opening circle are that students use vernacular movement that is low to the ground and has rhythm in the feet.

Traveling Rhythm

Shift to a song with a more layered rhythmic structure and/or complex melody. Create a short rhythmic footwork phrase that can be repeated as a base to get started and begin traveling anywhere in the space, executing the rhythm in the feet, encouraging interaction with fellow students. Perhaps a bounce in the knees, dropping the weight into the floor, and allowing the torso to respond to the reverberation of movement in the legs is emphasized. Offer suggestions to choose from to add to the complexity of the rhythms, such as steady rhythm in the feet with fluid arms, use of the torso, and/or vocals that mimic elements of the music. Or direct the students to "find a friend" to travel through the space with, encouraging them to alternate between a lead and follow role. This encourages conversation through movement and creates a sense of shared ownership using the tradition of call-and-response.

Phrase Work

Build a longer traveling phrase across the floor as the main portion of class. In this process, students are able to work on repetition, which builds functional motor learning in the language nuances of jazz, while also challenging them to learn new material quickly.[4] To build the phrase, try starting with a movement combination that is shorter in length, perhaps consisting of syncopated rhythm in the feet, juxtaposed with fluid arm movements while mixing in kicks and turns. This phrase is repeated each side at least three times, with limited or no feedback, giving students the opportunity to integrate the sequence in their bodies. Next, provide targeted feedback focusing on the concepts that students are struggling with, such as rhythm in the feet or using the pelvis to drive movement. Then give students the chance to complete the phrase twice more with the music in order to incorporate the feedback. Once the students have the phrase, perhaps shift the spatial location, having students start at any place in the room, facing any direction, and improvise their traveling pattern and/or inserting movement improvisation. This gives students the chance to improvise both space and movement inside of structure, and to interact with their classmates, speaking in the language of jazz by creating a sense of community and shared awareness.

ENGAGING WITH HISTORY

Another important approach to support students' movement language literacy of jazz dance is to include a component of theory into studio practices. When students engage with the history of the form, it helps rewire everyone's habits, while drawing attention to jazz dance's movement aesthetics and historical lineage from a scholarly standpoint. This gives students a chance to practice speaking about jazz as a specific art form with its own history, language, and value systems. This, in turn, helps them become bilingual movers through study of culture.

Some ways to do this are to incorporate readings and video viewings on the history, evolution, and current practices of jazz dance into coursework requirements. It works well to design assignments that give students one or two questions to consider as they read an article or view a video. For instance, try assigning the articles "Jazz Dance as a Continuum"[5] in conjunction with "Jazz Dance Styles,"[6] and ask students to come to the next class meeting prepared to discuss how the continuum of jazz dance relates to the continuum of United States culture. For an online discussion post about Carlos Jones's "Jazz Dance and Racism,"[7] you might ask students to discuss whether the following statement from the article rings true for them and explain why or why not: "Teaching and creating jazz dance in such a manner that the African aesthetic is intrinsic in the process is crucial and necessary."[8] These types of assignments can help students gain new perspectives about the stand-alone physical language of jazz dance, and build their cultural literacy by engaging with jazz dance scholarship.

ASSESSMENT METHODS

Once these shifts in studio instruction have been made, we want to know if students' ability to code-switch into the language of jazz dance has improved. Because the evaluation of technique in jazz class often relies on assessing principles designed for movement literacy in the language of ballet, assessing students in jazz class needs to be based on parameters in relationship to the language of jazz dance itself. Try creating criteria based on the communal, physical, verbal cues, or musical principles of jazz dance. Below are some baseline criteria centered on *how* the body is moving in the language of jazz: "Clear shifts of weight with bent knees in all ball changes; Clear rhythm in the feet throughout the combination in relationship to the musical phrasing; Clear groove in the torso; All traveling steps are driven by the pelvis; Arm movement has clarity of rhythm in relationship to the feet; and Interaction with fellow students through focus, or improvisation."

Using the above as a starting point, add elements such as clarity of articulation, spatial patterns, or specific use of focus and dynamics. It is useful to video and share these practical assessments with the student, providing each with written feedback on their progress in each category. All of the above strategies for shifting class content in your jazz class are jumping-off points to spark ideas. I also encourage conversation with students to see what is working for them, and what they might need more of as they continue learning the language of jazz.

Discoveries

I've been teaching jazz dance for the last two decades and can confidently say the biggest struggle has been getting students to understand groove and rhythm in their bodies. Imagine my surprise, then, when students I had been teaching for three years who struggled to "get down," and feel rhythm, found their groove after one semester. The process of retooling my classes has helped students on their own bilingual journey, one that they are excited to continue.

However, the most profound experience of redesigning my jazz classes was that students experienced transformative learning. Psychologically, many were deeply surprised, and some were upset, to discover they were unaware of their underlying assumptions and beliefs about jazz dance's movement language and people's history. As a result, student behavior transformed. They became hungry for more information, asking for more readings and class discussions on the history of jazz. They began using verbal cues with each other in class that were rhythm- and physicality-based. These two factors alone were enough to bring me immense satisfaction as a jazz dance professor. However, the most moving and potentially game-changing for the field of jazz dance was their conviction that they would teach the physical language of jazz dance from historical and cultural perspectives when they become jazz dance instructors. As an educator who came late in the game to the realization that jazz dance was a distinctive dance genre rather than a subset of ballet, watching students celebrate jazz dance in relationship to itself, want to have conversations that often brought about more questions than answers, and become committed to sharing their new knowledge with the world, has been one of the most profoundly rewarding experiences of my teaching career.

Conclusion

Jazz dance has its own movement language, complete with nuances, inflections, and meanings that stand on their own, without qualifiers. By thinking about jazz dance technique as an independent dance genre, teachers can reshape the narrative on why jazz dance needs to receive equal value to its counterparts in studio dance instruction. This is important in order to honor jazz dance aesthetic values, history, and the immense contributions of the African American people who created, evolved, and continue to evolve the form. It is my hope that my sharing these ideas will encourage other jazz dance educators to join me in participating in a paradigm of jazz dance instruction that honors its African roots and cultural legacies.

Notes

1. Patricia Cohen, "Jazz Dance as a Continuum," in *Jazz Dance: A History of the Roots and Branches,* ed. Lindsay Guarino and Wendy Oliver (Gainesville: University Press of Florida, 2014), 5–6.

2. *The Merriam-Webster Collegiate Dictionary*, 17th ed., s.v. "bilingual," www.merriam-webster.com/dictionary/bilingual.

3. Lindsey Salfran, "Jazz Dance Training: Contributions to a Well-Rounded Dance Education for College Students," *Journal of Dance Education* 19, no. 4 (October–December 2019): 144.

4. Virginia Wilmerding and Donna Krasnow, "Motor Learning and Teaching Dance," International Association for Dance Medicine and Science, 2009, 3, www.iadms.org.

5. Cohen "Jazz Dance," 3–7.

6. Lindsay Guarino and Wendy Oliver, "Jazz Dance Styles," in *Jazz Dance: A History of the Roots and Branches,* ed. Guarino and Oliver (Gainesville: University Press of Florida, 2014), 24–32.

7. Carlos Jones, "Jazz Dance and Racism," in *Jazz Dance: A History of the Roots and Branches,* ed. Lindsay Guarino and Wendy Oliver, 231–39 (Gainesville: University Press of Florida, 2014).

8. Ibid., 238.

18

Reframing the Jazz Narrative
in the High School Classroom

JESSIE METCALF MCCULLOUGH

When I first began teaching jazz at a performing arts charter high school seven years ago, I believed I was highly qualified. I had years of studio/competition experience as a dancer, teacher, and coach; had danced professionally for two major cruise lines; and much of my master's degree research centered on dance in musical theater. Unbeknownst to me, I was approaching jazz from a highly Eurocentric viewpoint, so deeply ingrained in the fabric of my jazz training that it served as an unconscious bias informing everything I embodied and taught.

Awareness of this bias became evident through my work in developing a high school jazz curriculum. Differing from studios, high school dance education requires the integration of national/state standards that often emphasize creation, connection, and reflection, especially as they relate to historical and cultural contexts.[1] In working to accommodate these standards, I began to research the history of jazz more deeply, realizing that the African American roots were shamefully underrepresented in my teaching pedagogy, appearing more like a footnote than the main event. This realization became a catalyst for the ongoing development of new teaching practices aimed at reframing the jazz narrative in my classroom to acknowledge more directly the African American vernacular roots of jazz.

As a White teacher in a predominantly White community, reframing jazz for my students and myself is a matter of the utmost importance. The desire to shift my perspective on jazz came out of a responsibility to myself, my students, and my community to be actively antiracist in my teaching practices.[2] Despite the sometimes seemingly endless workload of being a high school teacher, putting in the effort to reexamine embodied Eurocentric jazz practices and incorporate African American voices and aesthetics is paramount to twenty-first-century jazz dance education. While making this pedagogical shift is an ongoing process, it is one that can be truly transformative in the way it impacts students. High school dancers are on the verge of adulthood, in a stage of life that is highly influenced by developing self-awareness.[3] Students in predominantly White environments, like my own, may have limited knowledge of African American history. Rooted jazz practices provide the opportunity to help students learn about the African American contributions that have shaped U.S. culture and afford them the realization that alternatives to Eurocentric approaches are valid and valuable. In my experience, this leads students to begin the process of examining their own biases as they work to discover who they are.

The key to teaching jazz in high school is to develop a balanced pedagogy that factors in the variety of jazz styles utilized today, while incorporating vital and often missing West African and African American aesthetics into methodological frameworks.[4] The goal of this chapter is to offer strategies for reframing the jazz narrative in high school environments in pursuit of this balance. The examples provided are from my own teaching practice and experiences working in an American charter high school. Instructors should continually remind themselves that it will take time to adapt teaching practices and that continual revision should occur as knowledge is accumulated.

The High School Jazz Dancer

A sense of community is one of the foundational social elements of African American vernacular jazz and is also integral to student scholarship.[5] How a student feels while interacting in the classroom community has a marked effect on their ability to digest material. In my experience, the most effective learning happens in classrooms where students feel valued, respected, free to make mistakes, and are active participants, both mentally and physically, in their own scholarship.[6] Creating this community with a room full of teenagers can, however, be particularly challenging. While many dancers have been taught, through years of ballet-influenced etiquette, to respect all teachers, this respect often comes in the form of silence and the ability to stay in a specified location on the dance floor. High school dancers will, however, continue to roll their eyes, huff occasionally, cross their arms, and look upset until they feel a connection with the instructor and their peers. This connection is vital to shifting a student's approach to jazz. By engaging with the social elements of vernacular jazz, instructors can use their curriculum to develop this sense of community and create a highly effective learning environment.

There are additional commonalities that exist for this demographic that can make reframing the jazz narrative challenging. One of the greatest obstacles is the initial resistance I receive from some of my new students. While all dance students vary in their technical ability, exposure to jazz dance styles/environments, and length of study, many high school dancers have received previous training in private studios, particularly those that compete.[7] This experience often shapes their first interactions with jazz dance and can develop fixed ideas that can be difficult to reformulate, such as believing that ballet technique is the foundation of all jazz dance.

Another characteristic of this population is that part of their current stage of development is about identifying the ego, or discovering a sense of self.[8] When you combine developing a sense of self with lessons learned through participation in dance competitions, students can suffer from ego orientation and the illusion of knowing. *Ego orientation* is a strong "comparison with others and a desire to win."[9] Students with ego orientation can have lower self-esteem, suffer from performance anxiety, have a tremendous fear of making mistakes and an addiction to perfectionism.[10] These fears can greatly impact a student's ability to fully engage with new material. By reframing jazz as an African American vernacular tradition, my curriculum often diverges from the competitive styles they are familiar with. As they have a learned desire to equate quality dancing with Eurocentric models of perfectionism (pointed feet, vertical spine, stretched limbs), exploring jazz from a new perspective can be disconcerting.

This is amplified by the *illusion of knowing*, which is the belief that one has learned something when in fact one has not.[11] Competition students can cling to learned beliefs about jazz out of a desire for correctness. Competition rewards virtuosic movements, often referred to as "tricks," and teaches students that sharp, aggressive, sassy/sexy, movements are jazz.[12] Add to this a fierce loyalty to competition teams and coaches, and a top prize-winning jazz routine, and students may falsely believe that competition versions of jazz are "true jazz" and the instructor teaching new, sometimes contradictory ideas, is ill-informed. The combination of ego orientation, illusion of knowing, and new representations of jazz can then result in *cognitive dissonance*, where the new, contradictory information makes students feel uncomfortable.[13] In trying to alleviate this cognitive dissonance, students can either change their approach or may double down on their studio training by "find[ing] fault with the new information."[14] The latter results in *confirmation bias,* which is a "tendency to seek information that confirms rather than discredits current beliefs."[15] When exploring vernacular jazz, students in my class sometimes struggle to make their own choices regarding movement possibilities in improvisation and movement creation activities. They often fill their improvisations and chore-ographies with the virtuosic movements valued in competition, striving for a previously learned version of "correctness." Musicality can also pose difficul-ties, as these students have learned to value precision over individuality and musical interpretation.

Students are also impacted by exposure to jazz portrayals in the media. Many of these examples are highly commercialized (stylistically adapted to sell a product), and often utilize Eurocentric technique.[16] These portrayals inform student expectations of jazz and influence what studios teach, rein-forcing a belief that commercialized representations of jazz are most valuable and uphold students' illusion of knowing.[17] As a result, the way instructors talk about competition and media influences can affect student growth and content comprehension. Today's students love the versions of jazz they see on TV/competition stages, and if teachers denigrate these styles of jazz, students can rebel by disengaging. For many dancers in high school, sense of self can be synonymous with the label of "dancer." When instructors contradict previous dance training, question favorite TV shows, or accidentally belittle competi-tion teams, they are not only questioning something students are passionate about, but they are also indirectly questioning their students' sense of identity. This does not mean that teachers should avoid questions regarding the state of jazz dance in studios and media today, but, rather, they should try to create a community where the instructor's choice of language and the student's abil-ity to feel safe questioning previously held beliefs about jazz work together to instill in the student a more well-rounded knowledge of jazz dance.

The key to addressing these student concerns is to develop a sense of com-munity. Once students feel as though they are valued members of their class-room community, they will begin to take ownership of their own learning and will, in most cases, engage willingly with new ideas and concepts.[18] When in-structors utilize African American social concepts and aesthetics to approach jazz, the community organically develops. Below are some strategies to help jazz instructors currently utilizing predominantly Eurocentric/commercial-ized jazz styles shift their curriculums in pursuit of a more balanced pedagogy.

SHIFTING PERSPECTIVES

Teachers aiming to reframe students' knowledge of jazz need to be aware that high school students may shut down if they feel their previous understandings are being invalidated. This does not mean pretending that the Eurocentric viewpoint is the lens through which jazz should be qualified. Rather, it is about helping students create pathways for new information that can shift their perspectives.

One way I address this is through dialogue about dancer training. Words are powerful, and the way instructors talk about dancer training can impact how a high school dancer, developing a sense of self, feels in the environment and about themselves. It is easy for a teacher to say, "jazz dance is not about tricks," but it is hard for the high school dancer to accept this when their current exposure to jazz tells them otherwise. Without meaning to, a dance instructor may accidentally criticize a student's current training or allude to it as "lesser." For example, a teacher might imply that competition dance is not artistry, making those students whose understanding of artistry has been built on winning medals lose trust in the instructor and feel isolated from the community. Instead, teachers should use phrasing that leaves space for student ideas while also offering new information. One could modify the previous statement by stating that "some styles of jazz, competition for example, place value on virtuosic movements, while the style currently being learned places value on . . ." This simple shift in the presentation of information demonstrates that jazz is a complex art form and offers students the opportunity to reexamine perspectives, while keeping the instructor from seeming to disparage students' beliefs about jazz.

Another tactic I use is the tool-belt concept.[19] In this strategy, students are asked to visualize a tool belt around their waist, but instead of hammers and nails, they have the dance styles, teachers, and classes they have been exposed to throughout their lives. The more tools on the belt, the more knowledge they have to draw from when creating choreography, embodying a new style, or auditioning for a job. The goal is to help students feel that their previous training is valid, while placing an emphasis on jazz that is rooted.

It is also helpful to reexamine Eurocentric classroom structures that might inhibit the feeling of community. Many Western dance classrooms today are highly influenced by the etiquette and environmental expectations of ballet: no talking, stay in lines, face the mirror. While many of these rules are designed to show respect, they can hinder attempts to create a community that values individuality and exploration. Reducing instructor hierarchy is a great

FIGURE 18.1. Jessie Metcalf McCullough teaching jazz. Photo by Eric Young.

first step to developing a more communal environment and allows students to see instructors as leaders in the community rather than outsiders passing judgement. Reducing instructor hierarchy might include participating in improvisation exercises with the students, sharing stories and experiences, physically relocating to a new position in the room, or turning to face students while demonstrating, rather than teaching into the mirror.[20] Additionally, allowing students the opportunity to vocalize what they are learning helps develop connection and provides opportunity for reflection. As an instructor, hearing students express their thoughts offers me an opportunity to provide additional information or offer alternative lines of reasoning.

ROOTING STUDIO JAZZ

Today, studio-based jazz is notorious for using Eurocentric elements because they align with competition expectations.[21] These elements include a primary reliance on ballet vocabulary; overemphasis of a high relevé and a vertically straight torso; initiation of movement from the upper body rather than the feet and pelvis; and/or defining jazz dance as sharp, aggressive, or sexy. Most new students at my school who have trained at local studios enter the space with all the aforementioned elements highly informing their understanding of jazz. This is to be expected, as the propagation of ballet-informed jazz in studios is cyclical. Students learn it, go to college where there is often little jazz representation, and then become teachers themselves, relying on their studio training to inform what they teach.[22] Moreover, most of my new students have little to no understanding of jazz history, often citing that their studios never mention it.

As a teacher, I have spent years trying to find ways to blend my embodied studio training with the aesthetics of African American vernacular jazz. One of the first steps I undertook was to spend time examining the Eurocentric techniques I taught through an Africanist kinetic lens.[23] These kinetic elements are intrinsic to African American vernacular forms and are foundational to jazz technique. My logic was that, while highly Eurocentric, today's jazz styles, if jazz at all, should have evolved from African American jazz traditions and therefore theoretically should still consist of some Africanist kinetic elements. Realizing this, I adapted my teaching pedagogy to emphasize the Africanist aesthetics as integral to jazz technique. For example, I am a certified Giordano technique instructor, and there are a number of Africanist kinetic elements already present in this technique, such as initiation with the pelvis; use of asymmetry; emphasis on being grounded; inclining of the torso; and use of flat-footed movements and isolations.[24] When teaching, I articulate their presence and ask students to prioritize these elements when executing movements. Shifting the verbal and physical focus required my students to rethink their ideas on technique, breaking from the Eurocentric ideal as most valuable.

I then began to include and prioritize more of the Africanist kinetic elements and regularly integrate authentic jazz movements into class combinations and choreography. For example, taking a triple step down into the ground rather than allowing dancers to lift up as they would in a chassé, or having students do a boogie forward into a pirouette. Additionally, I draw attention to Eurocentric practices by identifying movements that students think are jazz but that are actually ballet in origin, such as a pirouette with a parallel passé (students truly believe that the parallel makes it jazz). Once students can identify the Africanist kinetic elements and have embodied African American vernacular movements, I ask them to explore how to make a movement more jazz and less ballet. We then discuss and embody our findings, collectively learning more about true jazz aesthetics. One of the benefits to this approach is that it teaches students to equate jazz technique with African American aesthetics through movements they are already familiar with.

Another way I root studio jazz is to utilize authentic and contemporary jazz music regularly, ensuring I draw awareness to musical interaction and engage with syncopation, polyrhythm, and body percussion. Many of my students have little to no experience with jazz music, most equating the ability to recognize counts or dance to lyrics as having musicality. When first implementing jazz music, I feared my students would think it was outdated, but to my surprise, they have loved it. Learning to actively listen to music and use it to inform movement choices encourages students to see musicality and rhythmic embodiment as valuable techniques.

IMPROVISATION

Improvisation is another important vernacular jazz component commonly missing from Eurocentric jazz methodologies. I often start classes with a quick, structured improvisational warm-up that allows for integration of Africanist social elements, providing students the chance to be innovative, connect with their bodies, and shift into a "jazz feeling" both mentally and physically.[25] This change has been paramount to promoting a sense of community as students interact and explore movement capabilities together. Improvisations can be particularly effective if coupled with musical interpretation and/or the utilization of Africanist kinetic elements and African American vernacular movements.[26] Studio jazz dancers who are trained to perform predetermined movement may initially find improvisation uncomfortable as they have lacked experiences in generating movement from a place of individuality. To help alleviate discomfort, mix and match the configurations of improvisations through use of various student communities (e.g., one large class circle, smaller four-to-five-person circles, pairs, follow-the-leader). Offer improvisational prompts that guide students away from virtuosic movements by prioritizing innovation and acknowledging brave choices outside the Eurocentric jazz vocabulary. Consequently, students with an addiction to perfectionism, framed by competition standards, will feel reinforced by new benchmarks of achievement.

REFRAMING THE DISCUSSION

One of the benefits of establishing a strong sense of community is the development of trust in the instructor, which breaks down student resilience to new ideas and provides space for the instructor to deconstruct jazz biases. Reframing class discussions and presentations so they give credit to the African

American community is essential to culturally responsible jazz practices. For me, this has manifested in a number of ways:

- Reconstructing history presentations to position the African American perspective at the forefront, such as examining the Jazz Era through the lens of the Harlem Renaissance.
- Being mindful that references to iconic dancers, key events, and visual examples prioritize African Americans.
- Requiring students to identify African American aesthetics in dance analysis and being mindful that students examine works by African American choreographers.
- Developing research and creative assignments that engage students with the African American roots of jazz.

Additionally, I connect jazz education to important social topics. For example, having students learn about diasporas in discussing why jazz is an African American tradition, and introducing/exploring cultural appropriation by examining how Whiteness impacted the evolution of jazz.[27] I have found that education regarding cultural appropriation, in a predominantly White community, is not only necessary, but it tends to motivate students to acknowledge the importance of giving credit to the African American community and subsequently shift their perspectives on jazz.

Another important part of this equation is to provide students with opportunities to challenge their own preconceived notions of jazz. This goes beyond a simple expression of learning to a deeper reflection and works best when paired with an assignment that requires them to critically examine their understandings. One way I facilitate this is through the jazz-tree project. Completed after an introduction to jazz history, I show students the jazz-tree visual from *Jazz Dance: A History of the Roots and Branches*.[28] We discuss how the tree represents the history of jazz, its roots, trunk, and many offshoots. I then challenge my students to think about how *they* would organize jazz in a visual. They can choose to create their own version of a tree, or they can envision something completely new. After personal investigation, they design a visual representation of their idea to present in class. Once created, we sit in a communal circle and share. While the task of developing the "tree" forces students to critically examine their understanding of jazz styles, the presentation portion allows students to question, affirm, and challenge their own ideas as well as those of their peers. It also provides me a chance to help students identify Eurocentric biases that may be influencing their opinions. When done in a supportive community, expressing deep reflections is a fantastic tool for shifting student perspectives on jazz.

Final Note

One of the greatest lessons I have learned in trying to balance my jazz curriculum is that it is important to be open with students about the process of shifting my own perspective. Sharing new information as we learn and discussing why this change was important is key to modeling antiracist behavior and reinforcing the validity of African American vernacular jazz. Balancing does not mean completely abandoning Eurocentric approaches. It means prioritizing the African American foundation through integration into teaching practices. Balancing jazz curricula takes time and commitment to the authenticity of jazz, but connecting jazz to its roots is a vital step toward moving it into the future.

Notes

1. "National Core Arts Standards," State Education Agency Directors of Arts Education, 2014, www.nationalartsstandards.org.

2. "Talking about Race," National Museum of African American History and Culture, Smithsonian, https://nmaahc.si.edu/learn/talking-about-race/topics/being-antiracist.

3. Jeanne Ellis Ormrod, *Essentials of Educational Psychology* (Upper Saddle River, NJ: Pearson Education, 2006), 228–30.

4. My comments regarding "missing West African and African American aesthetics" are supported by conversations I had at National Dance Education Organization's conference "Jazz Dance: Hybrids, Fusions, Connections, Community," Salve Regina University, Newport, Rhode Island, July 30–August 2, 2019.

5. Patricia Cohen, "Jazz Dance as a Continuum," in *Jazz Dance: A History of the Roots and Branches,* ed. Lindsay Guarino and Wendy Oliver (Gainesville: University Press of Florida, 2014), 5.

6. Personal observation supported in Barbara McCombs, "Provide Developmentally Appropriate Choices," in *Developing Responsible and Autonomous Learners: A Key to Motivating Students* (Washington, DC: American Psychological Association, 2019), www.apa.org/education/k12/learners?item=7.

7. Elsa Posey, "Dance Education in Dance Schools in the Private Sector: Meeting the Demands of the Marketplace," *Journal of Dance Education* 2, no. 2 (2002): 46, https://doi.org/10.1080/15290824.2002.10387207.

8. Ormrod, *Essentials of Educational Psychology.*

9. Bonnie E. Robson, "Competition in Sport, Music, and Dance," *Medical Problems of Performing Artists* 19, no. 4 (December 2004): 161.

10. Ibid., 164

11. Ormrod, *Essentials of Educational Psychology,* 102.

12. Lindsay Guarino, "Is Dance a Sport? A Twenty-First-Century Debate," *Journal of Dance Education* 15, no. 2 (2015): 78, https://doi.org/10.1080/15290824.2015.978334; Cohen, "Jazz Dance as a Continuum," 3.

13. Ormrod, *Essentials of Educational Psychology,* 187–88.

14. Ibid., 188.

15. Ibid., 36

16. Definition of "commercial jazz" found in Lindsay Guarino and Wendy Oliver, "Jazz Dance Styles," in *Jazz Dance A History of the Roots and Branches,* ed. Guarino and Oliver (Gainesville: University Press of Florida, 2014), 28.

17. Karen Schupp, "Dance Competition Culture and Commercial Dance, Intertwined Aesthetics, Values, and Practices," *Journal of Dance Education* 19, no. 2 (2019): 63, https://doi.org/10.1080/15290824.2018.1437622.

18. Chris Watkins, "Classroom Learning Communities: A Review of Research," *London Review of* Education 3, no. 1 (March 2005): 51, https://doi.org/10.1080/14748460500036276.

19. Concept courtesy of Bethany J. Hansen.

20. Denise Purvis, email to author, November 10, 2019.

21. Schupp, "Dance Competition Culture and Commercial Dance, Intertwined Aesthetics, Values, and Practices," 59.

22. Tamara Thomas, "Making the Case for True Engagement with Jazz Dance: Decolonizing Higher Education," *Journal of Dance Education.* 19, no. 3 (2019), https://doi.org/10.1080/15290824.2018.1451648.

23. Cohen, "Jazz Dance as a Continuum," 5–6.

24. Certified through the Nan Giordano Certification Program®, www.giordanodance.org/ngcp.

25. Idea suggested by Lindsay Guarino as part of an online course "Jazz Dance Theory and Practice," NDEO Online Education, March 2019.

26. Cohen, "Jazz Dance as a Continuum," 5–6.

27. MTV News, "Decoded: 7 Myths about Cultural Appropriation DEBUNKED!," YouTube, November 11, 2015, www.youtube.com/watch?v=KXejDhRGOuI.

28. Kimberly Testa, *Jazz Dance Tree,* image, in Wendy Oliver, introduction to *Jazz Dance: A History of the Roots and Branches,* ed. Lindsay Guarino and Oliver (Gainesville: University Press of Florida, 2014), xv. Permission to use this image for educational purposes was granted by Romi Gutierrez, University of Florida Press, email to author, March 19, 2018.

19

Countering Cultural Dissonance in a Graduate Jazz Dance Course

PATRICIA COHEN

As a jazz dance educator who focuses on jazz dance in cultural and historical perspective, I am always intrigued and sometimes concerned with my students' reactions, both to the material I present and to my person. I am a White woman teaching an essentially African American art form. Our many students of color, whose experiences in dance and life are substantially different than mine, bring a unique perspective to the studio and to our discussions of race, social justice, and the appropriate dissemination of this most American art form. I emphasize the cultural context and pedagogy of jazz dance. Technique, per se, is less important, except in its descriptor function and/or as exemplars of certain eras and styles. My intention here is to analyze, explain, and disseminate an approach to the jazz dance class through the lenses of Critical Dance Pedagogy and racial awareness.

My university exists in the heart of a major, multicultural city known for its access to the arts. Our student body is comprised of people from all parts of the United States and countries beyond. In most years, fewer than half identify as White, one-quarter to one-third are African American, one-quarter are Asian, and the remainder are Latinx. They range in age from their mid-twenties through their fifties. All the students in our program, which privileges scholarship, pedagogy, and artistry equally, are candidates for the master's degree (MA) in dance education. Because technique classes abound in our city, we neither require on-campus technique classes, nor do we favor any particular dance genre. Our students already do or eventually will teach in K–12 urban situations, in the private sector, and in higher education. Some may be teaching artists, dance with small companies, or develop their own not-for-profit performance groups. As emerging scholars and dance educators, they inform the field of their experiences in the classroom and studio via conference presentations.

COURSE OVERVIEW

"History, Culture, and Pedagogy of Jazz Dance" is a required one-semester course for most MA candidates in our program. Assuming that "all dance is culturally informed,"[1] the course explores vernacular and theatrical jazz dance in historical and cultural contexts, with emphasis on pedagogy across teaching environments through movement and shared research. Students engage in experiencing and deconstructing pedagogical approaches to vernacular movement, jazz dance technique, improvisation, and academic content. In addition to the specific student learning outcomes articulated in the course syllabus, my overall pedagogical goals for the course include students' ability to:

- analyze, demonstrate, and teach jazz dance as a particularly American art form rooted in Africanist aesthetic and vernacular movement, and equal to other dance forms;
- explain contemporary and theatrical jazz dance techniques through historical and sociocultural lenses;
- integrate improvisation in jazz dance classes in all sectors;
- integrate knowledge of teaching methodologies into the jazz dance class experience;
- redefine pedagogical assessment from technical proficiency to inclusion of social and kinetic elements of jazz dance;
- consider the impact of racism in American history through the lens of jazz dance and music;
- accept and utilize reciprocal teaching and learning, in which lived knowledge is deeply appreciated and respected; and
- advocate for the value of jazz dance as an evolving American art form.

I present jazz dance as a continuum in which students are urged to ask, "Where's the jazz" as determined by the Africanist social and kinetic elements outlined in *Jazz Dance: A History of the Roots and Branches*.[2] Students learn to identify and embody the signifiers of jazz, whose hallmarks include an Africanist aesthetic, rhythmic connection to the music, improvisation, and dynamic play,[3] spontaneity, call-and-response, self-expression, elegance, and control.[4] In her influential *Digging the Africanist Presence in American Performance*, Brenda Dixon Gottschild elucidates five principles of the Africanist aesthetic: (1) Embracing the conflict—encountering and accepting the

FIGURE 19.1. Briana E. Bunkley (*left*) and Christine DiBrita, graduate students, Dance Education Program, NYU/Steinhardt 2019. Photo by Patricia Cohen.

existence of opposites; (2) Polycentrism and Polyrhythm—the simultaneous existence of many movements and rhythms in various body parts; (3) High-affect juxtaposition—the overlay of varying moods; (4) Ephebism—a kinesthetic intensity, aligned with youthful power; and (5) "Aesthetic of the cool," Robert Farris Thompson's descriptor in which the "mask of the cool" covers a deep-seated energy or intensity.[5] Scholar and educator Julie Kerr-Berry analyzes these elements in an earlier chapter of this book.[6] Melanie George further extends the definition through her mantra, "jazz Is . . . musicality, improvisatory, community, individuality, agency, democracy, humanity."[7]

At our first weekly two-hour meeting, I ask students to choose one topic to research and present with which they are familiar and one that is less known to them. Topics include West African roots, Slavery/plantation distortions and blending, Ragtime, Jazz Age, Swing era, the Blues, musical theater, concert dance, popular and social dances of rock-n-roll through disco, hip-hop, and current trends in street dance. The jazz-tree image and kinetic and social elements described by Cohen[8] are analyzed and utilized throughout the course to determine "Where's the jazz?" Each week, students present their assignment-based research and teach a movement component. I then introduce movement phrases that exemplify the era and structured improvisations that may be based in authentic jazz, and/or inspired by text or visual art of the period. Discussions of colonization, appropriation, and racial perceptions are embedded in each class.

At the end of each session, students complete anonymous exit slips, which serve as self-evaluation as well as feedback to inform my pedagogical practice. Exit slips ask open-ended questions that address aspects of the class that were "most appreciated (I feel engaged with)," "least appreciated," and "most challenging (risk-taking) aspects of class." One question addresses new information that may impact their teaching, and additional space is allotted to "comments." Over the years, I have found that students disagree on "most appreciated" and "least appreciated" according to their individual prior experiences and expectations. The exit slips allow students to anonymously reveal their discomfort and/or validation regarding their racial preconceptions and prior knowledge. I offer general feedback to their often passionate comments via our university's online messaging system.

Cultural Dissonance or Confused Definitions?

Our students enter the program with expertise in one or more dance forms including American street dance, ballet, Bharatanatyam, Chinese classical dance, modern dance, tap dance, and West African dance. During our first class, we create a nonjudgmental space in which students are invited to share prior knowledge and perceptions of jazz dance. Most international and some American students' exposure to jazz dance is usually limited to Broadway and/or competition-style dancing, and they may define the term "classical jazz" as preparation for musical theater dancing. These students tend to reference the technical aspects of dance rather than social or community aspects.[9] Writer Lindsay Guarino has noted similar findings.[10]

Former students who are now colleagues in dance education reflected on the course's influence on their deepened understanding of racial constructs as manifest in the African American experience through dance. Most African American students, and others who took undergraduate Black studies courses, recognize jazz dance's African roots and connection to the African diaspora. Even so, some who have roots in African American communities are unaware that the rhythms and dances of enslaved peoples are connected to today's street and club dances via authentic, traditional vernacular, social dance forms developed by African Americans. Former student Michelle Cole told me that "vernacular jazz dance had felt like an exclusive club" to which she did not belong. She hadn't connected it with the "raw natural jazz dance" she had experienced.[11] Jessa Rose VanHerwynen wondered why she hadn't connected the vernacular to her cultural identity as a person of color. She "should have known."[12] Joya Powell said that learning about Ring Shout and Cakewalk "opened her eyes to the rooted connections to her knowledge of the African diaspora."[13] Afaliah Tribune, who learned hip-hop "on the back porch from her cousins," added that she "started thinking deeper about the roots of vernacular movement . . . (which) brought value to the dances the grownups did" when she was growing up.[14] In general, the students' prior perceptions of jazz dance reflect the White hierarchal environments in which most have been educated, regardless of skin color. They have accepted the status of performative arts and education as neutral, merit-based and color-blind, despite their lived and instinctual knowledge.[15] So had I.

Students who are steeped in ballet aesthetic often question the value of learning jazz dance, among other nonballet-related subjects. At least one student will claim that ballet is the foundation of jazz dance. Alexis Andrews reported that as a student, she was admonished, "Ballet dancers should never learn jazz" from a teacher who perceived jazz as hypersexualized and without artistic merit.[16]

Jazz Dance through the Lens of Critical Dance Pedagogy

Critical Dance Pedagogy (CDP) "asks students and teachers to investigate questions about the systems of power that dictate who perform, when and where."[17] In other writing, McCarthy-Brown expresses her concerns about White ownership of cultural heritages, asking: "Who dances these dances? Whose culture is affirmed through these dances? Who profits from them?"[18] Jazz dance is a culturally specific, kinesthetic practice that is inextricably bound to the African American journey in the United States, in which the power dynamic has been characterized by racial injustice and inequality. Jazz choreographer and author Carlos Jones asserts: "To discuss jazz dance and not acknowledge the issue of race greatly diminishes the truths that exist in the art form."[19] It was incumbent upon me to present jazz dance with truthfulness and integrity, with recognition of my own implicit biases, awareness of my Whiteness and my position in the hierarchy of my educational institution. By acknowledging my cultural outsider-ness, I exposed my presumed status as the authoritative source of all information in order to reveal the messy connection of jazz dance to an American legacy of racism and class hegemony. I sensed that some African American students questioned my authority to present a dance form that developed in their culture. When asked about their reaction to a White jazz dance teacher, several former students of color admitted their initial mistrust and/or misgivings. Ultimately, they accepted my knowledge and were grateful for having it shared with humility and integrity, or as Joya Powell put it, "because I included historical information in an authentic way . . . I was invested in it."[20] Whitley Green was comfortable because I understood White privilege in the university.[21]

Through movement and narrative, my course challenges these central issues. A former student now teaching in a conservatory-style high school troubles these questions every day, acknowledging that she began to consider issues of race and ownership of movement during our jazz dance course.[22] A student of European heritage, whose prior knowledge of jazz dance was limited to musical theater, synthesized information about colonization and marginalization in a culminating project that addressed social justice. Today, she incorporates her understanding of the origins of authentic jazz dance in her teaching.[23] A student from Colombia who had no prior knowledge of jazz dance almost immediately connected the social dances of her country to the African diaspora.[24] Danielle Staropoli finds that teaching jazz dance in her predominantly White school allows her to raise issues of race.[25]

As per the course syllabus, I anticipate that "students will demonstrate kinesthetic and cognitive knowledge of the jazz dance idiom in its historical/cultural context, develop and communicate a vision and rationale for its inclusion in an educational setting, differentiate and value the vernacular and theatrical threads of jazz dance, and demonstrate effective pedagogical approaches to the jazz dance class."[26] Implicit in this statement of learner objectives is consideration of the colonization and marginalization of jazz dance throughout its history. I teach from a place of informed perspective and deep respect for a culture that is not mine. In this, I have felt validated by scholars like Julie Kerr-Berry, who wrote: "I do not think that the amount of melanin in one's skin determines the right of delivery any more than I think it insures a better sense of rhythm. Rather, it is about experiences, upbringing, exposure, access and the like—and not about skin color. Problems arise when race becomes a measure of what constitutes a good teacher of certain content."[27] Kerr-Berry emphasizes the need for historical knowledge plus acknowledgment of the painful impact of race relations in the United States. As former student and now colleague, Afaliah Tribune, opined: "Knowledge doesn't belong to a specific race or color. You taught me about myself."[28] The counternarratives told by my students of color impact our shared teaching and learning by revealing cultural truths and fictions.

Pedagogy of Jazz Dance Contextualized

In this course, full participation is expected, even of the occasional guest. Everyone dances and/or participates to the extent of their ability, in the Africanist way of being a participant-spectator. A sense of community is projected through shared dancing, circles, and affirmations of one's individuality within the community. Jazz expert Karen Hubbard's inspiring experiential classes and published articles revealed truths about traditional vernacular dance that I have subsequently shared with my students. Her "interactive warm-up consists of individual expression in stylized walks, freezes, call-and-response, scatting-patting, limb and torso isolations and historical jazz dance vocabulary." This approach results in "increased historical awareness of black culture in the US and enhanced possibilities for expressiveness in terms of form . . . Lessons are planned with emphasis on style rather than technique."[29] We scatter across the floor rather than face the "Western" mirror. We make eye contact with each other rather than with ourselves in the mirror. Call-and-response is the principal teaching methodology. See it, do it, embellish it. Be in the groove. Drum-based rhythms and internal energetically driven dancing replace Eurocentric shape-based movement. We seek movement that is individualistic and expressive rather than formalized or idealized. We practice responding to the music, as well as to one another. Ring Shout and Cakewalk are introduced in the first classes. According to scholar Barbara Glass, the Ring Shout was "an amalgamation of several African circle dances, it is the oldest African American religious dance."[30] It was a counterclockwise circle dance that entailed clapping, shuffling, and stomping. This dance form led to the Cakewalk. It migrated from the plantations, after the abolishment of slavery from minstrelsy to the Black Broadway era.

At its best, jazz dance draws on people's lived experiences, which may be expressed individualistically. To foster embellishment and individual expression, we ask, "What if . . . ?" There is no judgment of movement choices or body type—we offer a safe space to explore one's individuality in relationship to the music. For a ballet or theatrically trained person, this is especially hard work. We avoid the French vocabulary of ballet and theater jazz. "Plié" is replaced by "bent knees"; "grand battement" is restated as "kick," and so on. We walk; we do not promenade. "Pirouettes" become "turns." Cakewalk is demonstrated, not broken down into separate steps. As Moncell Durden writes of hip-hop culture: "We need to be culturally sensitive to the values of other societies, communities, cultures, and subcultures and recognize that concert dance is not the only type of dance worthy of reflection and study. Social dance holds great importance, history, lineage, identity, and strength for the people who participate in it."[31]

Yet in academia and in private studios, we codify and teach social dance forms like Lindy or hip-hop, facing the mirror in a dance studio, although they were created in dance halls and on the streets, and are ever-evolving. In decontextualizing the dances, we diminish the very aesthetic elements on which they thrive, that is, community, conversation, individuality, and improvisation.

In the course, our conversations query and challenge the authenticity of dance that has been commercialized and/or staged as entertainment. We address appropriation as we experience, view, and contextualize the Cake Walk, Asadata Dafora's "Ostrich," the popular so-called animal dances of the early 1900s, the Big Apple, and the Twist. We ponder the racial stereotyping and economic implications of blackface in Minstrelsy. We note that an internet search of Charleston or Swing yields photos and videos primarily of White dancers, although those dances have African American origins. Deeper research eventually reveals authentic footage of Black people dancing, which allows comparing the vertical, fairly tightly held bodies of White dancers with articulated limbs and inclined torsos of grounded Black bodies.

Furthermore, it is essential that students understand that a culture is being appropriated as well as its particular dances. The long history of White appropriation of Black dances must be contextualized as a fascination with, and perhaps fear of, Blackness as an unknown, exotic, mysterious culture. If we can't be *of* the culture, the power inherent in Whiteness facilitates stealing and "cleansing" that which we desire, making it acceptable for White consumption. As scholar Danielle Robinson notes, unlike White Ragtime teachers, "African-American jazz teachers did not write manuals, open their own cabarets, or appear on sheet music covers. Rather, they had to remain "invisible"— while they opened studios, gave lessons, taught routines, and choreographed for theaters and clubs all over Manhattan."[32]

Assessment

Although the course functions within the university's Eurocentric mantle, and grades must be given accordingly, I avoid aspects of that value system in that traditional technique per se is not assessed. Rather, the vernacular form of jazz dance is made accessible to all, regardless of cultural background or dance training. Carlos Jones wrote: "The marker for excellent artistry rejects the African aesthetic for the European idea of beauty. Dropping the pelvis, rolling through the hips, and rebounding up through an articulated torso are replaced by a rigidly controlled torso with elongated arms and a leg extension. The reason for raising one aesthetic over another emerges from racial privilege favoring a White choreographer over others."[33]

"History, Culture, and Pedagogy of Jazz Dance" refocuses assessment to presentations and other assignments that evaluate understanding of the evolution of jazz dance in terms of its Africanist social and kinetic elements.

Pedagogical Integrity

It has been important to offer students authentic and embodied learning in jazz dance through my teaching, as well as our readings and viewings. Therefore, I invite people who have lived experience and expertise in aspects of jazz dance that I do not, particularly West African dance, hip-hop, and street dance forms. Students appreciate these exchanges, in that many feel culturally validated; all recognize that sharing power is acceptable in the classroom. Former students have reported that they are further empowered by presenting self-chosen topics of well-researched academic and experiential material each week. They thereby determine who gets to dance, who gets to teach, and who gets to lecture. The MA dance education program on whose faculty I serve is making valiant efforts to decolonize dance education through CDP approaches, and via a perspective that meets our diverse student population "where it is." Overall, our faculty reflects the composition of our student body, although the few full-time faculty are all White women. In addition, our diverse group of adjuncts plays a critical role in facilitating community discussions of race and privilege and in choreographic mentoring. To date, all our program's required courses have been taught by White people. At the time of this writing, however, Black and White dance educators are collaborating to teach two of a colleague's foundational and research courses during her leave of absence. Hopefully, this initiative has facilitated a fresh approach to hegemony in academia.

Recommendations

Based on outcomes from the "History, Culture, and Pedagogy of Jazz Dance" course for moving our program forward, and by extension, to all university dance and dance education programs, I recommend that dance faculty:

- consider the impact of racism, whether implicit or explicit, across the curriculum and (re)develop courses accordingly;
- make more non-Eurocentric courses like "History, Culture, and Pedagogy of Jazz Dance" required instead of elective;
- revise terminology that marginalizes non-White dance (Why do we refer to "Black dance" but not to "White dance?");
- embed the Africanist aesthetic in teaching and learning, in addition to Western-oriented pedagogies; and
- reorder the institutional hierarchy.

Jazz dance can be taught by qualified dance educators, regardless of skin color, with respect, knowledge, and a large dose of humility in recognizing and acknowledging the truths of historical wrongdoing. We must acknowledge and directly address issues of race in jazz dance and in academia.

Notes

1. Nyama McCarthy-Brown, *Dance Pedagogy for a Diverse World: Culturally Relevant Teaching in Theory, Research and Practice* (Jefferson, NC: McFarland, 2017), 23.

2. Patricia Cohen, "Jazz Dance as a Continuum," in *Jazz Dance: A History of the Roots and Branches*, ed. Lindsay Guarino and Wendy Oliver (Gainesville: University Press of Florida, 2014), 5.

3. Sheron Wray, "A Twenty-First-Century Jazz Dance Manifesto," in *Jazz Dance: A History of the Roots and Branches*, ed. Lindsay Guarino and Wendy Oliver (Gainesville: University Press of Florida, 2014), 12.

4. Jacqui Malone, *Steppin' on the Blues: The Visible Rhythms of African American Dance* (Urbana: University of Illinois Press, 1996), 2.

5. Brenda Dixon Gottschild, *Digging the Africanist Presence in American Performance* (Westport, CT: Greenwood, 1994), 13–17.

6. See Julie Kerr-Berry's essay in this book.

7. Melanie George, "Jazz Is . . . ," https://melaniegeorge.org/jazzis.

8. Cohen, "Jazz Dance as a Continuum," 3–7.

9. Daria Fitzgerald, interview by author, November 17, 2019.

10. Lindsay Guarino, "Jazz Dance Training via Private Studios, Competitions, and Conventions," in *Jazz Dance: A History of the Roots and Branches*, ed. Guarino and Wendy Oliver (Gainesville: University Press of Florida, 2014), 205.

11. Michelle Cole, telephone conversation with author, November 18, 2019.

12. Jessa Rose VanHerwynen, telephone conversation with author, November 18, 2019.

13. Joya Powell, telephone conversation with author, November 20, 2019.

14. Afaliah Tribune, telephone conversation with author, November 20, 2019.

15. Michelle Cole, Whitley Green, and Chanda Thornton, telephone conversations with author, November 18–23, 2019.

16. Alexis Arlene Andrews, interview by author, November 22, 2019.

17. McCarthy-Brown, *Dance Pedagogy for a Diverse World*, 10.

18. Nyama McCarthy-Brown, "Owners of Dance: How Dance Is Controlled and Whitewashed in the Teaching of Dance Forms," in *The Palgrave Handbook of Arts and Race in Education*, ed. Amelia M. Krache, Ruben Gaztambide-Fernandez, and B. Stephen Carpenter II (Cham, Switzerland: Palgrave Macmillan, 2018), 470.

19. Carlos Jones, "Jazz Dance and Racism," in *Jazz Dance: A History of the Roots and Branches*, ed. Lindsay Guarino and Wendy Oliver (Gainesville: University Press of Florida, 2014), 231.

20. Joya Powell, telephone conversation with author, November 20, 2019.

21. Whitley Green, telephone conversation with author, November 18, 2019.

22. Kate Diaz, telephone conversation with author, November 14, 2019.

23. Rita Bearden, telephone conversation with author, November 14, 2019.

24. Sylvia Henao, telephone conversation with author, November 19, 2019.

25. Danielle Staropoli, telephone conversation with author, November 18, 2019.

26. Patricia Cohen, "History, Culture and Pedagogy of Jazz Dance," course syllabus.

27. Julie Kerr-Berry, "The Skin We Dance, the Skin We Teach: Appropriation of Black Content in Dance Education," *Journal of Dance Education* 4, no. 2 (2004): 46.

28. Afaliah Tribune, telephone conversation with author, November 20, 2019.

29. Karen Hubbard, "Valuing Cultural Context and Style: Strategies for Teaching Traditional Jazz Dance from the Inside Out," *Journal of Dance Education* 8, no. 4 (2008): 112.

30. Barbara Glass, *African American Dance: An Illustrated History* (Jefferson, NC: McFarland, 2007), 32.

31. Moncell Durden, "Hip-Hop Dance as Community Expression and Global Phenomenon," in *Jazz Dance: A History of the Roots and Branches*, ed. Lindsay Guarino and Wendy Oliver (Gainesville: University Press of Florida, 2014), 191.

32. Danielle Robinson, "Oh, You Black Bottom! Appropriation, Authenticity, and Opportunity in Jazz Dance Teaching of 1920s New York," *Dance Research Journal* 38, no. 1/2 (Summer & Winter 2006): 19–20.

33. Jones, "Jazz Dance and Racism," 236.

20

Preparing a Lecture-Demonstration on the History/Styles of Jazz Dance for K–12 Students

LYNNETTE YOUNG OVERBY

It begins with the dance and leads to a more just and inclusive society.
Overby

In our K–12 schools, the students may never experience jazz dance, or only in relation to a musical theater performance. Since the history of jazz dance is connected to the history of the United States of America, jazz dance can provide knowledge and appreciation of our cultural heritage. This heritage, rich with the contributions of people from around the world, also includes issues of racial discrimination that directly and indirectly impact African and African American influences on American history and culture. In the book *Jazz Dance: A History of the Roots and Branches,* a large tree is described as an apt image of jazz dance: a tree has roots, a trunk, and branches, as does jazz dance. The roots include the foundation of West African dance and music brought by Africans to America. The trunk is represented by vernacular jazz dances that emerged in America including the Charleston and the Lindy Hop. The branches include the dance forms of hip-hop, tap dance, and musical theater. The tree is also affected by European influences.[1] If I were to add another important component to this figure, it would be dark but lightening clouds of racial oppression.

Many years ago, as one of a very few African American graduate students in a dance history class in the Department of Dance at George Washington University, I was given a new book to review and present to the class. The book *Black Dance from 1619 to 1970,* by Lynne Fauley Emery,[2] provided a timeline and description of the contributions of African Americans to dance in the

United States. The African foundation and the European influences shaped by cultural realities informed the creation of dances that were described in the text.

A year or so later, I was teaching in a K–6 school in Washington, D.C. I decided to create a dance history program with my fourth- and fifth-grade students that focused on the history of Black dance, as presented in the Emery text, and enhanced with stories and dance moves from my friends and relatives. The performance included the Cakewalk, a dance associated with slavery, and vernacular dances including the Charleston and the Lindy Hop. Other dances included tap dance to music of Louis Armstrong, and the Negro Danced Spiritual in the spirit of the work of Edna Guy. The program continued with popping and locking and concluded with musical theater danced to music from the Broadway show *The Wiz*. The entire program was narrated with an emphasis on the historical context of the dances. The students took their danced living history to several D.C. public schools, providing many children with a glimpse into the rich history of African American culture through the lens of dance and music.

Since that first foray into combining history with dance, I have presented variations of this program in other venues including productions and lecture-demonstrations at Howard University, Michigan State University,[3] and the University of Delaware.[4] The content of the lecture-demonstrations has included American jazz dance, defined as "work that is rooted in the African vernacular that highlights rhythm and syncopation,"[5] and African American concert dance, identified as embodying and highlighting an African diaspora heritage.[6] Sources for the creation of these programs have included books, journal articles, videos, and personal communication.

Racial oppression is an important part of the narrative of African American dance.

Throughout a lecture-demonstration, the cultural constraints and influences can be emphasized in the narration as introduction to the dances. For example, during the program, the Cake Walk may be explained as a parody of the White slave masters' dances. When the use of drums was banned in 1730 for enslaved African Americans, it prompted them to transform the drumbeats into body rhythms, clapping, stamping, and tapping. A narrator may introduce vernacular dances by explaining how the Charleston and the Lindy Hop were a product of African rhythms and movements with influences from European social dances and concert dance forms. Students learn about the impact of imposed state and federal policies that caused economic and educational discrimination by segregating African Americans into separate schools and neighborhoods, and how this segregation of communities of color fostered the development of vernacular dance and music, including hip-hop.

When the program ends, students will have many questions about the dances, the dancers, and the history and racial issues. When a lecture-demonstration on the history of jazz dance is created and implemented in this way, we are presenting work not from a color-blind perspective but, rather, a color-conscious perspective.[7] There is much for the K–12 student to comprehend—the dances, the history, the cultural constraints, and the positive outcomes that emerged from oppressive conditions.

In developing a jazz dance lecture-demonstration designed for school-age students, goals may include (1) providing students with knowledge of the rich history of African American dance in America; (2) connecting the African American dance experience to the culture of racial inequities; and (3) introducing African American dance as an integral part of American history and culture.

The remainder of this chapter will focus on the nuts and bolts of preparing, implementing, and assessing a jazz dance lecture-demonstration program that resides in a university dance department.

PREPARING A JAZZ DANCE LECTURE-DEMONSTRATION

Community Engagement as a Framework

In the university setting, community engagement promotes the development of co-created, co-implemented, and co-assessed projects that make meaningful connections between academic and community goals.[8]

The first step in developing community engagement projects is to ensure that there are mutually beneficial outcomes for the community and the student or faculty member.

The first step can be achieved by focusing on community and university needs.

- Community needs: Focus on the educational standards of the fifth- to eighth-grade students or eleventh-grade students as this is the time that American history is taught in schools.
  Also, focus on the arts standards that will be met through this program.
- University needs: Focus on the mission of the department and the university. Many have statements about the need to apply disciplinary knowledge to community needs and challenges. Diversity is

also included in many mission statements. The production should include an application of disciplinary knowledge (dance) within a community setting.

Design Excellent Projects

Lecture-demonstrations typically take place for approximately forty-five minutes with time for questions at the conclusion of the program.

Contents of a Lecture-Demonstration on African American Dance:
- Choreographed dances based on research of YouTube videos, books, articles, and websites to gain knowledge of the specific dances and their connection to African American history.[9]

Sample Dance Program (fifth-grade students)
- A narrative introduction should occur before each dance. Information about racial discrimination and constraints may be shared that will place the dances within the context of U.S. history. The dances are reflective of a specific time period.
  - Dances of Enslaved Africans
    - Ring Shout
    - Cake Walk
  - Vernacular Dances of the 1920s through 1940s
    - Charleston
    - Lindy Hop
  - Tap Dance—using music of the 1940s such as "It Don't Mean a Thing," by Duke Ellington.
  - The Negro Danced Spiritual—An example of African American concert dance in the spirit of Edna Guy[10]
  - Vernacular Dances of the 1960s to 1970s (Twist, Jerk, Mashed Potato)

FIGURE 20.1. Ring Shout. Photo by Dan Dunlap.

- Hip-Hop
- Audience Participation
  - Students are invited onstage to participate in one or more aspects of the performance[11]

Contents of a Sample Jazz Dance Styles Lecture-Demonstration (secondary students)
- Jazz Dance Styles (Dances)
  - Lindsay Guarino and Wendy Oliver, "Jazz Dance Styles," chapter 5 in *Jazz Dance: A History of the Roots and Branches* (2014).[12]
  - Specific dances can be found on YouTube and in films, including dancers from 1800s to hip-hop available on DVD.[13]

Narration that introduces each dance, will provide context and connections to U.S. History:
- Introduction to Jazz Dance (Narration)
  - Sample Program on Jazz Dance Styles
    - Tap Dance
    - Theatrical Jazz Dance
    - Afro-Caribbean Jazz Dance
    - Broadway Jazz/Musical Theatre Jazz Dance
    - Hip-Hop Dance
    - Street Jazz Dance
  - Audience Participation
    - Students are invited onstage to dance

Design Educational Materials to Accompany the Production/ Lecture-Demonstration

The educational standards for history[14] and dance[15] focused on specific grade levels should be used to design appropriate information, lessons, and activities.

Educational materials should be included to provide (*a*) information about the history and development of each of the dances in societal context; (*b*) a photo of the jazz dance tree; (*c*) a list of resources, for example, videos, books, articles, and lesson plans. "Understanding Resilience through the Ring Shout Dance" was a lesson created by University of Delaware ArtsBridge Scholar that could accompany a lecture demonstration on the history of Jazz Dance.[16]

Design Appropriate Assessments

With a focus on the grade levels fifth, eighth, or eleventh, African American dance content will fit easily into the curriculum. Pre and post questions should be developed to assess the knowledge of the artistic and historical content of the production.

Sample Questions for African American Dance in America (1800s–Present Day):

What are the origins of the Cake Walk dance? Describe why perform-ing the Cake Walk was a reaction to being enslaved.

Who was Edna Guy? What was her major contribution to African American concert dance?

List and describe three African American vernacular dances. Include the decade of their creation.

Why do you think the Ring Shout is a Circle Dance? (Circle Dance is a genre of dance in many cultures around the world.) What could the circle formation represent in this culture?

What does the story behind the song "Move Daniel" tell us about U.S. Slave culture?

Develop Reflections for Performers

After the performance of the lecture-demonstration, the performers should reflect on the performance through a blog site or by maintaining an electronic or paper journal. After each performance, the dancers can respond to the fol-lowing sample prompts:

How do you feel about your performance today?

Describe one incident related to your performance (positive or negative).

How will you build upon the knowledge you gained to maintain or improve future performances?

Contact the School

A jazz dance lecture-demonstration focused on African American contribu-tions to the history of America through dance fits in well with the priorities of schools. The students will learn about the consequences of a segregated and discriminatory society through an uplifting and embodied tale.

By contacting the State Department of Education, you can receive a list of schools in the area. Determine the list of schools that will be the appropriate audiences for the lecture-demonstration content. Find out the contact person for the school, who may be the principal or the PTA president. Try to speak to the contact person by phone to determine their interest in the program. After speaking to someone who expresses interest in the project, follow up the call with an email message and by sending the brochure with all pertinent information, including potential dates and times for the program. If a school indicates interest in the program and selects a date, follow up with a contract that stipulates the needs of the performer and space and time considerations.

Consider Dissemination of Outcomes

Other dance educators will be interested in the contents of the lecture-demonstration and the student response to the program. Publications like the *Journal of Dance Education* and/or *Dance Education in Practice,* both from the National Dance Education Organization, are appropriate. Presentations to state, national, and international organizations also give the presenter an opportunity to share examples and meet other presenters who have similar programs. Dissemination to schools may include information for schools to share online or in newsletters. Lessons and curricula materials can also provide follow-up support for the teachers and schools.

The Marketing

Determining why touring a jazz dance lecture-demonstration is important will be the first step in successful marketing. Development of a short mission statement, logo, brochure, and website will promote the production.

When I directed a lecture/demonstration touring company at Michigan State University, I would send a brochure to local schools during the summer prior to the beginning of the school year informing them of the upcoming production with dates and costs. The brochure, although it did not have the specific content, aligned the proposed content with state and national educational standards. I believe this was a key component of the success we experienced for the tour bookings. Starting in July with the first mailings, the entire fifteen-week tour would be reserved by September 1.

By first creating a meaningful mission statement, the lecture-demonstration is grounded in specific vision and outcomes:

Who are you?
What do you do?
When are you available?
Where do you perform?
Why do you dance in this way?[17]

Sharing our Legacy Dance Theatre: Mission Statement and Impact

Sharing our Legacy Dance Theatre (SOL) is a company that performs dances inspired by African American historical content.[18] I formed this company as an umbrella for a series of arts-based social-justice productions. The company tours throughout the year under the sponsorship of the University of Delaware Community Engagement Initiative, Department of Theatre, and the Delaware Division of the Arts. Since 2012, the company of students and community members has performed for more than fifty thousand children and adults in Delaware, Virginia, Texas, Washington, D.C., South Carolina, and in South Africa, Australia, and Belize. In addition to the performances, SOL performers provide educational programming so that everyone can see, hear, and experience the power of the arts.

Brochure

The materials produced for the touring company should be visually captivating, with descriptions that promote interest and enthusiasm about the group. Excellent-quality photos, a stunning logo, and mission statement on fine-quality paper are important. The brochure should include a brief description of the production. Testimonials from past audience members and school personnel, including students and teachers, are also important to include in the literature. The brochure should include detailed information. In each school performance, the audience will see forty-five minutes of dance followed by ten minutes of time for audience questions. The company performs on a stage or in a gym or multipurpose room and provides its own sound and props. Teachers will also receive an educational packet with resources and sample lesson plans. Dressing rooms, a sound system, and three lavaliere microphones are needed for the production.

A word of caution from Ella Magruder about brochures: "A brochure serves as an introduction to your company but does not substitute for the personal contact that your booking manager or you make by phone or in person . . . Most people will just glance at a brochure. Make sure the brochure is distinctive and that your reader/viewer can understand quickly what you are saying, and sees only the best visual representation of your dance company."[19]

Website

Today, websites are essential to the marketing of a successful company. An ebrochure or photos and description can be sent to contacts with a link to a well-organized website. The website may also include dance clips, resources, testimonials from satisfied audiences, as well as opportunities to give donations and book programs.

A Day in the Life of a University Touring Company

The alarm goes off—5:00 a.m.! Time to prepare for the lecture-demonstration on African American dance history at Gains Elementary School. Gains is about forty-five minutes from the university. By 6:30, all of the dancers have arrived at the van and are loading props and costumes. With map in hand, I follow the directions to the school, while the dancers nap in their seats.

Approximately one hour later we arrive at the school. The cafetorium has a microphone, and the janitor has mopped the floors.

7:45 a.m.—Dancers warm up, and then begin spacing the dances. The audio equipment is tested, and the props are placed in their proper locations.

8:30 a.m.—The dancers are changing into their costumes and preparing for the production.

9:00 a.m.—The Gains Elementary School students are in place ready for the program to begin.

9:45 a.m.—The program concludes, and the performers take a bow, then introduce themselves. The students ask questions about the dancers and about the production.

10:00 a.m.—The students leave the cafetorium.

10:30 a.m.—Three of the dancers lead a class in an experiential workshop on the "Ring Shout" based on the production.

11:30 a.m.—The dancers go the cafeteria to have lunch with the students. The Gains Elementary students cheer as they enter the room.

12:30 p.m.—Everyone boards the van for the ride back to the university, completing a written reflection on the experience and feeling good about another opportunity to share the arts and history with young people.

Financial Considerations

Since I am primarily addressing artistic directors who are a part of universities, the information on financing is directly related to this group. In this section, I will discuss budgeting, grant writing, and fundraising.

Creating a Budget

In creating your budget, determine what it will cost to perform, assess, and disseminate products from the show.

Paying performers could be in cash or for school credit. If the program is a part of a community engagement experience for students, they should be required to complete reflections and connect their experience to their future careers in writing, photos, and blogs.

Grant Writing

Universities often have pots of money in several different offices. Grant writing will be essential in obtaining university and external funds. Internal funds could come from Community Engagement offices, Diversity offices, as well as dance, theater, or Black American studies departments.

Because universities are likely to be nonprofit entities, state and national arts organizations are likely targets, as are local foundations and businesses.

When approaching funding sources, first contact someone in the organization. At the university, the director or department head; in an external organization, the program director. Also, be certain to view the forms and read the information on requirements for the grant.

Grant writing takes time and effort. Grants require meeting specific internal and external deadlines necessary for submission through the university research office. Collecting pre-post survey data requires human-subject approval from the university institutional research office for ethical considerations. A well-written grant proposal has many positive benefits, including the requirement to prepare a clear compelling case for why the lecture-demonstration should receive funding.

Table 20.1. Sample budget of demonstration tour

REVENUE FROM TOUR	
$400 per performance for 20 performances	$8,000
DEBITS FROM TOUR	
Transportation (university van)	-$1,000
Costumes	-$1,000
Brochures and website maintenance	-$500
Research assistant	-$500
Video production	-$1,000
Payment to dancers (5), $30 per performance for 20 performances	-$3,000

Fundraising

Fundraising is also an option. The GoFundMe sites provide an opportunity to request funding support from family, friends, and acquaintances. Again, a well-established and attractive website with testimonials, videos, and educational materials may encourage individuals to support the program.

The Jazz Dance Lecture-Demonstration Is Ready!

The impact of the lecture-demonstration on jazz and African American dance styles and history is significant. Through this performance, a child may for the first time be able to connect their history to the rich cultural heritage of jazz dance. They may see, for the first time, university students passionately involved in sharing the message of history and art. Because of this program, a child may decide to study dance and/or history and, more importantly, see a way forward as a student in higher education.

The university students will benefit by moving out of their comfort zones and entering public schools as an educator/entertainer. I have seen many students transformed by the process—they are no longer just students but ambassadors of knowledge.

The artistic director of the lecture-demonstration will benefit by becoming a community-engaged scholar, creating a program that has impact on both the university student and the school-age students and teachers. I must admit, getting up at 5:00 a.m. on a cold winter morning and traveling to a school takes quite a commitment, but the rewards are many!

Creating a jazz dance–focused lecture-demonstration acknowledges the contributions of an oppressed people to the world of dance. Furthermore, by situating these specific dance forms within a historical context, K–12 students and the university students see more than the dance, and more than the history; they experience the creativity, determination, and achievements that begin with the dance and continue with a deepening appreciation for a more just and inclusive society.

NOTES

1. Lindsay Guarino and Wendy Oliver, *Jazz Dance: A History of the Roots and Branches* (Gainesville: University Press of Florida, 2014).

2. Lynne Fauley Emery, *Black Dance from 1619 to 1970* (Hightstown, NJ: Princeton Book Co., 1988).

3. Lynnette Y. Overby and Dixie Durr, "Dance in America: An African American Journey," paper presented at the Annual Conference of the Midwest Popular

Culture and Midwest American Culture Association, East Lansing, Michigan, October 1993.

4. Lynnette Y. Overby, Jennifer O. Shanahan, and Gregory Young, *Undergraduate Research in Dance* (New York: Routledge, 2020).

5. Gill Wright Miller, "The Transmission of African-American Concert Dance and American Jazz Dance," in *Jazz Dance: A History of the Roots and Branches,* ed. Lindsay Guarino and Wendy Oliver (Gainesville: University Press of Florida, 2014), 165.

6. Ibid.

7. Robin Prichard, "From Color-Blind to Color-Conscious," *Journal of Dance Education,* 2019, doi: 10.1080/15290824.2018.1532570.

8. Lynnette Y. Overby, "Jazz Dance as a Gateway to Community Engagement," in *Jazz Dance: A History of the Roots and Branches,* ed. Lindsay Guarino and Wendy Oliver (Gainesville: University Press of Florida, 2014), 217–27; Lynnette Y. Overby, *Public Scholarship in Dance* (Champaign, IL: Human Kinetics, 2016).

9. "They Danced to Tell the World about Living," Dancetime Publications, https://dancetimepublications.com/product-category/afro-american-history/.9; "Hellzapoppin' in Full Color," colorized with DeOldify, 2020, www.youtube.com/watch?v=dSAOV6XEjXA; *The Spirit Moves: A History of Black Social Dance on Film, 1900–1986,* "Part 1: Jazz Dance from the Turn of the Century to 1950."

10. Susan Manning, *Modern Dance, Negro Dance: Race in Motion* (Minneapolis: University of Minnesota Press, 2004).

11. Lynnette Y. Overby, "Ring Shout: Same Story Different Countries," www.youtube.com/watch?v=TniNKv6hSpk.

12. Lindsay Guarino and Wendy Oliver, "Jazz Dance Styles," in *Jazz Dance: A History of the Roots and Branches,* ed. Lindsay Guarino and Wendy Oliver (Gainesville: University Press of Florida, 2014), 24–31.

13. "They Danced to Tell the World about Living," Dancetime Publications, https://dancetimepublications.com/product-category/afro-american-history/.9.

14. "History/Social Studies," History/Social Studies, Common Core State Standards Initiative, www.corestandards.org/ELA-Literacy/RH/.

15. "National Core Arts Standards," Home, National Core Arts Standards, 2014, www.nationalartsstandards.org/.

16. Marielle Kraft "Understanding Resilience through the Ring Shout Dance," 2017, www.sharingourlegacy.org.

17. "Sharing Our Legacy Dance Theatre," Home, 2018, www.sharingourlegacy.org.

18. "Sharing Our Legacy Dance Theatre," Home, 2018, www.sharingourlegacy.org.

19. Ella Magruder, *Dancing for Young Audiences* (Jefferson, NC: McFarland, 2013), 54.

To Topple, Not Maintain

Changing Pedagogical Practice in the College Jazz Dance History Course

KAREN CLEMENTE

The history of jazz dance is rich, diverse, provocative, and far-reaching. The study of jazz dance history should be no less than that. Many of us who are teaching in colleges and universities today are the products of colonized curricula (from the private studio to academia) and continue to propagate the same information that we were taught. We either assume or perceive false barriers to any genuine curricular revision that espouses a full-fledged acknowledgment of the key element of jazz—African aesthetics. While we may indeed be teaching in colleges that have entrenched systems of pedagogy, now is the time to topple past practice and look to a future in which the core of dance curriculum content includes the heritage of African aesthetics and a connection to the African diaspora. This chapter describes a jazz dance history course taught at a liberal arts college that reflects ongoing efforts at decolonization in the dance program curriculum.

Ursinus College Dance Program Curriculum Change

At Ursinus College, in Collegeville, Pennsylvania, the dance major program has existed for approximately fifteen years, and in the last several years, the curriculum has been revised. Inspired by the research of Julie Kerr-Berry and Nyama McCarthy-Brown, supported by the faculty and administration of the college, and reflecting a changing demographic of dance students, the revised curriculum addressed four areas: technique classes, auditions, dance history courses, and dance concert pieces. In the two dance-history-specific courses— "History of Jazz Dance" and "History of Modern Dance"—the Africanist aesthetic is at the core of the syllabi, focusing on African American dancers and choreographers who have been given short shrift in history books. This chapter focuses on the pedagogical practice of the "History of Jazz Dance" course, including (1) a brief description of the course; (2) course content and student reaction; and (3) strategies for launching a process for change.

A REFLECTION OF QUEST: THE OPEN QUESTIONS/OPEN MINDS CORE CURRICULUM

The "History of Jazz Dance" course description is as follows:

> This course investigates the unique origin and evolution of jazz dance in America. The course will follow the chronological development of jazz dance, including: African dance and music source material; African American vernacular dance forms; the relationship to jazz music; the contributions of specific choreographers and styles; and the impact of popular entertainment, such as vaudeville, musical theater, films, television, and music videos. Students will develop an understanding of jazz dance in the United States as related to socio-political and cultural contexts in the 20th century and the beginning of the 21st century, including a study of race and gender relations and the dynamics of power and privilege. Throughout the course of the semester, students will have the opportunity to embody basic jazz dance movement principles of rhythm, improvisation, and musicality.[1]

The course was originally offered as part of the dance major/minor curriculum and as a component of the college-wide diversity course offerings; the last two times (2017/2019) the course ran in conjunction with the Ursinus Music Department's "History of Jazz" course. Students in both courses came together for combined lectures by the dance and music faculty and, in 2017, also co-produced a two-day jazz festival on campus. The festival was partially funded by the U-Imagine Center on campus that supports experiential, innovative, and entrepreneurial pedagogy. In 2019, the course was offered during the inaugural year of Ursinus's new Quest: Open Questions/Open Minds core curriculum that is centered on four questions: "*What should matter to me? How should we live together? How can we understand the world? What will I do?*"[2] The core questions set up a fertile classroom environment for the type of discourse that needs to occur to address issues of race, power, White privilege, and appropriation that are part of an authentic inquiry into jazz dance history. The course, then, challenges students to investigate their own experience against the backdrop of an evolving social climate, with issues of diversity and inequality at the forefront.

COURSE CONTENT: SELECTED COURSE LEARNING EXPERIENCES

The "History of Jazz Dance" course focuses on the Black American roots of jazz dance, with attention to social consciousness. Selected course learning experiences include:

Required Course Textbook and Other Required Reading

The primary required course text is *Jazz Dance: A History of the Roots and Branches,* edited by Lindsay Guarino and Wendy Oliver,[3] with additional, required supplemental readings. Two readings supplement the course text and set up the swing lessons using an interdisciplinary approach that includes historical and technical perspectives from both music and dance. These are Brenda Dixon Gottschild's "Legacy: All That Jazz," from *Waltzing in the Dark: African American Vaudeville and Race Politics in the Swing Era,* which discusses the effects of the swing aesthetic on the social, cultural, and political aspects of American life from the 1920s through the mid -1940s;[4] and an excerpt from Marshall Stearns and Jean Stearns's *Jazz Dance: The Story of American Vernacular Dance* on the origins of the Shim Sham, a tap and jazz dance standard.[5] Thomas DeFrantz's "African American Dance: A Complex History," from *Dancing Many Drums: Excavations in African American Dance,* provides a context for the landscape of jazz dance scholarship prior to 2002, investigating the relationship of vernacular dance to "art dance," while highlighting the problematic aspect of stereotypical and static definitions of jazz dance.[6] Jacqui Malone's chapter "Keep to the Rhythm and You'll Keep to Life: Meaning and Style in African American Vernacular Dance," from her *Steppin' on the Blues: The Visible Rhythms of African American Dance,* provides a specific reference point for viewing historical dance video footage by identifying what she describes as the "six definitive characteristics of African American vernacular dance . . . *rhythm, improvisation, control, angularity, asymmetry, and dynamism.*"[7]

Course readings are the foundation for inquiry-based classroom learning experiences. During the last time the course was offered, one such classroom experience included a Skype session with Carlos Jones, author of "Jazz Dance and Racism,"[8] in a discussion of key points from the essay that have implications for teaching jazz dance today. The virtual session with Professor Jones was a highlight of the semester, as students remarked over and over again that having access to the author of a required reading brought the chapter to life for them. In preparation for the session, students were asked to consider the following questions:

1. Why is the definition of jazz dance, as described by Jones, enigmatic?
2. Though jazz dance was clearly rooted in an African American aesthetic, in what ways was the Black presence systematically omitted in the early part of the twentieth century?
3. How is the African aesthetic in jazz dance portrayed as less important than the European aesthetic in the 1960s example of the British television series *Ready Steady Go*?
4. As jazz dance technique was codified in the latter half of the twentieth century, how did the European aesthetic take precedence over the authentic roots of jazz?
5. What solutions does Jones suggest to counteract racism as jazz dance continues to evolve?

Additional questions and new themes emerged in the hour-long session with Jones; students were engaged in a conversation that was relevant not only to their study of jazz dance history but to their everyday lives. In this assignment, students were clearly encountering the core curriculum questions of *What should matter to me?* and *How should we live together?* as they discussed the marginalization of key jazz dance icons and discussed strategies to counteract similar racist omissions in the future.

Another extension of the course text is a lecture that I developed entitled "Rhythm, Race, and Rip-off: Tap Dance in the 1930's and 1940's" that expands upon Susie Trenka's "Vernacular Jazz Dance and Race in Hollywood Cinema."[9] In that lecture, I show film clips of African American tap dancers (e.g., Nicholas Brothers, Jeni LeGon, and Bill Robinson) and then discuss the beauty and power of the Africanist performance aesthetic that was most often relegated to stereotypical portrayals and not fully acknowledged for its brilliance and genius. Here, students are introduced to film clips that they have not previously seen and to artists who have been on the fringe of their experience. They are genuinely surprised and amazed that they have never experienced most of the artists' work, even if they had some prior exposure to tap and jazz dance history. Here, as well as with other aspects of the course content, the core curriculum question of *How can we understand the world?* is addressed, as the study of jazz dance history becomes the window into understanding the sociocultural history of the United States in the twentieth and twenty-first centuries.

Combined Classes

Content addressed in the combined dance and music classes has been: minstrelsy, swing music and dance, bebop, 1980s jazz dance, and hip-hop. Specifically, for the combined class period on the topic of minstrelsy, students watch "Gumbo (Beginnings to 1917)" from the Ken Burns documentary *Jazz*[10] and read "Jim Crow, Juba and the Minstrels" and "Late Minstrelsy and the Soft-Shoe Shuffle," from *Black Dance* by Edward Thorpe.[11] During the class session, students and faculty engage in difficult discussions concerning the nineteenth- and twentieth-century tradition of minstrelsy, its dehumanization of African American people, as well as its proliferation of harmful racial stereotypes, and the preponderance of such in contemporary times (e.g., Halloween costumes, political figures in racist photos, jewelry and fashion items, etc.). Many students in the most recent class admitted that they had no knowledge of the history of blackface and of the tradition of minstrelsy and, prior to the class session, no historical context for present-day experience. The conversations proved to be invaluable to an authentic study of the roots of jazz and its relationship to human experience.

In a later swing dance session, I use authentic jazz dance movement learned firsthand from African American dancers Frankie Manning and Karen Hubbard. Prior to the dance class, students watch and discuss the following film clips: Savoy Ballroom: Benny Goodman vs Chick Webb (Battle of the Bands);[12] Lindy Hop movies: *Keep Punchin'* (1938), with "The Big Apple" danced by Whitey's Lindy Hoppers;[13] "Frankie Manning Tribute Video";[14] and *The Swing Thing* BBC documentary directed by Alan Lewens.[15]

Following the dance class, we discuss the music and dance of the swing era, and how they make one "feel" in the body, pointing out that the cross-disciplinary learning of the course provides students with the opportunity to experience swing music in its original context, combining music and dance. Without the experiential "knowing" found through dancing, the swing class would be missing the primary component—the feel of swing in the body. We also discuss the complicated history of race relations at the Savoy Ballroom in Harlem, New York, focusing on the issue of "giving credit where credit is due" with regard to Chick Webb's band topping Benny Goodman's band in the momentous evening entitled "The Battle of the Bands."[16] Last, we talk about the decline of swing dance as jazz music evolved into the bebop era, making way for a sound that was predominantly for listening. (Note: the informed jazz dance scholar can bring illumination to the historical misunderstanding that jazz dance completely diminished during the bebop era by selecting, among other examples, Dizzy Gillespie's film *Jivin' in Bebop* [1946][17] for classroom viewing.) Overall, the opportunity to combine dance and music classes and work with a music colleague who has expertise in jazz music history has led to a core curriculum "linked inquiry" designation for the courses; such courses are a requirement for all students at the college.

Guest Artist Classes

Throughout the semester, students watch footage of many styles of jazz dance, encompassing a range of jazz dance artists. They also experience jazz dance guest-artist classes. Classes have included African dance, tap dance, authentic/ vintage jazz dance, Neo-jazz, Luigi jazz style, and hip-hop. Students enjoy the guest classes that give them the opportunity to embody numerous styles; one student commented after a Luigi master class that she enjoyed taking the class since it was close to her first love, ballet. This opens up a conversation about the European influence on jazz dance, especially with regard to terminology, and how most of the students' experience in jazz dance is based on a European-based norm. At the end of the course, as part of a final exam review, students participate in a "cocktail party," each one being assigned a particular jazz dance artist studied throughout the semester. Students assume the role of the artist and talk candidly about aspects of racial inequity that concerned them about the artists' careers. Imagine the following two scenarios: Katherine Dunham asking Jack Cole about his privileged position of having a training studio on the Columbia Studios lot;[18] and Eleanor Powell expressing her apologies to Jeni LeGon who lost her MGM contract due to "out dancing" Ms. Powell in public.[19]

Attendance at Off-Campus Events Grounded in an Africanist Aesthetic

Students and the course professor attend live dance performances in nearby Philadelphia that are grounded in an Africanist aesthetic. A recent highlight was attending a performance of Dawn Marie Bazemore's *Letters* (a performance piece consisting of letters the artist wrote to people she considered "unreachable") and *The Browder Project* (the artist's collaborative work that tells the story of Kalief Browder, who was unjustly imprisoned at Rikers Island for a crime he did not commit, and later died due to suicide brought on by extreme trauma).[20] The students prepared for the performance by reading

Bazemore's article "Dance and Activism: The Practice and Impact of Sociopolitical Concert Dance"[21] and by investigating the Kalief Browder Foundation, which is dedicated to "eliminating racial disparities that permeate the "Justice System.""[22] A postperformance talk-back moderated by dance scholar Brenda Dixon Gottschild began with the prompt: "think of a time when you were accused of something that you didn't do."[23] Audience members considered that question and discussed the power of the Kalief Browder piece. A particularly poignant aspect of the evening was Akeem Browder's participation in the talk-back as he discussed his work with the Kalief Browder Foundation that honors his brother's legacy. Upon returning to the classroom, students in the jazz dance history course continued the discussion of the performance, relating the movement and thematic motifs to course content encountered throughout the entire semester. Students raised the issue of the effects of racism on everyday life and claimed the importance of dance as an agent for social change. In a tangible way, students were addressing the core curriculum question, *What will I do?* as, beyond describing the impact of socially conscious dance, they also discussed their future role in addressing racial inequality through such organizations as the Kalief Browder Foundation. The proximity of Ursinus College to Philadelphia is important for encouraging students to experience professional performance pieces that enhance their experience of dance. Providing opportunities for off-campus experiences is a priority for a dance program that wishes to diversify and inspire.

Action Strategies to Topple Current Practice

Changing an Individual Mind-set

To begin to change current practice, dance educators need to first be willing to ask themselves: Am I willing to change? Am I willing to give up "coverage" of a range of curriculum content that heretofore I believed was "necessary" to the teaching of jazz dance history? Am I willing to shift focus to the African American artists who undoubtedly were the nexus of the jazz dance genre and give less emphasis to the White artists considered the "pillars" of jazz dance technique? Notice if you have reservations or feel resistance while encountering such questions. Answering these questions with integrity and based on current research in the field is fundamental to making a true change.

Addressing Change at the Student Level

Students often replicate what they are taught. Create an exciting environment that highlights Africanist, authentic jazz dance. Share the autobiographies of African American jazz dance artists whose stories have not been told. Screen vintage film footage and discuss the work of seminal artists. Invite guest teachers to your classroom/studio who will genuinely inspire students in creating a new aesthetic. When ideas flop, try something else. The work speaks for itself and will eventually take hold with students. This is a given.

Addressing Change at the Departmental Level

All dance curriculum in higher education is ultimately shaped by the professors who teach the courses. Take an inventory of degree requirements and existing courses, proceeding toward a justice-based curriculum overhaul. If you encounter pushback at the departmental level, produce current pedagogical research that substantiates your desire for a more equitable curriculum that centers African diasporic dance forms. Find allies in the department and across the college (students, faculty, and administrators) who will support your cause.

In the revision of the dance curriculum at Ursinus College, in addition to teaching dance history courses from an Africanist aesthetic, the most recent set of requirements that relate to technique courses includes a deemphasizing of the Western dance canon; now, a student may choose a combination of three different genres (including African, jazz, modern, ballet, hip-hop, and special topics, such as tap) to meet the Dance program requirements. Dance faculty work with students to design a technical training program that works for their interests and future goals. The prospective student audition process also does not privilege European dance forms; in fact, over the past four years, the dance scholarship audition began with an African dance technique class.

The Ursinus College Dance Program also produces concerts that include Africanist roots-based dance pieces, including an annual African dance residency, jazz and tap dance pieces, and hip-hop. Student choreographers also have created dance in the vernacular jazz idiom, perhaps as a result of their expanded understanding of the jazz dance genre, which, earlier, may have been marginally understood or misrepresented in their precollege dance studio training. This approach to concert dance helps to diversify offerings and increase exposure to dance that reflects the African diaspora.

FIGURE 21.1. Jackie Henigan, Kevin Harris, and Justine Cinalli (*left to right*) perform *Swing, Eva, Swing!* by choreographer Carlos R. A. Jones at Ursinus College, November 2019. Juliana Wall Photography.

Addressing Change at the Institutional Level

Moving beyond your department, make your voice heard across your institution. Assistance may come from obvious places; at Ursinus College, this is the African American and Africana Studies Program and the Institute for Inclusion and Equity. Look for ways to partner with programs, departments, centers, and offices at your institution that may not be as visible, but that value diversity and want to actualize calls for an inclusive curriculum. As stated earlier, the new Ursinus Quest core curriculum grounded in four questions provides a fertile soil for growing curricular programs that ask students to consider what matters to them, how they should live together, how they can know the world and what will they do in the future. The "History of Jazz" course is a good fit at Ursinus, where a reenvisioning of the entire curriculum is in process—a process that values an inquiry approach to education, providing meaningful content that assists students in deciphering core questions from a socially conscious perspective. Look closely at your particular institution for ways in which a jazz dance curriculum can provide rich learning experiences across the campus. Specifically, volunteer for service on committees that have institutional diversity and inclusion on their agenda; align your jazz dance curricular offerings with that agenda, focusing on racial equity as the priority for curricular issues related to jazz dance.

At Ursinus College, the process of toppling the Western canon of dance in order to bring about equity with regard to dances of the African diaspora is ongoing, but not without challenges. Students and faculty may want to cling to their past understanding of the nature of dance, most probably because it is familiar and feels most comfortable. For the majority of students, however, the new approach is a rich experience and one that most closely mirrors the world around them. By continuing to center the curriculum in an Africanist aesthetic, we reflect the bedrock of American dance in its authentic state.

Notes

1. "Ursinus College," www.ursinus.edu/academics/theater-and-dance/courses/.

2. "Ursinus College," www.ursinus.edu/academics/catalog/open-questions-core-curriculum/.

3. Lindsay Guarino and Wendy Oliver, eds., *Jazz Dance: A History of the Roots and Branches* (Gainesville: University Press of Florida, 2014).

4. Brenda Dixon Gottschild, "Legacy: All That Jazz," in *Waltzing in the Dark: African American Vaudeville and Race Politics in the Swing Era* (New York: St. Martin's, 2000), 203–30.

5. Marshall Stearns and Jean Stearns, *Jazz Dance: The Story of American Vernacular Dance* (New York: Macmillan, 1968), 195–96.

6. Thomas F. DeFrantz, "African American Dance: A Complex History," in *Dancing Many Drums: Excavations in African American Dance,* ed. DeFrantz, 11–17 (Madison: University of Wisconsin Press, 2002).

7. Jacqui Malone, *Steppin' on the Blues: The Visible Rhythms of African American Dance* (Urbana: University of Illinois Press, 1996), 32.

8. Carlos Jones, "Jazz Dance and Racism," in *Jazz Dance: A History of the Roots and Branches*, ed. Lindsay Guarino and Wendy Oliver, 231–39 (Gainesville: University Press of Florida, 2014).

9. Susie Trenka, "Vernacular Jazz Dance and Race in Hollywood Cinema," in *Jazz Dance: A History of the Roots and Branches*, ed. Lindsay Guarino and Wendy Oliver, 240–48 (Gainesville: University Press of Florida, 2014).

10. *Jazz: A Film by Ken Burns*, dir. Ken Burns (PBS, 2001).

11. Edward Thorpe, "Jim Crow, Juba and the Minstrels," and "Late Minstrelsy and the Soft-Shoe Shuffle," in *Black Dance,* 40–49 (New York: Overlook, 1990).

12. "Savoy Ballroom: Benny Goodman vs Chick Webb (Battle of the Bands)," www.youtube.com/watch?v=EbamDNDoJuo.

13. Lindy Hop movies: *Keep Punchin'* (1938), with "The Big Apple" danced by Whitey's Lindy Hoppers, www.savoystyle.com/big_apple.html.

14. "Frankie Manning Tribute Video" (Swing Bud Films, 2009), www.youtube.com/watch?v=m34eD21QzUw.

15. *The Swing Thing* documentary, dir. Alan Lewens (BBC 4), www.youtube.com/watch?v=Anob9IMBE70.

16. "Savoy Ballroom: Benny Goodman vs Chick Webb (Battle of the Bands)," www.youtube.com/watch?v=EbamDNDoJuo.

17. Dizzy Gillespie, *Jivin' in Be-Bop,* documentary (Starry Night Video, 1946).

18. Jones, "Jazz Dance and Racism," 237.

19. Trenka, "Vernacular Jazz Dance," 243.

20. Dawn Marie Bazemore/#dbdanceproject, www.dbdanceproject.com, www.performancegarage.org/2019-dancevisions.

21. *Tarrytown (NY) Dancer-Citizen*, http://dancercitizen.org/issue-1/dawn-marie-bazemore/.

22. Kalief Browder Foundation, www.kaliefbrowderfoundation.com/.

23. Brenda Dixon Gottschild, postperformance talk-back moderator for a performance of *Letters and the Browder Project* by Dawn Marie Bazemore, Philadelphia, April 2019. www.dbdanceproject.com.

Monique Marie Haley, River North Chicago Dance Company 20th Anniversary (2009). Erika Dufour Photography, Inc.

V

The Future of Jazz Dance

The future of jazz dance in the twenty-first century will necessarily be related to the future of race and race relations in the United States. Two chapters give consideration to the challenges and opportunities for jazz dance within this race-conscious framework. The first, written by White authors Lindsay Guarino and Wendy Oliver, follows three different themes, including the discussion of jazz as a Black American art form; interconnections between jazz music and jazz dance; and the future of jazz studies in the academy. The second chapter is a personal statement by Black choreographer/educator Carlos Jones, explaining his understanding of how race and colonization have shaped his own development as an artist, and how he has come to terms with that. He closes with a call for change throughout the jazz dance field.

In a field where the very way we work is defined by our humanity, we as artists can be progressive in our calls for equity and justice. Together, let's move advocacy to action.

22

Connective Threads

Jazz Aesthetics, Jazz Music, and the Future of Jazz Dance Studies

LINDSAY GUARINO AND WENDY OLIVER

The study of jazz is the study of a Black American art form; its language is inextricably connected to the African American experience and distinctive due to racial tensions that manifest as aesthetic elements. Although it has been widely documented that jazz is a product of cultural transmission, West African at its roots with varying amounts of European and Latin American influences depending on the time, place, and style,[1] there are elements unique to jazz that make the form distinctly different from West African or European dance forms. Understanding exactly *what it is* that is different is the real conundrum.

Perhaps the reason jazz has been so difficult to define is because conversations about race, and between races, have never sat comfortably in American discourse. At the end of the first episode of the Ken Burns's PBS documentary titled *Jazz*, Wynton Marsalis attempts to talk about the connection between jazz and race. After contemplating, "well, race is a . . . ," he pauses for fourteen seconds. The gravity of the silence is laden with emotion, giving credence to his experience as a Black jazz musician:

> Race is like, for this country, it's like, the thing in the story, in the mythology, that you have to do for the kingdom to be well. And it is always something you don't want to do. And it is always that thing that is so much about you confronting yourself, that is tailor-made for you to fail dealing with it. And the question of your heroism, and of your courage, and of your success at dealing with this trial is: can you confront it with honesty, and do you confront it, and do you have the energy to sustain an attack on it? And since jazz music is at the center of American

mythology, it necessarily deals with race. The more we run from it, the more we run into it.[2]

Jazz dance, like jazz music, has largely ignored the role of race within the art form. Practitioners and appreciators need to acknowledge and understand the underlying racism inherent in the form in order to understand jazz clearly and approach it responsibly.

In "Five Premises for a Culturally Sensitive Approach to Dance," Deidre Sklar asserts that all movement is the embodiment of cultural knowledge: "It is time to deal with movement in a culturally sensitive way and to give movement a more central place in the study of culture and culture a more central place in the study of movement."[3] To get to the center of jazz, to define it from the inside out, is to confront the great injustices that birthed the jazz language. From its most inhumane origins grew a language of democratic freedom. The defining characteristics of jazz are there, in the paradox, an essence only to be uncovered through a process of self-examination. To see jazz is to confront

FIGURE 22.1. Decidedly Jazz Danceworks' Natasha Korney and Kaleb Tekeste (2013). Photo by Trudie Lee Photography. Courtesy of DJD.

ourselves, as Marsalis said, regardless of race or origin. Jazz is, as Melanie George lists in her Jazz Is . . . Dance Project mantra, humanity.[4]

A twenty-first-century definition of jazz dance exposes previously concealed truths and interrogates mainstream narratives that shape public perceptions. The way into the center of this "American mythology" is only revealed by listening to the Black perspective, past and present. As jazz musician and scholar Lewis Porter called for decades ago, one must "view things from the black perspective as much as possible . . . it is crucial to make the attempt, not for some vague reason of fairness but for the very specific reason that one simply cannot understand many important historical and musical facts if one looks at them entirely from a non-black cultural viewpoint."[5]

Pat Taylor bears witness to this truth to be uncovered at the core of jazz in her chapter in this volume, "The Duality of the Black Experience as Jazz Language," when she identifies the dynamic tension of jazz as a reflection of "the oppositional forces and realities of daily Black life." With this in mind, what separates jazz from other dance forms is in the dynamic extremes born from the lived experience of Blackness. Tension and release. Resistance and freedom. Hot and cool. Oppression and democracy. As Taylor describes herself and her company members, "we are dutifully and inspirationally aware and conscious of [the lived experience of Blackness], and we seek it out as an expressive ideal."

A rooted understanding of jazz is steeped in respect and tradition, body and soul. In "Must Be the Music," LaTasha Barnes shares: "As a result, my body has developed to instinctively respond to the visceral call of the music with consideration of traditions as well as the *seemingly* ingenious possibilities that manifest within me. In doing this, I convey my truth through movement in the moment." With music as a portal and a reverence for the elders that created the jazz form, she considers herself a "conduit" and a "tradition-bearer." Converging the visceral, or embodied, with that which comes from deep within, is what Brenda Dixon Gottschild calls "soul power" in her book *The Black Dancing Body.*[6] When performers are doing "what they are supposed to do,"[7] as exemplified by Barnes and explained by Gottschild, they "act as mediators and conduits between the observer and the intangibles manifested in the words, music notes, or dance steps of their medium."[8] This sacred space is where the body manifests spirit through *soul power*.

Gottschild names the Africanist aesthetic as the means for expressing the spirit in African American expressive performance styles. By digging down into the soul, the spirit is released through "radical juxtaposition of unanticipated elements; call-and-response; polyphony and syncopation; ephebic energy; and the balance between hot and cool."[9] The Africanist elements explored and expressed throughout this book, languaged in different ways by different authors, all act as gateway to the intangible spirit—the essence of jazz that is inherently Black. E. Moncell Durden confirms this in his chapter, "The Morphology of Afro-Kinetic Memory: A Provocative Analysis of Marginalized Jazz Dance," when he writes: "From my position as a Black dancer, I know there exist impalpable elements that lie beyond physical movement. They are intangibles that tether jazz dance to an African American experience and hold a deep structural cellular memory of African aesthetics, traditions, and rituals." At the core of jazz dance, Africanist aesthetics and the African American experience are indivisible. To dig deep and express truth (*soul power*) in jazz, the continuum of Africanist aesthetics informed by the essence and lived experience of African Americans is the vital thread.

Africanist elements are equally palpable in jazz music; their presence speaks to the "deep structural cellular memory" described by Durden while taking on a uniquely African American aesthetic feel. An essential ingredient that defined jazz as separate from its roots and early influences, or what is recognized in West African and European folk music, according to American jazz critic and musicologist Marshall Stearns, is swing. In *The Story of Jazz*, he describes the original jazz rhythms as "fairly simple" in contrast to West African rhythms.[10] And yet, "Theorists tell us that there is no limit to the complexities that can be superimposed upon march rhythm—and that is what jazz is doing."[11] While a jazz player accents around the continuous rhythm, it sets up "a contrasting tension which is released when, by means of more unexpected accents, he catches up . . . It's also a kind of rhythmic game. The effect on the listener varies: he may want to sing, dance, shout, or even hit somebody. Somehow he wants to express himself."[12] In the pedagogy section of this book, Karen Hubbard states that the main identifying feature of jazz dance is swing: "For all of the bodily actions and rhythmic nuances to come together as jazz dance, the quality *swing* must be a consistent element." The dancer, as both listener and instrument, embodies the contrasting tensions—or duality—connecting the uniqueness of jazz rhythms and its resulting physical expression to the Black American experience.

Rooted jazz dance and jazz music use the same language, sharing the same early history, sociocultural concerns and implications, and aesthetic underpinnings. And yet the two mediums entered the academy separately, the scholarship disjointed. As jazz music forged ahead, making headway for jazz research and education, it seems that jazz dance became all but stuck. The rich dialogue that could have ensued between music and dance in jazz studies never occurred, and jazz dance succumbed to a crisis of identity. As the dancing evolved in the late twentieth century, it distorted and flattened as it was forced into submission by the dominant culture, forgoing the qualities within jazz that created a distinctly jazz essence and upheld Black American cultural values. The absorption of jazz into a more mainstream American identity made the dance more confusing with each passing year. Dancers assume the moniker "jazz" without ever dancing to jazz music. Jazz musicians took notice, assuming that *their* jazz language was not *ours*.[13] With little collaboration between jazz musicians and dancers, minimal jazz dance scholarship, and few programs dedicated to nurturing jazz as equal to Western theatrical dance forms, jazz dance became more ambiguous while jazz music grew in stature and recognition both nationally and globally.

In 1988, jazz music historian and critic Lewis Porter noted that "jazz research seems to be coming of age in the academic world."[14] He saw a dramatic increase in jazz scholarship, commitment to jazz as an academic subject, and overall investment in the status of jazz as an art form. This was not without consequence for Black jazz musicians. American educational institutions marginalized Black Americans throughout history; hegemonic systems formed by White-supremacist views provided inroads for White jazz musicians to become gatekeepers within the academy, while limiting access for Black American youth to learn and play their music.[15] Regardless, in the late twentieth century, jazz music became anchored within American universities, and institutes, journals, festivals, and educational programs became widespread.

It might be precipitous to say that jazz dance is having its "coming-of-age" moment in the academic world today, but there is definitely movement in that direction. This moment comes more than thirty years after Porter noticed a similar pivotal time in jazz music in 1988, writing: "There is a growing commitment to jazz as an academic subject, and colleges are actively seeking qualified teachers. The positions always require teaching other subjects in addition to jazz, but progress is clearly being made."[16] It is worth noting that, at the time of this book's publication, similar progress is evident in calls for jazz dance and historically marginalized dance forms within the academy.[17] When reflecting on the widespread efforts at decolonization in dance program curricula, scholar and artist-educator Cynthia Oliver responded, "I don't know that America as a whole is ready for it, but it feels like institutions are finally ready to look at the ways inequity has historically been established and continues through the systems in place."[18] While "artists of color have been doing this work for a really long time,"[19] today's efforts are organizing artists across racial lines with a sense of urgency.

It is not only artists who are calling for marginalized histories and practices to be brought front and center. The call for change in the academy cuts across disciplines, as advertisements for tenure-track positions in a variety of Black-focused areas signals an increased interest in Black representation on campuses nationwide. In a January 2021 issue of the "Jobs" section of the *Chronicle of Higher Education*, a search of some relevant terms was conducted through the *Chronicle*'s online search function.[20] Searching all full-time, tenure-track listings in academia with two different search terms yielded the following figures: Black studies, 75 listings; African American studies, 90 listings. A few examples of the full-time professor listings were Black studies at SUNY, New Paltz, and University of Oregon; Black queer studies at the University of Texas, Austin, and Black children's literature at University of California at San Diego. Providence College advertises three different interdisciplinary tenure-track positions that marry Black studies with modern languages, sociology and anthropology, and health policy and management. Black studies departments are also a logical link for jazz dance in academe, as they have been for jazz music and other Black-originated art forms.

By forging connections to jazz music programs, Black studies programs, and African diasporic studies, jazz dance may be able to more easily "unearth" or reveal its roots. While some university dance programs have a strong focus on African diasporic dance, far more programs focus predominantly on ballet and contemporary dance. In this situation, the roots of jazz dance and other Black forms may get only a cursory mention, or alternatively, may be deeply explored, but in only one or two courses. The movement to diversify dance curriculums and faculty could be enhanced and accelerated through interdisciplinary work among departments and programs that study race, racism, and the arts in ways that intersect. Some programs and institutes have been created specifically for this purpose, for instance, the Berklee Institute of Jazz and Gender Justice, and Harvard University's Creative Practice and Critical Inquiry doctoral program, founded by musicians and activists.[21]

In his article "Jazz Has Always Been Protest Music: Can It Meet This Moment?" music writer Giovanni Russonello suggests that there is a problem in the academy, where jazz music, like jazz dance, has become divorced from its Black American roots. Nicole Mitchell, head of the Jazz Studies Program at the University of Pittsburgh, noted of her earlier experience in the New School's jazz program this fundamental problem: "At the center of the teaching would always be the idea that jazz is not about race. And it absolutely is. It was absolutely about where people weren't allowed to go, which made them travel in their music."[22] A new group called the We Insist! Collective released a statement in August 2020 listing demands for jazz institutions: "Educational institutions must commit to revamping their curriculums around an antiracist understanding ... A Black Public Arts Fund must be created to help increase the representation of African American students in jazz programs. And educational institutions should work in partnership with 'grass-roots local community organizations,' recognizing where the music has historically grown."[23]

Jazz music and jazz dance in the academe must acknowledge and embrace the Black American roots of the art form, and be publicly committed to the development of explicitly antiracist, historically informed spaces for jazz dance to thrive in the future.

Another potential model for Black dance in academe, including jazz dance, are the curricula and underlying values in historically Black colleges and universities (HBCUs). HBCUs celebrate diasporic cultural heritage in myriad ways on campus, including through dance. Researchers Wanda Ebright and Gary Guffey state that HBCU dance programs have developed "their institutional visions and missions in a manner that offers students an experience of American higher education in dance, while honoring how the African diaspora persists in and through these experiences."[24] Dance curricula at these institutions center diasporic dance forms such as jazz and West African dance, while also offering Eurocentric forms including ballet and modern dance. Ebright and Guffey's research shows that it is easier to find graduated levels of diasporic forms at an HBCU than at a PWI (primarily White institution), and that diasporic forms are also more likely to be required than at a PWI. They also point out that most HBCU dance faculty have been trained in diasporic dance forms, unlike instructors at PWIs.[25] The authors reference the Dance 2050 Vision Document, created by members of the National Dance Education Organization, noting that by the midpoint of this century, things will look different: "Dance units and programs within academia provide opportunities to study and perform diverse styles, idioms, and genres of global dance technique and choreography, and they promote the diverse cultural values expressed through these global dance practices. All forms of dance are seen as global dance forms."[26]

If this is the case, then a variety of dance genres, especially including African diasporic forms such as West African dance, Afro-Caribbean dance, tap, jazz, and hip-hop, will be in demand. This prediction is based on ideas related to population change, as well as diversity, equity, and inclusion initiatives. The Brookings Institute states that the so-called "minority population" will become the majority in or around 2045 in the United States.[27] As a result, more students of color will be attending primarily White institutions. Secondly, higher education is awakening to the idea that it is desirable to have a more inclusive curriculum and faculty in order to serve not only students of color, but White students. An education that does not include the histories or art forms of (currently) minority populations is incomplete.

Based on anecdotal evidence and job postings on various websites, it appears that PWI have begun tenure-track hiring in these areas. This will meet the interests of their students, as well as fulfill their institutions' quests for diversity, equity, and inclusion within the curriculum, in dance and beyond.[28] Ebright and Guffey emphasize that HBCUs could serve as models for the successful inclusion of diverse dance genres, honoring the Black experience, yet also including ballet, modern, and other forms originating from outside the African diaspora. This diversity of experience allows HBCU graduates to be extremely prepared to meet the challenges of teaching within either PWIs or HBCUs, or becoming professional dancers in a variety of contexts.

Academe is not the only place where change is needed. In addition to establishing tenure-track lines and programs within universities, the dance world at large needs to become educated about the roots of jazz dance and its accompanying racial tensions. Professional jazz dance companies that connect to the roots of the form must be acknowledged and supported by grant-giving organizations, just as ballet and modern companies have been. Jazz dance training in studios and schools needs to stop perpetuating Eurocentric biases that position ballet as the foundation for jazz, and should teach jazz in its historical and social contexts. Jazz dance companies and choreographers should be seriously considered as potential winners of important prizes and awards, such as those given by Capezio and the MacArthur Foundation. Jazz dance should figure more prominently in prestigious national dance festivals, such as those at Jacob's Pillow or the American Dance Festival.

The desire for jazz to become a better-understood and more respected art form is driven by the need to recognize its African roots. However, naming the roots as West African and the essence as Black American does not exile all other races from participation in the jazz form. Instead, it reveals and revitalizes it, allowing all to engage with jazz steeped in tradition and respect leading to future innovation. The democratic and improvisatory spirit that makes the jazz language universally American is only universal because, as Ralph Ellison said to a Harvard audience in 1973, "You cannot have an American experience without having a black experience."[29] In a land of immigrants, American White people identified deeply with jazz, explains writer Gerald Early in the film *Jazz*: "And so many people felt kinda displaced . . . you had this music that kinda captured some feeling of that. I think that that was part of its amazing appeal is that it spoke to feeling out of sorts, and out of joint, and malad-justed."[30] In 1951, a group of psychiatrists wrote on their hypothesis that those who are drawn to jazz, consciously or not, are so because it's "a way of express-ing resentment toward the world in general."[31] Jazz is, essentially, a language of courage and protest. Billy Siegenfeld confirms this nature when he writes, "Being free to speak one's inside voice requires taking a stand apart from what is conventionally approved of."[32] In that spirit, jazz grants entry and access to those who identify with the shared humanity of the jazz language, in connec-tion to its roots via lived experience as individuals.

> *Your thoughts, your wisdom.*
> *If you don't live it, it won't come out of your horn.*
> Charlie Parker[33]

The future of jazz depends on this shared humanity. Through jazz, universal truths can be realized, communities can heal, and the future can be more fair, just, and equitable.

NOTES

1. Lindsay Guarino and Wendy Oliver, *Jazz Dance: A History of the Roots and Branches,* ed. Guarino and Oliver (Gainesville: University Press of Florida, 2014).

2. Ken Burns, *Jazz,* episode 1: *Gumbo* (PBS, 2000).

3. Deidre Sklar, "Five Premises for a Culturally Sensitive Approach to Dance," in *Moving History/Dancing Cultures: A Dance History Reader,* ed. Ann Dils and Ann Cooper Albright (Middletown, CT: Wesleyan University Press, 2001), 30–32.

4. "Jazz Is . . . Dance Project," Melanie George, https://melaniegeorge.org/jazzis.

5. Lewis Porter, "Some Problems in Jazz Research," *Black Music Research Journal* 8, no. 2 (Autumn 1988): 199–200, www.jstor.org/stable/779352.

6. Brenda Dixon Gottschild, *The Black Dancing Body* (New York: Palgrave Mac-millan, 2003), 222–23.

7. Ibid., 223.

8. Ibid.

9. Ibid.

10. Marshall W. Stearns, *The Story of Jazz* (New York: Oxford University Press, 1956), 4.

11. Ibid.

12. Ibid., 5–6.

13. Staff at the Newport Jazz Festival, in conversation with author Lindsay Gua-rino, Summer 2016.

14. Porter, "Some Problems," 195.

15. Giovanni Russonello, "Jazz Has Always Been Protest Music: Can It Meet This Moment?" *New York Times*, September 3, 2020, www.nytimes.com/2020/09/03/arts/music/jazz-protest-academia.html.

16. Porter, "Some Problems," 195.

17. Observations from job postings.

18. Rachel Rizzuto, "Artist, Scholar, Teacher: Cynthia Oliver Has Created a New Model for the College Dance Educator," *Dance Teacher Magazine*, December 2, 2020, www.dance-teacher.com/cynthia-oliver-illinois-2649098103.html.

19. Ibid.

20. The same search on the American Association of Blacks in Higher Education website resulted in twenty-four full-time Black studies positions, and nineteen full-time African American Studies positions (https://jobs.blacksinhighered.org/).

21. Russonello, "Jazz Has Always Been Protest Music."

22. Ibid.

23. Ibid.

24. Wanda Ebright and Gary Guffey, *Dance on the Historically Black College Campus: The Familiar and Foreign* (New York: Springer International, 2019), 118.

25. Ibid., 120.

26. National Dance Education Organization, "Vision Document for Dance 2050: The Future of Dance in Higher Education," 2013, 13, https://s3.amazonaws.com/ClubExpressClubFiles/893257/documents/Final_Ratified_DANCE2050_Vision_as_of_12–23–14_242087547.pdf?AWSAccessKeyId=AKIA6MYUE6DNNNCCDT4J&Expires=1610721155&response-content-disposition=inline%3B%20filename%3DFinal_Ratified_DANCE2050_Vision_as_of_12–23–14.pdf&Signature=oErekMvXTCBFN6I4ZnDu4m4exhI%3D.

27. William Frey, "The U.S. Will Become 'Minority White' in 2045, Census Projects," March 24, 2018, www.brookings.edu/blog/the-avenue/2018/03/14/the-us-will-become-minority-white-in-2045-census-projects/.

28. Ebright and Guffey also make this point anecdotally in their book *Dance on the Historically Black College Campus*, 51.

29. Gottschild, *The Black Dancing Body*, 234.

30. Burns, *Jazz*, episode 3: "Our Language" (PBS, 2000).

31. Stearns, *The Story of Jazz*, 297.

32. Billy Siegenfeld, "Performing Energy: American Rhythm Dancing and the Articulation of the Inarticulate," in *Jazz Dance: A History of the Roots and Branches*, ed. Lindsay Guarino and Wendy Oliver (Gainesville: University of Florida Press, 2014), 275.

33. Stearns, *The Story of Jazz*, 305.

23

My Truth, My Self, Our Way Forward

CARLOS R. A. JONES

Consider this . . . Many jazz dance practitioners whose premier culture flowers from the African diaspora and who have experienced dance through a Whiteness lens reside in a dance body that is colonized. It is practically inescapable. This is particularly true for African American dance artists, those from the diaspora whose ancestors trace back to generations of enslavement. The degree of colonization varies greatly from Black body to Black body and is dependent on personal experience with/in generational place, codified methods, K to 16+ dance education, chosen performance venue or any combination of these. I stand truthfully in a colonized body, having experienced all of these during my life as an architect of jazz dance.

My body—OUR Black and Brown bodies—are very much the jazz experience in America. Resembling jazz dance, the African roots are embedded in our DNA. Our bodies are the trunks standing in the amalgamated glow of the American experience and often dissociated from our heritage. Countless times unknowingly . . . often unwillingly. Many of us have traversed colonized movement systems, navigated Eurocentric training methodologies, and participated in aesthetic reprogramming only to be abandoned among the branches in poorly fitted techniques. We have been stranded there, forever altered and untethered to our jazz heritage . . . you know, the rooted one. Under the auspices of training and refinement, we are stripped of our intrinsic groove and in many cases, provided little to no agency in navigating the overbearing Whiteness in the branches . . . our mangled aesthetic sensibility in tow. Here is the snap back. The African American jazz practitioner created a home in the foreign branches and in most cases cleared a view in the branches to interact with our roots as we see fit. We embraced the predominant European-influenced techniques as we freely call on the aesthetics and techniques of our African ancestry. The African American jazz dancer creates a passport through technique, and it is used liberally to travel back and forth while allowing space for a multitude of blended destinations along the way.

My technique passport is frayed. I use it extensively, far more consciously than I did in my early years as a dance artist. Two decades ago, the articulation of this understanding would surely not have happened. Investigations of self and a recalibration of my viewpoint brought me to this space where I embrace my colonized existence. The movement that feels symbiotic to my body is neither entirely Africanist nor Europeanist. In fact, my movement is also Asian and Latinx. I am an amalgamation of my VERY American experiences. In any teaching or choreographic project, I carry my technique passport and take off, landing in any destination at any time. I do so respectfully and responsibly, noting to my students or dancers the lineage of the technique and the significance of how it has shaped the dance. I have always been a technique shifter. The difference? Now, I do so consciously and with respectful agency.

At the time of this writing, the United States is being asked to reconcile its complacency with racism and to dismantle ideologies and practices that have ordained Whiteness as supreme. Coincidentally, or not, a global pandemic has forced us to sit still and take stock of the inequities happening to Black and Brown people. Many citizens, here I am specifically speaking about White citizens, have expressed powerful disdain for the unabridged and dehumanizing actions of individuals who have taken oaths to protect. They are aghast at the unmitigated gall of an elected public entity, whose chief responsibility is to administer justice, refusing equitable treatment to Black and Brown people. Why not be equally insulted at the systemic assassination of Black culture? Jazz dance, an undeniably African American cultural gemstone, has been a victim of Whiteness for over a century.

To my White colleagues and friends in jazz dance, here is the call to provide reparations to jazz dance. Yes. It will challenge everything you know to be true. Your foundation will be rocked. We are two decades into the twenty-first century. Let's get to work and leave the contentiousness behind. This is not a zero-sum game. To my Black and Brown brothers and sisters in jazz dance, here is the call to step out of the fog of the colonized mind-set, own your truth, and boldly champion the Africanist aesthetics. Jazz dance needs your agency. If you identify with neither of the aforementioned communities, here is your call. Do the scholarship and then advocate for equity in jazz dance. Indifference is the hotbed for aggression. Your culture is next. The discussion has been unveiled. The call has been made. Jazz dance in the twenty-first century awaits.

FIGURE 23.1. Decidedly Jazz Danceworks' Dezjuan Thomas (2016). Photo by Trudie Lee Photography. Courtesy of DJD.

Decidedly Jazz Danceworks, Natasha Korney and Sabrina Comanescu with Jonathan McCaslin (drums), Rubim de Toledo (bass), and Carsten Rubeling (trombone) in "Cumbia and Jazz Fusion" from *Better Get Hit in Your Soul* (2019), by artistic director Kimberley Cooper. Photo by Scott Reid. Courtesy of DJD.

Appendix I

Jazz Music Glossary

WENDY OLIVER, RUBIM DE TOLEDO, AND JOANNE BAKER

Responsibly studying, teaching, and creating jazz dance involves a parallel investigation into jazz music. Jazz music, like jazz dance, is a uniquely African American art form, commonly thought to have developed first in New Orleans, Louisiana. Historian Marshall Stearns posits that two key elements throughout the 1700 and 1800s were primarily responsible for the early development of this music form: private *vodun* (also known as voodoo) ceremonies, and public performances in Congo Square: "The first preserved African music—and especially rhythm—in the midst of its rituals; and the second forced the same music . . . out into the open where it could easily influence and be influenced by European music."[1] From 1724 into the 1880s, Congo Square in New Orleans was a gathering place for people of African, French, and Spanish descent, where African-based music and dance served as the foundation for an eventual blending with European-derived movement and songs.[2]

According to Stearns, some of the elements that give jazz music its distinctive quality are rhythmic complexity, a blue tonality (a scale using a lowered third and seventh note), call-and-response, falsetto break (a high-pitched cry based on the field or street holler), and the improvised drum solo.[3] All of these derive from West African music. As African American musicians began to adopt European-style instruments such as the piano, trumpet, and trombone, the musicians imbued them with their own musical styles, which were expressive of African musical aesthetics.

Key elements foundational to the jazz form can be known and understood through both music and dance. Dancers, educators, and choreographers can find infinite sources of inspiration from the distinctive features of jazz music.

FIGURE I.1. Holla Jazz performing *FLOOR'D* (2018). Dancer: Sarah Tumaliuan. Musicians: Gerald Heslop, Raymond Blake, Iain Green, Brian Huntley, Jan Morgan, Sabine Ndalamba, Micheal Redhead, Bruce Skerritt, Felicia Wirahardja, Terry Woode. Photographer: Tamara Romanchuk.

Deep listening and full embodiment, in connection to the social and kinetic elements from West African, African American, and vernacular jazz dance, can ignite the more elusive aspects of the jazz experience. It is important to note that the genre is vast and continues to grow. An in-depth study can take a lifetime.

This glossary of jazz music terminology is an entry point to begin this study. In addition, you will find a timeline of jazz music followed by related genres/ cousins of jazz,[4] a list of distinctive jazz sounds, and a short reading list. These entries are not meant to be comprehensive but instead to open the door to the study of jazz music as it intersects with rooting your jazz practices.

JAZZ MUSIC TERMINOLOGY

accent: A stress on a particular note or beat, usually indicated by volume or attack.[5]

articulation: The manner in which a musician produces a note. This can mean short or long, refer to the note's attack or decay, and can include timbre, bends, and dynamics.

bar or measure: A grouping of beats. The number of beats within each grouping is dependent on the time signature.

beat: A musical pulse or basic unit of time. Example: the 4/4 time signature has 4 beats. (Note: Many of the following terms are interpreted differently within classical music theory.)

    backbeat: The emphasized beats in a measure. Example: in 4/4 time beats 2 and 4 are the usually the backbeats. The beat we clap our hands or snap our fingers to. However, in a half-time feel, the backbeat could be beat 3.

    downbeat: The first beat of a measure. In some contexts, the downbeat refers to all the beats in a measure as opposed to the upbeats (see "upbeat").

    offbeat: An unaccented beat or portion of a beat in a musical measure.

    upbeat: The upbeat occurs between the beats. Example: In 4/4 time the upbeats are the eighth-note subdivisions on the "ands" (1 and 2 and 3 and 4 and).

bend: When a musical note is steadily altered in pitch, either higher or lower.

blues: A musical genre, ancestral to jazz, R&B, and rock-and-roll. (See "Related Genres" section below.)

blues form: A form normally consisting of 12 bars, characteristically based on the I, IV, and V chords of a key.

blues scale: A six-note scale widely used in the blues, jazz, R&B, and rock-and-roll that creates a characteristic "blue," "blues," or "bluesy" sound. (See "blues" and "blues sound").

blues sound (or to play bluesy): A style of playing, with typical associated harmonies, using certain blues scales, riffs, and grace notes. Also, a feeling that is said to inform jazz, R&B, and rock-and-roll.

break/solo break: A brief solo passage occurring during an interruption in the accompaniment, usually lasting one or two bars and maintaining the underlying rhythm and harmony of the piece.

bridge: The contrasting middle section of a tune, for example, the B section of an AABA song form.

call-and-response: A solo voice or instrument sings or plays a melodic line or chant, which is then echoed by a group of voices or instruments. A musical term referring to the alternation between two musical voices in a work, particularly that between a solo singer (the "call") and a group chorus (the "response").

clave (*cla*-vay): An African rhythm often used in Latin music. The clave rhythm enforces tension-and-release and forward momentum.

crescendo and decrescendo: Crescendo refers to when a musician or ensemble gets louder throughout a musical phrase. Decrescendo is when they get softer.

dynamics: The volume and/or energy of a musical section within a composition.

fade or fade out: Slowly getting softer; typically, at the end of a song.

falsetto: A high-pitched series of notes made by a voice or instrument (typically the saxophone) sung or played outside of the instrument's normal range. This technique allows a singer or saxophonist to extend their tonal range upward.

fill: An ad-libbed series of notes, typically at the end of a phrase, which sets up a transition to a new section. Typically played by the drums but can include any instrument.

form: (1) The organization of a composition or arrangement; (2) (harmonic/melodic structure): Traditional jazz pieces utilize a repetitive structure of melody and harmony comprised of sections. These sections are often labeled A, B, or C. One complete structure is labeled a "chorus."
Common forms include:

> AABA
> ABAC

> Or can be:

> 12-bar blues
> 16-bar tune

> song form: The traditional jazz song employs the overarching structure comprised of several choruses. The most common form is:

> > *melody/head—soloist—additional soloist or soloists—reinstatement of the melody/head*

The form of a tune may also include an intro, use of interludes, and an outro or tag. Note: Other structures exist in contemporary jazz, and this structure can be significantly modified or expanded on.

groove: The "feel" of a piece of music. The rhythmic element that the listener can attach to, typically presented by the rhythm section. This can be referred to as the groove, feel, or "beat" of a song.

harmony: When two of more voices or instruments play simultaneously but not the same pitches.

head: The first (and last) chorus of a tune, in which the song or melody is stated without, or with minimal, improvisation.

improvisation: The spontaneous expression of musical elements (melody, rhythm, accompaniment, etc.) in a performance and a characteristic element of jazz music. Improvisation can happen as an individual soloist or in a collaborative and collective ensemble environment. Each jazz musician transmits their musical and artistic voice through improvisation. This expression is unique to each improviser and is an evolving element of a jazz musician's artform. The soloist spontaneously composes musical phrases using melody, rhythm, and articulation. Collectively, the rhythm section, through its improvised accompaniment, serves to support the soloist in many ways. The rhythm section adds the rhythmic, harmonic, and structural foundation for the soloist to improvise over. As well, the rhythm section aids the soloist by supplying dynamics, energy, and momentum. This collaboration can go both ways where the soloist entices the rhythm section, and simultaneously the rhythm section informs the soloist.

in the pocket: A term used when musicians are locked in with one another to achieve a sense of togetherness and groove.

intro & outro: Elements of song form. Intro—the beginning of the piece that sets up the feel, key, and tempo of the piece. Outro—the ending of the song.

melody: A set series of varied notes that create a phrase or pattern that can be sung or played by a single instrument. The melody of a song is the main theme of the piece. In jazz, often called the "head."

musical phrase: A grouping of musical bars/measures that creates a mini-completion within the composition, coming to a natural pause where (1) one might breathe if singing, or (2) a new phrase begins.

note: A single tone made by a musical instrument or voice. The building blocks of rhythms and melodies.

In 4/4 time, note values are assigned as follows:

A whole note = four beats
A half note = two beats
A quarter note = one beat
Two eighth notes = one beat
Three triplets = one beat
Four sixteenth notes = one beat

polyrhythm: Two distinct rhythmic patterns played simultaneously.

rhythm: A pattern of beats/notes.

rhythm section: The instruments and players in the band that typically provide the accompaniment of a song as opposed to the melodic content. This always refers to the drums and bass and often includes the piano, guitar, and percussion.

subdivision: Note values within the beats. In 4/4 time, an eighth-note subdivision would be two notes per beat. A triplet subdivision would be three notes per beat, and a sixteenth-note subdivision equals four notes per beat.

swing: The characteristic rhythmic feel in jazz music where the eighth-note subdivisions are not interpreted as equal. Generally accepted as having evolved from a triplet-based feel retained from elements of West African rhythm.

syncopation: (1) A cornerstone of jazz music and all African-based music of South and North America; (2) the unexpected accent of an "off-beat"; (3) a displacement of the regular/expected accenting in music.

tag: A musical device used as an arranging technique to create an ending where the last phrase of a song is repeated and played three times.

tempo: Speed; how fast or slow the music is performed.

timbre: The sound coloring or quality that makes a voice or instrument distinctive, separate from pitch, rhythm, or volume. For instance, each jazz singer has their own distinctive timbre.

time: The tempo or rhythmic pulse of a song. Playing "in" time refers to playing rhythmically correctly and maintaining the tempo. Playing out of time refers to playing rhythmically inaccurately.

　　half time: When a song's tempo is slowed to half its original tempo.

　　half-time feel: When the musicians play as in half time, but the tempo of the song continues to be counted the same as the original tempo.

　　double time: When a song's tempo is doubled.

　　double-time feel: When the musicians play as in double time, but the tempo of the song continues to be counted the same as the original tempo.

time signature: Two numbers at the beginning of a notated piece of music, where the top number indicates how many beats per measure, and the bottom number indicates what type of note gets one beat. In 4/4 time, there are four beats to the measure, and the quarter note gets one beat.

unison: When two or more voices or instruments play together and play the same pitches, as opposed to playing in harmony (different pitches).

TIMELINE OF JAZZ MUSIC

early jazz: Generally described as Dixieland, ragtime, and stride piano styles from New Orleans occurring before the swing era. Sometimes referred to as traditional jazz.

ragtime: A style of piano music developed around the turn of the twentieth century, with a march-like tempo, syncopated right-hand melody, and an "oom-pah" left-hand accompaniment.

Dixieland: Sometimes referred to as hot jazz or traditional jazz, based on the music that developed in New Orleans at the start of the twentieth century.

swing/big band: A style developed out of New Orleans jazz of the 1910s, securing its place along the jazz timeline in the late 1920s through the early 1940s. Comprised of an orchestra or band of more than ten members, swing is characterized as having a driving rhythm, simple structure, clear melodies, and, above all else, danceability.

bebop: The style of jazz developed by young players in the early 1940s. Small groups were favored, and simple standard tunes or just their chord progressions were used as springboards for rapid, many-noted improvisations using long, irregular, syncopated phrasing. Bebop is typically played at a fast tempo and showcases a musician's improvisational and technical ability.

hard bop: The style of the late 1950s. Still essentially bebop, the style used hard-driving rhythmic feel and vehement, biting lines and harmony drenched with urban blues, rhythm and blues, and gospel. Original compositions were stressed over the old standards used in bebop.

post-bop: A general term for many developments in jazz after the 1950s. Post-bop saw a breakaway from standard jazz form, feels, and harmony favoring new compositions by jazz musicians rather than standard repertoire.

cool jazz: A jazz style characterized by moderate volume, quiet rhythm sections, low vibrato, and sometimes improvised counterpoint, ca. 1950s. Can be described as an aesthetic approach to jazz contrasting the aggressive approach to bebop.

modal: A style of improvisation and jazz composition utilizing a single tonality or chord for many measures at a time instead of many alternating chords within complex chord progressions. This approach allows the improviser to focus on melody, phrasing, and the use of space, timbre, and dynamics, ca. 1950s.

free jazz: A jazz style emerging in the 1960s that emphasized creative expression over the confines of conventional rhythm, form, standard harmony, or jazz bebop vocabulary.

fusion: A group of styles of jazz that merged post-bop music with soul, rock, Latin, other global musical genres, and funk in an amplified form. Characterized by the use of electric guitar, synthesizers and electric pianos, bass guitar, and rock-and-roll drum setups.

smooth jazz: A later development of fusion in which elements of R&B and pop music were distilled and refined by the formulas and constraints of radio to become bright and recognizable melodies (though ironically often recorded with audiophile sensibilities in mind). Recent smooth jazz owes little to jazz and might be better seen as instrumental pop music.

acid jazz: Music for dancing, first heard in the 1980s, that combines elements of soul, jazz, funk, and hip hop, and mixes acoustic and electric instruments.

Related Genres/Cousins of Jazz

blues: A style of Afro-American secular music originating in the southern states rooted in African American work songs and spirituals. The blues is characterized by call-and-response, the 12-bar blues pattern, and the usage of the pentatonic or blues scale. The blues genre is regarded as a central stylistic influence on jazz, R&B, and rock-and-roll music.

boogie woogie: A style of piano playing very popular in the 1930s. Blues, with continuous repeated eighth-note patterns in the left hand and blues riffs and figures in the right hand.

funk: A loose term for music that draws from blues or gospel-based harmony, rhythm, and melody. Funk-based music is often modal and very riff-based (using distinctive repetitive motifs). It features syncopated bass, drum, and guitar parts to create an intricate and highly danceable groove. As well, funk music is characterized by the use of horn sections and shouted vocals.

funky: A term generally used to describe African American-influenced grooves that have a strong beat and are highly danceable.

Latin jazz: Afro-Cuban, Brazilian, or other South American–derived musical styles incorporating jazz improvisation, form, and harmonic structures. These styles can include jazzified versions of the Samba, Bossa Nova, Salsa, Songo, Rumba, Bolero, or Tango.

R&B: An abbreviation of "rhythm and blues." An African American popular music style emerging in the 1940s influenced by blues, boogie woogie, jump blues, and jazz. To some, the term "R&B" is used as a "catchall" label for soul, funk, and other African American popular musical genres.

DISTINCTIVE SOUNDS OF JAZZ

blue notes: Very expressive notes that musicians use to create nuances resembling early African American vocal styles. These notes are typically outside of the conventional theoretical norms. Often, they are microtonal, or tones outside the typical Western tuning system, and employ the bending and sliding of pitches. This sound has become characteristic of the blues, jazz, African American contemporary musical styles, and even rock-and-roll.

mutes: Brass instruments, like the trumpet and trombone, use mutes (cone-shaped devices that fit into the bell of a brass instrument) to alter the sound of their instrument. Most notably used in big-band jazz, some of the common mutes are the plunger, blucket, and harmon. The harmon mute is a quintessential sound of the cool jazz trumpet.

scatting: Singing using abstract syllables rather than words. Typically improvised.

stop time: Rhythmic "hits" providing stops or breaks for soloists to be featured.

Stride Piano: A style of piano playing (ca. 1917–30) with a strong left-hand pattern that rapidly moves between bass notes and chords, and uses a wide range of pianistics to decorate melodies and create variations on themes.

trading fours or eights: When two improvisers trade phrases. This is often four-bar or eight-bar phrases. As well, this commonly occurs between soloists and the drummer.

vocalese: The setting of lyrics to originally instrumental melodies. Most widely used to add lyrics to bebop melodies.

vocalize: When vocalists sing melodies but do not use lyrics. Instead, they use syllables like "oohs" and other vowel sounds. This differs from scatting, as scatting is typically improvised.

RESOURCE LIST

Film and Online

Blues, dir. Martin Scorsese, film series, PBS.
Jazz, dir. Ken Burns, documentary, PBS.
Jazz at Lincoln Center YouTube channel, website.
Tradition Is a Temple, dir. Darren Hoffman, documentary, self-distributed.

Books and Magazines

DownBeat. Monthly magazine.

Giddins, Gary, and Scott DeVeaux. *Jazz*. New York: Norton, 2009.

Schuller, Gunter. *Early Jazz: Its Roots and Musical Development*. New York: Oxford University Press, 1986.

Stearns, Marshall. *Story of Jazz*. New York: Oxford University Press, 1956.

Stein, Sammy. *Women in Jazz: The Women, the Legends, and Their Fight*. New York: Eighth House, 2019.

Wheeler, Lisa, and R. Gregory Christie. *Jazz Baby*. Boston: HMH Books for Young Readers, 2007. Children's book.

Notes

1. Marshall Stearns, *The Story of Jazz* (New York: Oxford University Press, 1956), 44.

2. Takiyah Nur Amin, "The African Origins of an American Art Form," in *Jazz Dance: A History of the Roots and Branches,* ed. Guarino and Oliver (Gainesville: University Press of Florida, 2014).

3. Stearns, *Story of Jazz,* 4–15.

4. Wharton Center, *Lansing State Journal,* www.lansingstatejournal.com/story/sponsor-story/wharton-center/2015/07/16/wharton-varying-styles-jazz-road-map/30249361/; www.thejazzpianosite.com/jazz-piano-lessons/jazz-genres/swing-music-explained/; https://ccnmtl.columbia.edu/projects/jazzglossary/s/.

5. Sources consulted for the glossary include: www.merriam-webster.com/dictionary/offbeat; www.britannica.com/art/swing-music; Naxos Records website, www.naxos.com/education/glossary.asp#; www.jazzinamerica.org.

Appendix II

Experimenting with Time Signatures

VICKI ADAMS WILLIS, JOANNE BAKER,
AND JAMIE FREEMAN CORMACK

Jazz is rooted in African cultures in which music and dance have historically been experienced as a single, unified, and indivisible expression, saturated with essential complex rhythms and, indeed, polyrhythms. Today, jazz movement becomes authentic when it connects deeply to the spirit, soul, and intrinsic groove of the music, with the time signature being the foundation of each groove. This foundation establishes a specific lilt that can inhabit our bodies and compel us to move. Each time signature presents its own world of possibilities to embrace and mine.

As jazz artists and teachers, it is vital that we commit to the exploration of a variety of jazz genres and grooves and in doing so we develop and evolve our musical ear, which in turn deepens and enhances our range of expression. The exploration of less common time signatures can shift us (and our students) out of our comfort zones and into new ways of moving.

Jazz music provides countless versions of original tunes from throughout its history that are constantly being interpreted and reinterpreted in endless ways. This list is merely the tip of the iceberg when considering the myriad options available in unusual time signatures. It cites specific artists whose versions we deem "danceable" and that allow for solid recognition of each time signature. The list is by no means complete and is simply a resource to be used as an entry point for exploration. Although primarily comprised of jazz offerings, we have also included other genres from its periphery where the playful nature of time has spoken to us.

3/4 Time

Table II.1. Music in 3/4 time

Title	Composer	Artists
Gravy Waltz	Ray Brown	Ray Brown & the Oscar Peterson Trio
		Bill Henderson
Spam-boo-Limbo[a]	Dan Berglund	Esbörn Svensson Trio (E.S.T)
	Magnus Öström	
	Esbörn Svensson	
Someday My Prince Will Come	Frank Churchill	Bill Evans Trio
All Blues	Miles Davis	Miles Davis
Waltz for Debbie	Bill Evans	Bill Evans Trio
Sophie Rose-Rosalee	Wynton Marsalis	Wynton Marsalis Quartet
Rolling with a Dub	Ari Roze	Ari Roze

Note: [a] 6/8 African or Afro-Cuban clave pattern underneath.

5/4 Time

Table II.2. Music in 5/4 time

Title	Composer	Artists
Long as You're Living	Oscar Brown Jr.	Elizabeth Shepard
Far More Drums	Dave Brubeck	Dave Brubeck Quartet
Far More Blue	Dave Brubeck	Dave Brubeck Quartet
Take Five	Paul Desmond	Dave Brubeck Quartet
Cuerpo y Alma (Body and Soul)[a]	Johnny Green	Esperanza Spalding
Bridge	Amon Tobin	Amon Tobin
Goblins	Ashley Turner	Ash Walker
	Milo O'Halloran, Andre Dane Lance	
Sunflowers	Wynton Marsalis	Wynton Marsalis Septet
Tonight	Magnus Zingmark and Oscar Simonsson	Koop

Note: [a] A 5/4 variation on a standard 4/4 tune.

6/4 and 6/8 Time

Table II.3. Music in 6/4 and 6/8 time

Title	Composer	Artists
Maori Blues	Dave Brubeck	Dave Brubeck Quartet
Pick Up Sticks	Dave Brubeck	Dave Brubeck Quartet
26	Brad Mehldau	Brad Mehldau Trio
Minuana	Pat Metheny	Pat Metheny Group
Group Shot	Buddy Rich	Buddy Rich Big Band
Afro Blue	Mongo Santamaria	Dianne Reeves
		Mongo Santamaria & The Cal Tjader Quintet
Minuana	Pat Metheny	Pat Metheny Group
Footprints	Wayne Shorter	Giovanni Hidalgo

7/4 Time

Table II.4. Music in 7/4 time

Title	Composer	Artists
Unsquare Dance	Dave Brubeck	Dave Brubeck Quartet
Seven Up	Don Ellis	Don Ellis
Yesterdays	Corey Kendrick	Cory Kendrick Trio
Got Me Wrong	Brad Mehldau	Brad Mehldau Trio
Suspect Seven	Rubim de Toledo	Rubim de Toledo

9/8 Time

Table II.5. Music in 9/8 time

Title	Composer	Artists
Blue Shadows in the Street	Dave Brubeck	Dave Brubeck Quartet
Fool for You	Curtis Mayfield	The Impressions
Ginger Spice	Ron Miles	Ginger Baker

MIXED-TIME SIGNATURES

Table II.6. Music in mixed-time signatures

Title	Composer	Artists	Time Signatures
Urban Nomad	Geof Bradfield	Geof Bradfield	7/4 & 4/4
Three to Get Ready	Dave Brubeck	Dave Brubeck Quartet	3/4 & 4/4
Kathy's Waltz	Dave Brubeck	Dave Brubeck Quartet	4/4 & 3 /4
Blue Rondo a la Turk	Dave Brubeck	Dave Brubeck Quartet	9/8 & 4/4
Sunshine Superman	Donovan	Emilie Claire Barlow	7/4 & 4/4
Espera	Esperanza Spaulding	Esperanza Spaulding	7/4 & 4/4
Golden Lady	Stevie Wonder	Kurt Elling	7/4 & 4/4

12/8 TIME

Table II.7. Music in 12/8 time

Title	Artists
It's a Man's World	James Brown
At Last	Etta James

FIGURE II.1. Holla Jazz performing *FLOOR'D* (2018). Dancers (*left to right*): Raoul Wilke, Miha Matevzic, Hollywood Jade. Musicians: Gerald Heslop, Raymond Blake, Iain Green, Brian Huntley, Jan Morgan, Sabine Ndalamba, Micheal Redhead, Bruce Skerritt, Felicia Wirahardja, Terry Woode. Photographer: Tamara Romanchuk.

Appendix III

Music Inspiration

Over the journey of working on this book, there have been many conversations about jazz dance and music. Everyone agrees that music is important to the art form. How music is accessed, however, varies along the continuum. Styles that are rooted in the Africanist aesthetic are reliant on a symbiotic relationship between dance and music. The authors have shared some of the music choices they use in their teaching, choreography, and performance. The list is not exhaustive. It is offered as an entry to researching music that dovetails smoothly with rooted jazz dance practice. The selections are listed by the first name of the artist and then by song.

Table III.1. Music inspiration

	Song	Artists	Album/CD/DMP	Genre of music (if known)
1	Amtrak Blues	Alberta Hunter	*Amtrak Blues*	vocals
2	Sweet Georgia Brown	Alberta Hunter	*Amtrak Blues*	vocals
3	Come Down	Anderson .Paak	*Malibu*	Hip-hop/Funk
4	The Thrill Is Gone	B.B. King	*Greatest Hits*	vocals
5	You Don't Know Me	B.B. King & Diane Schuur	*Heart to Heart*	vocals
6	Pow	Beastie Boys	*The In Sound from Way Out*	Funk
7	Moten Swing	Bennie Moten	*Bennie Moten: 1929– 1932/Band Box Shuffle* (album)	Swing
8	King Porter Stomp	Benny Goodman	*Best of Ken Burns Jazz*	instrumental
9	Sing Sing Sing	Benny Goodman	*Essential Benny Goodman*	instrumental
10	St. Louis Blues	Bessie Smith	*Essential Bessy Smith*	vocals
11	Bumble Bee	Big Mama Thornton	*Ball N' Chain*	vocals

	Song	Artists	Album/CD/DMP	Genre of music (if known)
12	Bring It on Home	Big Mama Thornton	Ball N' Chain	vocals
13	Gary's Theme	Bill Evans	*You Must Believe in Spring*	Jazz
14	Night & Day	Bill Evans	*Everybody Digs Bill Evans*	Jazz
15	I Don't Want You on My Mind	Bill Withers	*Still Bill*	R&B Blues
16	Railroad Man	Bill Withers	*Justments*	R&B Blues
17	Strange Fruit	Billie Holliday	*Billie Holliday: Ken Burns Jazz*	vocals
18	Lush Life	Billy Strayhorn & Duke Ellington	*Masters of Jazz—Billy Strayhorn*	vocals
19	Take the A Train	Billy Strayhorn & Duke Ellington	*Masters of Jazz—Billy Strayhorn*	instrumental
20	Fake	Brand New Heavies	*Brother Sister*	Funk
21	Ten Ton Take	Brand New Heavies	*Brother Sister*	Funk
22	Jambalaya	Brenda Boykin	*See Ya Later*	Jazz
23	Perm	Bruno Mars	*24K Magic*	Pop
24	Trombone Shorty	Buckjump	*For True*	Jazz
25	Blues for Basie	Buddy Rich	*Buddy Rich: From the Sticks*	instrumental
26	Come on in My Kitchen	Cassandra Wilson	*Blue Light 'Til Dawn*	Blues
27	Run the Voodoo Down	Cassandra Wilson	*Travelin' Miles*	Jazz
28	Seven Steps	Cassandra Wilson	*Travelin' Miles*	Jazz
29	Sky and Sea	Cassandra Wilson	*Travelin' Miles*	Jazz
30	Hog Callin' Blues	Charles Mingus	*Oh Yeah*	Jazz
31	Parkers Mood	Charlie Parker	*Best of the Complete Savoy & Dial Studio—Charlie Parker*	instrumental
32	Old Devil Moon	Chet Baker	*Chet Baker Sings: It Could Happen to You*	Jazz
33	Tin Tin Deo	Clark Terry & Chico O'Farrill	*Spanish Rice*	Jazz Funk
34	The Rebirth of the Fat Lola	Club Des Belugas	*Night over Rio*	Dance & DJ
35	Straight to Memphis	Club Des Belugas feat. Brenda Boykin	*Free*	Electronic

	Song	Artists	Album/CD/DMP	Genre of music (if known)
36	Basie Boogie	Count Basie	*Flappers & Dappers: Cocktail Party Mix*	instrumental
37	Jumpin at the Woodside	Count Basie	*Basie Is Back*	instrumental
38	Street Life	The Crusaders feat. Randy Crawford	*Street Life*	Jazz
39	Sugah Daddy	D'Angelo	*Black Messiah*	R&B Funk
40	When We Get By	D'Angelo	*Brown Sugar*	Jazzy R&B
41	Blue Rondo A La Turk	The Dave Brubeck Quartet	*Time Out*	Jazz
42	Take Five	The Dave Brubeck Quartet	*Time Out*	Jazz
43	Three to Get Ready	The Dave Brubeck Quartet	*Time Out*	Jazz
44	Unsquare Dance	The Dave Brubeck Quartet	*Time Further Out*	Jazz
45	The Crossing	David Murray Octet	*Octet Plays Trane*	Jazz
46	Flowers for Albert	David Murray Octet	*Murray's Step*	Jazz
47	Pretty Eyes	Dee Dee Bridgewater	*Love & Peace: Tribute to Horace Silver*	vocals
48	Soulville	Dee Dee Bridgewater	*Love & Peace: Tribute to Horace Silver*	vocals
49	I Can't Give You Anything But Love	Diana Krall	*When I Look in Your Eyes*	Jazz
50	Deed I Do	Diana Krall	*All for You: A Dedication To the Nat King Cole Trio*	Jazz
51	Manteca	Dizzy Gillespie	Any version from any album	Latin Jazz
52	Tin Tin Deo	Dizzy Gillespie	*The Champ*	Latin Jazz
53	Gillespiana Suite: Toccata	Dizzy Gillespie Alumni Allstars	*Dizzy's World*	Jazz
54	Groovin' High	Dizzy Gillespie and Charlie Parker	Any greatest hits	Jazz
55	The Mooche	Duke Ellington	*Best of Ken Burns Jazz*	instrumental
56	Perdido (and other selections)	Ella Fitzgerald	*Twelve Nights in Hollywood (Live)*	vocals
57	Blue Suede Shoes	Elvis Presley	*Essential Elvis Presley*	vocals
58	Hound Dog	Elvis Presley	*Essential Elvis Presley*	vocals
59	Charleston	Enoch Light	*Roaring 20s*, vol. 2	instrumental

	Song	Artists	Album/CD/DMP	Genre of music (if known)
60	Don't Sweat the Technique	Eric B & Rakim	*Don't Sweat the Technique*	Hip-hop
61	All selections	Ethel Waters	*American Legends: Ethel Waters*	vocals
62	In the Mood	Glenn Miller	*Essential Glenn Miller*	instrumental
63	I Will Survive	Gloria Gaynor	*I Will Survive: The Anthology*	vocals
64	Marvin Gaye	Got to Give It Up	*Marvin Gaye: 15 Favorites*	R&B
65	Sookie Sookie	Grant Green	*Alive*	Jazz Funk
66	1960 What?	Gregory Porter	*1960 What? The Remixes*	Jazz
67	Freestylin'	Greyboy	*Freestylin'*	Jazz Funk
68	Singles Party	Greyboy	*Freestylin'*	Funk
69	Who's Gonna Be the Junkie	Greyboy	*Freestylin'*	Funk
70	Mister Magic	Grover Washington Jr.	*Mister Magic*	Jazz
71	Chameleon	Herbie Hancock	*Head Hunters*	Jazz Funk
72	Watermelon Man	Herbie Hancock	*Head Hunters*	instrumental
73	Bus Stop	The Hollies	*The Hollies: Greatest Hits: Live*	vocals
74	Bonita	Horace Silver	*Cape Verdean Blues*	instrumental
75	Baby Workout	Jackie Wilson	*Greatest Hits*	R&B/Soul
76	Reet Petite	Jackie Wilson	*Greatest Hits*	R&B/Soul
77	Liberty City	Jaco Pastorius	*Word of Mouth*	Jazz
78	Super Bad	James Brown	*20 All-Time Greatest Hits*	R&B
79	Canned Heat	Jamiroquai	*Center Stage (Motion Picture Soundtrack)*	Dance
80	Little L	Jamiroquai	*A Funk Odyssey*	Funk
81	Virtual Insanity	Jamiroquai	*Virtual Insanity*	Funk
82	Made for Now	Janet Jackson	*Made for Now*	Pop
83	Together Again	Janet Jackson	*The Velvet Rope*	Pop/ Rock
84	Let's Get Loud	Jennifer Lopez	*On the 6*	Pop
85	The Lotus Blooms	Jeremy Eliis	*The Lotus Blooms*	Electronic Funk
86	Coming to You	Jill Scott	*Woman*	Soul and R&B
87	Feeling Good	Joe Sample & Randy Crawford	*Feeling Good*	Jazz

	Song	Artists	Album/CD/DMP	Genre of music (if known)
88	Giant Steps	John Coltrane	*Giant Steps*	instrumental
89	My Favorite Things	John Coltrane	*My Favorite Things*	Jazz
90	Olé	John Coltrane	*Olé Coltrane*	Jazz
91	Doctor Jazz	John Gill's Dixieland Serenaders	*Take Me to the Midnight Cakewalk Ball*	instrumental
92	Take Me to the Midnight Cakewalk	John Gill's Dixieland Serenaders	*Take Me to the Midnight Cakewalk Ball*	instrumental
93	What'd I Say	John Scofield	*That's What I Say (John Scofield Plays the Music of Ray Charles)*	Jazz
94	Love Got in The Way	Kandace Springs	*Kandace Springs*	R&B
95	Can't Take My Eyes off of You	Lauryn Hill	*The Miseducation of Lauryn Hill*	Soul and R&B
96	Burnin' Coal	Les McCann	*Much Les*	Jazz
97	Doin' That Thang	Les McCann	*Much Les*	Jazz
98	Ain't Misbehavin'	Louis Armstrong	*Louis Armstrong: The Definitive Collection*	Jazz
99	St. Louis Blues	Louis Armstrong	*Best of Ken Burns Jazz*	instrumental
100	Uptown Funk	Mark Ronson feat. Bruno Mars	*Uptown Funk*	Pop
101	Blow Gabriel	McIntosh County Shouters	*Slave Shout Songs from the Coast of Georgia*	vocals
102	Move Daniel	McIntosh County Shouters	*Slave Shout Songs from the Coast of Georgia*	vocals
103	In the Closet	Michael Jackson	*Dangerous*	Pop
104	Soko	Michael Markus	*Magbana*	instrumental—drums
105	All Blues	Miles Davis	*Kind of Blue*	Jazz
106	Black Satin	Miles Davis	*On the Corner*	Jazz
107	Freddie Freeloader	Miles Davis	*Kind of Blue*	Jazz
108	Flamenco Sketches	Miles Davis	*Kind of Blue*	instrumental
109	Django	The Modern Jazz Quartet	*Pyramid*	instrumental
110	Any selection	Multiple artists	*Flappers & Dappers: Cocktail Party Mix*	instrumental
111	Any selection	New Orleans Own Dukes of Dixieland	*Timeless: The Classic Collection*	vocals & instrumentals

	Song	Artists	Album/CD/DMP	Genre of music (if known)
112	Do I Move You?	Nina Simone	*Sings the Blues*	Vocal Blues
113	Strange Fruit	Nina Simone	*Nina Simone: Anthology,* disc 1	vocals
114	Akiwowo, Shango, etc	Olatunji	*Drums of Passion*	instrumental—drums
115	Dixieland One-Step	Original Dixieland Jazz Band	*The Complete Original Dixieland Jazz Band (1917–1936)*	instrumental
116	Ostrich Walk	Original Dixieland Jazz Band	*The Complete Original Dixieland Jazz Band (1917–1936)*	instrumental
117	Lady Marmalade	Labelle	*Nightbirds*	vocals
118	Maya	Philip Hamilton & Peter Jones	*Voices*	vocals & instrumentals
119	Soul Bossa Nova	Quincy Jones	Big Band Bossa Nova	Jazz
120	It's Your World (The First Take)	R. Kelly feat. Jennifer Hudson	It's Your World (The First Take)	R&B
121	Calypso Breakdown	Ralph MacDonald	Saturday Night Fever (The Original Motion Picture Soundtrack)	Salsa
122	Let the Good Times Roll	Ray Charles	*Ray Sings, Basie Swings*	vocals
123	You and I	Rick James	*Come Get It*	R&B Funk
124	On the Street Where You Live	Rickie Lee Jones	*It's Like This*	Jazz
125	Various blues selection	Robert Johnson	*The Compete Recordings*	vocals
126	Greensleeves	Roy Haynes	*Fountain of Youth*	Jazz
127	Jingo	Santana	*Santana*	Latin-influenced rock
128	Oye Como Va	Santana	*Abraxas*	Rock
129	The Look of Love	Sergio Menedes feat. Fergie	*Encanto*	Jazz Funk
130	Waters of March	Sergio Menedes feat. Ledisi	*Encanto*	Jazz
131	Various blues selections	Sonny Terry & Brownie McGhee	*Sonny and Brownie*	vocals
132	Don't You Worry 'Bout a Thing	Stevie Wonder	*Innervision*	Latin-influenced R&B

	Song	Artists	Album/CD/DMP	Genre of music (if known)
133	Higher Ground	Stevie Wonder	*Innervision*	Soul and R&B
134	I Wish	Stevie Wonder	*Songs in the Key of Life*	Soul and R&B
135	Breakout	Swing Out Sister	*It's Better to Travel*	Pop
136	Ain't Too Proud to Beg	The Temptations	*Getting Ready*	R&B
137	Anatomy of a Murder	Terrence Blanchard	*Jazz in Film*	Jazz
138	Money Jungle	Terri Lyne Carrington	*Money Jungle: Provocative in Blue*	Jazz
139	Don't Leave Me This Way	Thelma Houston	*Motown: The Complete No. 1's*	R&B
140	Locomotive	Thelonious Monk	*Straight, No Chaser*	Jazz
141	Straight No Chaser	Thelonious Monk	*Straight, No Chaser*	instrumental
142	Proud Mary	Tina Turner	*All the Best—The Hits*	Pop
143	Falling Down A Mountain	Tindersticks	*Falling Down a Mountain*	Alternative
144	Opus One	Tommy Dorsey	*Swing: Best of the Big Bands*	instrumental
145	Down to the Nightclub	Tower of Power	*Bump City*	Funk
146	Hurricane Season	Trombone Shorty	*Backatown*	Alternative rock
147	Tukka Yoot's Riddim	Us3	*Hand on the Torch*	Rap & Hip-hop
148	Batuco No Chao	Various artists	*Brazil Classics 2: O Samba*	International
149	Charleston	Varsity Eight	*Dance! Dance! Dance!*	instrumental
150	Birdland	Weather Report	*Heavy Weather*	Jazz
151	Teen Town	Weather Report	*Heavy Weather*	Jazz

CONTRIBUTORS

Joanne Baker graduated from the University of Waterloo (Honors, BA Dance) and has been a part of the Decidedly Jazz Danceworks (DJD) organization in Calgary, Canada since 1993, both as a performer and educator. Currently DJD's dance school principal and arts in education coordinator, she is dedicated to the art of jazz dance and exploring its rich history.

LaTasha Barnes is a New York City–based internationally recognized and awarded dancer, educator, and tradition-bearer of the African American social dance forms of Jazz, Lindy Hop, Waacking, House dance and Hip-Hop. Her ethno-choreological work aims to bridge the gap between communities of practice and academia while inspiring the cultivation of an authentic sense of self through creative expressions.

Cory Bowles is a multidisciplinary artist and educator from Nova Scotia, Canada. He makes movies, theater, music, and choreography and has created over 70 works for stage and screen. In 2009, Decidedly Jazz Danceworks commissioned Bowles to write the poem *I Am Jazz* for its 25th Anniversary concert.

Karen Clemente is professor of dance and the co-director of the dance program at Ursinus College. She is the former co-artistic director of the Feet First Dance Center in Phoenixville, PA and a contributor to curriculum guidelines and academic standards for arts education at the Pennsylvania Department of Education. Her most recent research centers on 1920s–1940s era jazz and tap dance artists of the Paramount Theatre in New York City, with a focus on tap dance artist Ralph Brown.

Patricia Cohen is on faculty in the NYU/Steinhardt Dance Education Program, where she created and teaches a required course, *Jazz Dance: History, Culture & Pedagogy*. She has presented jazz workshops at national and international conferences, contributed two chapters to *Jazz Dance: A History of the Roots and Branches,* and serves on the editorial board of the NDEO journal, *Dance Education in Practice.*

Brandi Coleman is assistant professor of jazz dance at Southern Methodist University and was a performing member, rehearsal director, and associate artistic director of Jump Rhythm® Jazz Project, founded and directed by Billy Siegenfeld. As a teaching artist, she has led more than 40 choreographic and teaching residencies at universities throughout the United States and internationally, and received an Emmy Award for her performance in the documentary, *Jump Rhythm Jazz Project: Getting There.*

Kimberley Cooper is artistic director of Decidedly Jazz Danceworks (DJD) in Calgary, Canada. DJD was founded in 1984 with a mandate to create an awareness of, and encourage respect for, the integrity, spirit and traditions of jazz through performance and education. Cooper began her DJD career as a dancer (1989–2013), then resident choreographer and artistic associate (2001–2013); she is now the second artistic director in DJD's history (since 2013).

Jamie Freeman Cormack is a Calgary, Canada-based dancer, teacher and choreographer whose jazz studies have taken her around the world. She was a dancer with Decidedly Jazz Danceworks (DJD) from 1994 to 2001 and is currently the director of the organization's Professional Training Program.

E. Moncell Durden is a dancer, educator, historian, author, documentarian, and professor of practice at Glorya Kaufman International School of Dance at the University of Southern California, specializing in pedagogical practices of Afro-Kinetic memories. His book, *Beginning Hip- Hop Dance,* was published by Human Kinetics in 2019.

Melanie George is the founder of Jazz Is . . . Dance Project and *JazzDanceDirect.com*, and an associate curator at Jacob's Pillow. A scholar and teacher of neo-jazz style, she has contributed writing on jazz to Jacob's Pillow's archives and podcast, and *Jazz Dance: A History of the Roots and Branches*. Melanie is a featured consultant in the film *UpRooted: The Journey of Jazz Dance.*

Lindsay Guarino is associate professor and chair of music, theater, and dance at Salve Regina University in Newport, RI, where jazz and social justice are central to the dance major curriculum. She co-edited *Jazz Dance: A History of the Roots and Branches* with Wendy Oliver and appears in the film *UpRooted: The Journey of Jazz Dance*, which she also consulted on. Lindsay developed Jazz Dance Theory and Practice for NDEO's Online Professional

Development Institute and has planned and hosted two jazz conferences for the organization.

Monique Marie Haley teaches jazz dance curriculum as an assistant professor of dance at Western Michigan University in Kalamazoo, Michigan, and is a concert jazz dance and musical theater choreographer and performer. She was the first African American woman to join the former contemporary jazz company River North Dance Chicago, in 2001, and danced with them for nine years. Professor Haley holds an MFA in Dance from the University of Wisconsin-Milwaukee and is the creator of the *Diasporic Encounter Method* (DEM), which centers African ethos, cultural values, and ritual in jazz dance pedagogy.

Adrienne Hawkins, MFA Dance'76 from Connecticut College, has been on the faculty of all the major universities in the Boston area, and has been artistic director of Impulse Dance for over thirty years. She has taught, performed and choreographed nationally and internationally for over forty-five years.

Karen W. Hubbard, associate professor at UNC Charlotte, holds a BA, MA, and certificate in African/Kenyan Studies as a Fulbright-Hays Scholar. Her jazz dance embodied/theoretical research spans five decades beginning with professional training/performing in NYC. Karen has taught workshops/master classes to educators and students throughout the US, SA and the BWI, and she was one of the scholars consulted for the groundbreaking PBS *Free to Dance* series and the recently released film *Uprooted*.

Carlos R. A. Jones is professor of musical theater and dance at the State University of New York College at Buffalo, where his current position is associate dean of the School of Arts and Sciences. He spent his early career as a performer, where he worked in concert dance, musical theater, television and film, including *The Drew Carey Show*, *The Nanny*, *Dance with Me* and *Uptown Girls*, and has choreographed nationally for Broadway legend André De Shields, SNL veteran Ellen Cleghorn, and television icon Carol Burnett, among others.

Julie Kerr-Berry is professor and chair of the Department of Theatre & Dance at Minnesota State University, Mankato (MSUM). Her scholarly work focuses on the intersections of dance, race, and history specific to how

Whiteness operates in all three arenas. She is editor emerita of the *Journal of Dance Education* and a recent recipient of a Distinguished Faculty Scholar Award at MSUM.

Jessie Metcalf McCullough is a certified instructor of the Giordano Jazz Technique (NGCP®) and is currently on the dance faculty at Salt Lake School for the Performing Arts. A US-UK Fulbright Award recipient for dance (2012–2013), she holds a BS in dance performance from Southern Utah University and an MA in dance studies from Roehampton University in London.

Wendy Oliver, MFA, EdD, is professor of dance in the Department of Theatre, Dance, and Film at Providence College, where she teaches dance and women's and gender studies. She co-edited *Jazz Dance: A History of the Roots and Branches* with Lindsay Guarino, has edited six additional books, authored *Writing about Dance,* by Human Kinetics, and in 2020, edited a Special Issue of *Journal of Dance Education* entitled *Race and Dance Education.* She received the National Dance Education Organization's Dance Education Researcher Award in 2019.

Lynnette Young Overby is professor of theater and deputy director of the community engagement initiative at the University of Delaware, and is the author of over 40 publications, including twelve edited or authored books. She is the artistic director of the Sharing our Legacy Dance Theatre, a company that creates and presents multidisciplinary performances based on African and African American History, and was the 2018 recipient of the National Dance Education Lifetime Achievement Award.

Paula J. Peters is assistant professor of dance and the dance program coordinator at State University of New York at Fredonia, where she teaches jazz, ballet, dance history, and kinesiology. She danced with Spectrum Dance Theater for fourteen years, holds a BFA in dance from Cornish College of the Arts, an MFA in Dance from University of Washington, and has presented research on jazz dance pedagogy nationally and internationally.

Pat Taylor is the artistic director/choreographer of Los Angeles–based Jazz-Antiqua Dance & Music Ensemble, founded in 1993 to celebrate jazz as a vital thread in the cultural fabric of African American history and heritage, and a defining element of the American experience. She holds an MFA in interdisciplinary arts (with a jazz aesthetics emphasis) from Goddard College, and is a frequent artist in residence across the United States and internationally.

Rubim de Toledo is assistant professor of jazz and contemporary popular music at MacEwan University in Edmonton, Canada, where he serves as the bass department head. His current research focuses on African rhythm as the foundation of contemporary bass performance. Rubim has been a frequent musical director for Decidedly Jazz Danceworks (DJD) in Calgary, Canada, since 2007.

Vicki Adams Willis is a Calgary, Canada-based choreographer and teacher who founded the jazz division in the Faculty of Fine Arts' Program of Dance at the University of Calgary in 1978, and co-founded Decidedly Jazz Danceworks (DJD) in 1984, where she continued in her role as artistic director for 29 years. She is currently enthusiastically embracing her founder-in-residence position with the organization.

INDEX

LiteFeet, 72

Lived experience, 9, 64, 65, 66, 83, 107, 108, 111, 115, 119, 127, 130, 133, 142, 194, 195, 230, 232, 263, 264, 269

Locking, 15, 123, 236

Lock-turn, 126

Lorde, Audre, 54

Luigi, 17, 31, 40, 48, 252

Male gaze, 157

Malone, Jacqui, 9, 172, 193, 249

Manning, Frankie, 25, 82, 91, 124, 251
  Big Apple, 74

Marginalization
  of African American people/culture, 24, 100, 141, 142, 177, 265, 266
  of jazz, 34, 52, 63–75, 229, 250, 264, 265, 266

Marsalis, Wynton, 154, 261, 286

Marshall, Kerry James, 147

Martin, John, 52

Masculinity, 150

Mashed Potato, 69, 72, 189, 238

Masterworks, 166

Mattox, Matt, 31, 40, 48, 58

McCarthy-Brown, Nyama, 247

McCullough, Jessie Metcalf, 213–223, *218*, 300

McIntyre, Dianne, 30

McKayle, Donald, 30, 37, 38, 39, 41

Media, jazz in, 21, 24, 46, 131, 166, 216

Meritocracy, and American culture, 57

Mess Around, 71

Methodological frameworks/teaching methodologies, 179, 190, 194, 214, 130

Middle Passage, 48, 67, 89

Middleton, Sam, 145

Miller, Norma, 25, 63, 74

Mimicry, 51

Mingus, Charles, 112–114, 290

Minns, Al, 82

Minstrelsy, 80, 190, 230, 231, 251

Mitchell, Nicole, 266

Modern dance, 29, 30, 31, 41, 44, 45, 46, 52,

53, 58, 120, 153, 163, 166–170, 172, 173, 182, 189, 227, 247
  in academe, 227, 247, 267
  compositional values, 30, 119, 120, 165, 167–170, 172, 173
  in jazz hybrid forms, 31, 189
  relative to jazz dance, 29, 30, 31, 41, 44–46
  technique, 53

Moloney, Sharon, 66

Monk, Thelonious, 145, 295

Monson, Ingrid, 23

Mooch, the, 8, 73, 291

Moreno, Rita, 38, 39, 41

Mosley, Walter, 144

Motif
  literary, 142
  musical, 9, 82, 143, 282
  movement, 3, 130, 253

Moulin Rouge, 28

Mr. TOL E. RAncE, 30

Music
  improvisation, 279
  live music in performance, 87, 136, 137

Musical accompaniment, 39, 172, 184, 185, 277, 279, 280, 281

Musicality, 14, 31, 88, 170–173, 196, 197, 199, 208, 216, 220, 226, 248

Musical theater, 4, 7, 37, 43, 167, 213, 226, 227, 229, 235, 236, 248, 299

Music glossary, 275–284

Music inspiration, 285–288, 289–295

Music videos, 29, 69, 157, 159, 248

Nae Nae, 66

Nagrin, Daniel, 132, 168, 169

Nash, Joe, 63, 183

National Dance Education Organization
  Dance 2050 Vision Document, 267

National Dancing Masters' Association, 65

Neo-jazz, 31, 252, 298
  See also George, Melanie; Jazz dance styles

New Jack, 123

Printed in the USA
CPSIA information can be obtained
at www.ICGtesting.com
JSHW022147240924
70151JS00003B/10

9 780813 080765